POISONOUS LIES

THE
CROYDON
ARSENIC
MYSTERY

To Roger
Best wishes
Diane

POISONOUS LIES

THE
CROYDON
ARSENIC
MYSTERY

DIANE JANES

The
History
Press

For Hector

First published 2010

The History Press
The Mill, Brimscombe Port
Stroud, Gloucestershire, GL5 2QG
www.thehistorypress.co.uk

British Library Cataloguing in Publication Data.
A catalogue record for this book is available from the British Library.

ISBN 978 0 7524 5337 8

Typesetting and origination by The History Press
Printed in Great Britain

CONTENTS

ACKNOWLEDGEMENTS

This book would not have been possible without extensive use of the facilities provided by the National Archives and the British Library Newspaper Section at Colindale, whose staff have provided me with their usual good service. I would also like to thank Chris Bennett and the team at Croydon Local Studies & Archives who have been unfailingly helpful and welcoming, as were the staff I encountered at the Wellcome Collection. I am grateful to Joan Self of the National Meteorological Archive and Jeremy Downer of Sutton & East Surrey Water Company, who swiftly provided me with the data I requested, and also for the help and information received from Lisa Lawson of Croydon Community Services, Lesley at Sevenoaks Library and various members of staff at J.B. Shakespeare Ltd.

Dr Sacha Kolar generously provided me with the benefit of his expertise in the field of pathology, Drs Ann and Barry Colville patiently answered my questions about symptoms, diagnoses and their collective experience of general practice and Dr John Bergin and his wife Pamela shared valuable insights about the life of a general practitioner in the 1920s.

I am greatly indebted to Mary-Virginia Christakos, her son Paul Christakos and to Hazel and Ben Cottis, who provided the photographs of the Duff and Sidney families which illustrate this book and who gave generously of their time and shared their memories of the people involved.

Peter Woolley came to the rescue yet again when a sketch of a long-vanished building was needed, and together with Erica Woolley provided a level of interest and support which goes beyond mere friendship. I would also like to thank Margaret and Eric Thomas and indeed all the friends and family who have put up with conversations about arsenic over the last three years.

Finally I must thank my husband Bill, whose love and encouragement makes everything possible.

CHAPTER ONE

A HAPPY, UNITED FAMILY

Mrs Violet Sidney breathed her last at around 7.20 on the evening of Tuesday, 5 March 1929.[1] She expired in the front bedroom of 29 Birdhurst Rise, South Croydon: a large Victorian villa complete with attics and cellars – the very place in which to stage a melodramatic murder mystery – and in a coincidence entirely in keeping with the set piece detective story which Violet's death was about to become, all the principal suspects were on the premises at the time.

There was Kathleen Noakes, the household servant who was responsible for providing all the meals at no.29 – a distinctly uncomfortable position to hold in a household whose address was shortly to become synonymous with poisoning. Moreover, far from being a trusted old family retainer, Mrs Noakes had only arrived on the premises six months earlier and was already working her notice. Another contender in this speculative list was Dr Robert Elwell, who had been present at the deathbeds of all three members of this unfortunate family whose deaths would shortly be perceived suspicious. In itself the presence of the family doctor was hardly remarkable, but Dr Elwell's involvement took on a particular significance in the light of a rumour that he was enamoured of Mrs Sidney's daughter, Grace Duff. Dr Elwell's partner, Dr John Binning, was also in the house, and although not considered a suspect at the time, Dr Binning was a major participant in the unfolding drama, and questions about his involvement would arise later.

Violet Sidney's two surviving children were at her bedside and, needless to say, they both stood to benefit under their mother's will – although it would later be suggested that her son Tom's real motive for murder could have been a desire to break free from his mother and start a new life in America. And finally, what of Violet Sidney's daughter, Grace? Grace would eventually emerge as the most favoured suspect of all – with many willing to believe her sufficiently avaricious or deranged, that over a period of just under a year, she masterminded the murder of three members of her immediate family.

Before her death, Violet Sidney had lived quietly in South Croydon for more than a decade. Ladylike, reserved and rather old-fashioned, Violet had attended the local church and run her household, tended her garden, received callers and made visits; to all intents and purposes a very ordinary, very private life. Yet within days of her death her name would be headline news and the lives of herself and her family would be illuminated in a blaze of publicity. Magazines and newspapers would speculate about them, whole books would be devoted to their fate; eventually they would be represented by actors and actresses in a medium which was then scarcely known – television. It would be suggested that Violet had been murdered by her beloved son Tom, or more frequently that she was done to death by her daughter Grace. There would even be speculation that she herself had murdered two members of her family, before taking her own life in a belated fit of remorse. Every theory was possible, because in spite of a series of inquests, a long police investigation, and massive public interest, the Croydon Arsenic Mystery has never been solved.

The Metropolitan Police's desperate attempts to pursue every lead are well illustrated by the reaction of Croydon detectives on receiving a letter from Utah some five years after the investigation had faltered to a halt. The author claimed to know something about the case and, in spite of the letter being written in blue crayon and couched in the vaguest of terms, Detective Inspector Morrish, who was by then in charge of the Croydon case, took this missive seriously enough to contact the American authorities in order to have the matter followed up. It transpired that the author was 'a mental patient' who made a habit of writing to various individuals (including ex-President Calvin Coolidge) claiming to be in receipt of answers to a variety of outstanding mysteries, courtesy of information received via dreams[2].

The Utah letter is just one of numerous crank communications which survive in the police files; letters came from as far afield as New York and the Leeward Island – news of the mystery had spread around the world and everyone apparently had a theory. The Croydon Poisonings swiftly achieved 'classic' status, with accounts appearing in one true crime compendium after another. As a murder mystery the case truly had everything – except a definitive solution. In 1975 Richard Whittington-Egan claimed to provide the answer in his book *The Riddle of Birdhurst Rise*[3] which confidently named Grace as the killer. More than thirty years later in the occasional television series *A Most Mysterious Murder*[4] Julian Fellowes concluded that the guilty party was Tom.

On the face of it, the Sidneys were an ordinary middle class family and Birdhurst Rise a quiet suburban enclave of respectability. No.29 had three main living rooms on the ground floor, together with a kitchen and scullery. Upstairs there were four generous size bedrooms and a dressing room on the first floor, a bathroom and WC on the half landing and two further bedrooms on the second floor. It was also a house of nooks and crannies, well provided with linen cupboards, pantries and cellars: premises which could be accessed via front, back and side doors, to say nothing of French windows into the garden[5]. By March 1929 only sixty-nine-year-old Violet Sidney and Mrs Noakes, the general domestic, were living there.

Violet Sidney had been born Violet Emily Lendy in Middlesex in 1859.[6] (In later life, her middle name became corrupted to Emelia, whether by accident or affectation is not known.) At the time of her birth her father, Captain Augustus Lendy, was the principal of the Sunbury House Military College and it was here that Violet grew up. In 1884 she married Thomas Stafford Sidney, a soon-to-be barrister four years her junior, with whom she had three children: Grace, born in 1886, Vera, born in 1888 and Thomas, born in 1889. For the duration of their marriage, Thomas and Violet lived in Enfield at a house called Carlton Lodge, but in the early 1890s Thomas left Violet for another woman. Although Thomas Sidney or his family continued to support Violet and the children financially, enabling Violet to live comfortably and send the children to boarding school, marital breakdown was a social disgrace and Violet must have felt the matter acutely.

Violet and her three children were said to have been exceptionally close. Certainly when the census was taken in 1911 all three of them were still residing with her at a house named Garleton in The Ridgeway, Enfield. Neither daughter was employed and Tom listed his occupation as 'entertainer, piano'. Garleton had thirteen rooms, not including kitchen, scullery or bathrooms and the cook and housemaid lived in. However, things were about to change, because two years earlier Grace Sidney had fallen in love with Edmund Creighton Duff, one of that vast band of men who, although born and raised in India, thought of himself as British and spent most of his adult life working in the Colonial Service in various parts of the Empire. He met Grace Sidney while on leave in Britain in 1909 and when he returned to Nigeria they began to correspond. During his next leave in summer 1911, he and Grace were married. On the face of it, Violet Sidney may have had cause to disapprove. Edmund Duff was forty-two to Grace's twenty-four, they had had little opportunity to get to know one another and, to cap it all, Duff had originally been introduced to Grace by Violet's despised errant husband, Thomas Sidney. When the time came for Edmund Duff to return to Africa, Grace stayed with her mother to await the arrival of the couple's first child, Kathleen Margaret, who was born in July 1912. At the end of Edmund's next leave in 1913, Grace travelled out to Africa with him and they spent nearly a year there, before Grace came home to have their second child, John, in 1914.

In the meantime, Violet's youngest, Tom, had also been globetrotting. His career as an entertainer had taken off to the degree that when war broke out in 1914 he was in the process of fulfilling a series of concert engagements in Australia, with fellow concert performer Peter Dawson.[7] At the outbreak of hostilities, Tom returned home to join up and do his bit, while sister Vera became a nurse. In the meantime, Grace had set up an establishment of her own as befitted a married woman, and by the end of the war, she and Edmund had a third child, Grace Mary (always known as Mary in order to distinguish from her mother). In spite of the difficulties of wartime travel, Edmund Duff managed to get back to Britain for leaves in 1916 and 1917.[8] In 1919 he resigned from the Colonial Service and 'came home' to England for good.

At the end of the war, family life reverted to familiar patterns. Tom Sidney picked up the threads of his old career and began touring again; while playing in the USA he met Margaret Neilson McConnell, the American girl he would go on to marry in 1922, but until his marriage he continued to live with his mother when in London. Violet had moved to 29 Birdhurst Rise in 1917 and it was to this house that Tom first brought his bride in 1923, while they looked for a place of their own. They eventually settled on no.6 South Park Hill Road, barely five minutes' walk from Violet's house, and this was still their home at the time of Violet's death in March 1929. Grace and Edmund also lived close by, initially a few hundred yards further north at 16 Park Hill Road, but in 1926 they moved down the road to rent 16 South Park Hill Road, only half-a-dozen doors away from Tom and Margaret Sidney. By now Grace had produced another daughter, Suzanne, born in 1921 and would go on to have a fifth child, Alastair, in April 1927. Tom and Margaret Sidney also had two children, Cedric, born in 1923, and Mary-Virginia, born in 1925.

Vera Sidney remained unmarried, and was still living with her mother as she approached her fortieth birthday. In 1917 Violet's three children had each received £5,000 legacies from their father's family, and this left Vera in a sufficiently comfortable position that she had no need to work – although she took occasional work as a masseuse, a legacy of her nursing days. Although devoted to Violet, Vera also had an active social life of her own; she was a keen golfer, with a membership at Croham Hurst Golf Club[9], an enthusiastic bridge player and regularly visited the theatre in the company of family or friends. Gregarious and likeable, to all intents and purposes she did not have an enemy in the world.

While Tom and Vera were doing well in their separate ways, their sister Grace had been less fortunate. Her £5,000 inheritance had been lost through bad investments and since leaving the Colonial Service, Edmund's earnings had been drastically reduced. In order to help make ends meet, the couple had been in the habit of letting part of their house to a paying guest or lodger. Violet considered Grace and Edmund not only extravagant, but also unwise to have had so many children – five in all – but Vera was more sympathetic and had generously offered to help with her nephew John's school fees. Nor were Edmund and Grace's misfortunes confined to financial matters. In 1919 their seven-year-old daughter Kathleen died after a failed operation to remove an intestinal blockage and, in 1924, they lost a second daughter, Suzanne, to tubercular meningitis – but worse was to come.

At the end of April 1928 Edmund Duff returned home from a few days fishing, feeling unwell. In less than forty-eight hours he was dead – heart failure following heat stroke was the inquest verdict. Grace was left a widow with three children: John age fourteen, Mary age twelve and baby Alastair. Now in an even more financially precarious position, she moved from South Park Hill Road to 59 Birdhurst Rise, where she endeavoured to let both the ground and top floors, while living on the first floor with herself and the children. She turned to her mother and sister for comfort, popping in even more frequently, now that she lived almost within sight of their front door.

Then in early 1929 another blow fell; Vera became ill, apparently with gastric influenza, and on 15 February she died, leaving Violet, who had always been closest to her younger daughter, inconsolable. Tom Sidney handled the funeral arrangements, utilising the services of J.B. Shakespeare, a family firm of undertakers still operating in Croydon today.[10] Vera was buried in the Queen's Road Cemetery, occupying a grave in the same large plot in which her brother-in-law Edmund Duff had been laid to rest some eight months previously. Violet was pronounced too ill to attend Vera's funeral and from then until her own death, not quite three weeks later, she never left the house again.

It had been a long, bitter winter; snow, frost, fog and icy pavements confronted everyone who ventured outside, with the cold weather even causing problems for those able to stay at home. Frozen water pipes led to so many bursts that water companies were forced to erect standpipes in many parts of London and the South East. Although the supply to Birdhurst Rise was not interrupted, Violet Sidney had to call a plumber out to deal with frozen pipes on several occasions throughout the winter, the last of these visits taking place only the day before she died. When company arrived for Sunday tea it was taken not at the table, but clustered around the drawing room fire, with the maid required to answer the front door to all callers, in order to protect Violet from the risks presented by cold draughts.[11]

However, although unwell over the preceding fortnight, Violet Sidney's condition had not been considered life-threatening until the hours immediately preceding her death. Moreover, there were some extremely peculiar circumstances to be considered – not least Violet's own dramatic declaration, 'I have been poisoned!' Thus, although to the world at large Violet Sidney's death initially appeared to be just one more tragedy in a run of family misfortunes, and although arrangements for her funeral went ahead (with Messrs Shakespeare again being called upon to provide a polished oak coffin with brass handles, to arrange for a service in St Peter's Church, followed by interment in the Queen's Road Cemetery on 11 March[12]) behind the scenes, affairs were moving in a very different direction.

In line with normal procedure in cases of unexpected death, the coroner had been informed and a post-mortem ordered. This was conducted by Dr Robert Bronte on the morning after Violet's death, Wednesday, 6 March. Dr Bronte sent some of the deceased's organs for analysis by Dr John Ryffel, the Home Office Analyst based at Guys Hospital.[13] On Friday, 8 March Dr Henry Beecher Jackson, the Croydon coroner, opened and almost immediately adjourned the inquest in somewhat enigmatic terms, informing the jury:

> I cannot say very much to you today as to the object of your enquiry. The deceased was Mrs Violet Sidney, who died somewhat suddenly on Tuesday, March 5. I am not in a position to put before you medical evidence as to the cause of death, as investigations are now being made.

After taking evidence of identification from Tom Sidney, Dr Jackson adjourned the inquest until 4 April.[14]

This first abortive act in the drama provoked no more than minor interest – 'Croydon Lady's Death – Coroner Adjourns Enquiry', announced the *Croydon Advertiser & Surrey County Reporter*, but the unusual length of the adjournment, coupled with various rumours which had begun to circulate, ensured that journalists would be keeping an ear to the ground, awaiting a possible escalation in the story.

They were not disappointed. By the time Violet Sidney's funeral went ahead on 11 March, a full-scale police investigation was already under way. Detective Inspector Frederick Hedges of Z division, Metropolitan Police, had been called in on the day after Violet's death, and he wasted no time in searching the house and removing a whole selection of articles he considered to be of potential interest in a possible case of poisoning – principally various liquid medications, or liquids which could have been deemed medicinal, such as a bottle containing a small amount of brandy. On the following day he took statements about the events leading up to Violet Sidney's death from Tom Sidney, Grace Duff, Dr Binning, the housekeeper Kathleen Noakes, and Frederick Rose the local chemist, who had provided various medications for the deceased. By 12 March he had extended these enquiries to encompass statements from Margaret Sidney, Dr Robert Elwell, and Arthur Lane, Violet Sidney's gardener and odd-job man. He had also received various samples of food and vomit retained after Violet Sidney's last illness, which he forwarded on to Dr Ryffel of Guy's Hospital for analysis.

By the time Inspector Hedges put together what was to be the first of many reports on the case to his senior officers, he had yet to receive firm confirmation of Dr Ryffel's analysis or Dr Bronte's conclusion as to the cause of death, but he already knew enough to state that, '…in all probability Dr Jackson will press for the exhumations of Vera Sidney and Edmund Duff…'[15]

There are strong grounds to suspect that Croydon journalists were getting their information direct from a member of the local constabulary: the *Croydon Times & Surrey County Mail* ran a story on 20 March headlined 'Three Members of One Family Dead – CID Investigation May Mean Exhumations'; while the *Croydon Advertiser & Surrey County Reporter* devoted two columns to the story on 23 March, explaining in detail how not only Violet and Vera, but also Edmund Duff had died suddenly, under the dramatic headline 'Three Deaths…Scotland Yard Called In'. In the event, exhumation orders were only applied for in respect of the recently deceased mother and daughter.

By now the national dailies had picked up the story. A double exhumation guaranteed headlines and on 23 March *The Times* was among those which ran the story, informing its readers that the post-mortem which had taken place at the Mayday Hospital Croydon, in the early hours of that morning, was conducted by Dr Bernard Spilsbury – a man whose name was already synonymous with sensational murder investigations. By the conclusion of this examination, said *The Times*, 'They were able, it has been stated, to determine the points which they had sought to ascertain.' And on that tantalising note, for the general public at least, the matter had to rest until the formal inquests began.

CHAPTER TWO

'DEVELOPMENTS EXPECTED IN THE NEXT FEW DAYS'

In the early part of 1929 the *Sunday Express* was running a series entitled 'Crimes Without Parallel' and on Sunday, 31 March the instalment happened to be 'The Poisoner with the Bedside Manner' – a lurid tale of Dr Pommerais, who used digitalis on his victim in nineteenth-century France. At that stage, of course, no one was openly printing the word 'poison' in connection with the Sidney case, but it hardly took a giant leap of intellect to arrive at the idea, with newspaper reports full of references to midnight exhumations and organs being sent for analysis. A number of newspapers stressed that the investigations were being carried out under a cloak of 'considerable secrecy', but this did not prevent word of the exhumation getting out, enabling a small crowd to gather outside the cemetery, presumably including at least one reporter who was able to offer what appears to be a first-hand report of the 'eerie scene' as council gravediggers set to work behind the hastily erected screens, with hurricane lamps providing the only illumination.[1]

The workmen reached Violet's coffin at 1 a.m. and Vera's, which lay directly beneath it, was raised shortly afterwards. As the coffins were lifted to the surface, those present, including the detectives and Sir Bernard Spilsbury, stood bareheaded at the graveside and the procession to the mortuary was led by two undertakers' mutes. Once at the mortuary, the coffins were opened and Tom Sidney identified his mother and sister, before Spilsbury commenced his post-mortem examinations.

The involvement of Scotland Yard and a high-ranking pathologist such as Spilsbury only served to underline the gravity of the situation. The Croydon coroner, Dr Henry Beecher Jackson, was already in constant touch with the police and Home Office and took the unusual step of handing over most of the local inquest work to his deputy, Mr E.S. Morey, in order to concentrate on the Sidney case.[2] Dr Jackson had ten years' experience as coroner, having been appointed on the retirement of his father, Dr Thomas Jackson, in 1919.[3] Exhumations were unusual enough to be memorable, so it is likely that Dr Jackson junior could recall an earlier exhumation which had taken place in Croydon, when his father had been the officiating coroner in 1907.

In some ways, this earlier case bore slight resemblances to the current one. The 1907 exhumation was in respect of Mrs Johanna Maria Blume, whose death the previous year at the age of seventy-six had originally been ascribed to a cerebral haemorrhage. Only in May 1907, when the main beneficiary under her will, Richard Brinkley, had been arrested for murdering Richard Beck and Mary Ann Beck, and for attempting to murder Kathleen Beck and Reginald Parker – all by poisoning – did alarm bells start to ring.[4] If Henry Beecher Jackson did recall the Brinkley case, then he may have quailed at the memory – Brinkley was tried for the murders of Richard and Mary Ann Beck, but police files reveal that he was also suspected of murdering not only Mrs Blume, but also a woman called Laura Glenn and a child of his one-time common-law wife, Emily George.[5] With talk already extending to three possible victims in this new case of alleged poisoning, small wonder that Dr Jackson put as much other work as possible on hold.

On the afternoon of 22 March he opened the inquest on Vera Sidney.[6] After the jury of ten men had been empanelled, Dr Jackson explained that when Vera Sidney died in February, a death certificate had been issued and the body buried without his knowledge or involvement. (There was, of course, nothing irregular in this, because Vera's death had been attributed to causes for which her doctor was happy to provide a certificate and there were no attendant suspicious circumstances.) Within minutes of the proceedings getting underway, the coroner initiated what was to be the first of many contentious spats, by stating that Vera's death had occurred in the early hours of 15 February.

'No, sir,' Tom Sidney spoke up from the back of the room. 'She died the previous evening.'

'We shall have to go into that further,' said the coroner. 'I have been informed that it was in the early morning.' He went on to explain that from information he had received, he had deemed it necessary to procure an order for the exhumation which had taken place that morning, but as he was not yet in a position to call any medical evidence, he intended to take only identification evidence and then adjourn the proceedings, which would be reconvened on 18 April.

After the excited headlines of the preceding days, this was something of a damp squib. The twice weekly *Croydon Times & Surrey County Mail*, whose Saturday edition print deadline was too early to include full details of anything taking place on a Friday afternoon, had already promised its readers a special edition of the paper, giving a full report of the inquest proceedings. The plan was shelved when the sensational revelations they clearly anticipated failed to materialise.[7]

Meanwhile the bodies of Violet and Vera Sidney lay in the mortuary at the Mayday Hospital. When the cemetery gates were closed on Thursday afternoon the grave had still been covered with funeral flowers, but later that night these had been moved aside in order to re-open the grave, which was afterwards roughly boarded over. The site of the exhumation became a source of curiosity, with dozens of people tramping into the cemetery to peer at the spot, some of them already waiting at the gates when they were opened on Saturday morning. Late on Sunday afternoon, accompanied by three cars containing police officers and members of the family, the two coffins were returned to the Queen's Road

Cemetery, where they were placed in the Chapel of Rest to lie overnight, before being re-buried the following afternoon. By Monday afternoon there were hardly any members of the public on hand to see the coffins lowered back into the ground without ceremony. Only the undertaker and a Scotland Yard detective stood at the graveside.

By now press and public were agog to see what would happen next. According to the *Croydon Times & Surrey County Mail*, 'developments are expected in the next few days,'[8] and when the inquest on Violet Sidney resumed on 4 April, there was not a seat to be had in the room. In spite of the attendant excitement, at that stage probably not even Coroner Jackson anticipated that this would be just the beginning of a long-running drama, which would dominate not only the local newspapers, but also the lives of all those involved, into the summer and beyond.

Dr Jackson opened by impressing upon the jury the importance of disregarding anything they had seen in the press.[9] Their verdict must be 'founded solely on the evidence you hear in this court'. For the same reason, Dr Jackson explained, he did not intend to give a long description of the events leading up to Mrs Sidney's death – this would emerge from the evidence. He then briefly summarised events as follows:

The deceased had not been very well for some weeks … her daughter … died in February and the deceased had grieved very much for her. Dr Elwell was the deceased's medical attendant and had been calling occasionally to see her. He called at 12.40 on 5 March … and found her rather better than she had been recently. After he left, Mrs Noakes the general servant went into the room to lay the table for lunch and saw her mistress pulling faces. Mrs Noakes asked her what was the matter and Mrs Sidney said the medicine she had just taken had left a nasty taste in her mouth. Dr Elwell had some days before prescribed a tonic and some tablets for the deceased … the deceased ate a little lunch and when Mrs Noakes went to clear the table, the deceased complained of feeling sick. Afterwards she vomited and had an attack of diarrhoea. Dr Elwell and Dr Binning and a specialist from London attended her, but she died the same evening. A post-mortem examination has been carried out and an analysis of the viscera[10] and other substances made and you will have evidence of the result of the examination.

The post-mortem and analysis evidence was not to be forthcoming that day, however.

The first witness to be called was Tom Sidney. The coroner began with some questions to establish the details of the deceased's family, affording Tom Sidney the opportunity to explain that his mother was a widow[11] with two surviving children, himself and Grace, and that a third child, Vera, had recently died. He explained that Vera had lived all her life with her mother, 'they were devotedly attached to one another.'

'As a matter of fact, you were a very happy family, were you not?' prompted Dr Jackson.

'Very,' replied Tom. He then moved on to explain that his mother had a servant living in, Mrs Kathleen Noakes. She had been with his mother only a few months, and about the time of his sister's death there had been some talk of her leaving, but he believed she had been persuaded to stay on. At this there was an interruption from the back of the court, as Mrs Noakes called out, 'I was leaving before Christmas.'

Tom Sidney then went on to say how, after the death of his sister, he had been concerned about his mother's health; initially he thought 'she might only last a few weeks'. Indeed the whole family had been anxious about her, fearing a heart attack or a stroke. His mother had been grieving deeply, he said, and had stated on a number of occasions that she could not live without Vera. Her last remaining close friend had also recently died and she had more than once told Tom that she had no one left in the world but her immediate family. It had been impossible to speak to her for very long without her breaking down. A stroke seemed a particularly strong possibility, as she had suffered with high blood pressure for some time and had recently complained of giddiness. In answer to questions about her mental health, Tom said that so far as he knew, his mother had never suffered from delusions, or mental illness, and there was no history of it in the family. She had never previously threatened or attempted to take her own life and as a member of the Church of England would consider it morally wrong to do so. He did not think she had taken her own life now.

He claimed to have been unaware that Dr Elwell had prescribed any medicine for his mother, although in the days immediately before her death, she had mentioned problems with constipation and that she had taken several aperients[12] for it, with senna pods finally doing the trick. Since Vera's funeral, he had generally called in on her for about twenty minutes every morning, usually seeing her in the dining room, as that was where she sat in the mornings. Latterly she had appeared to be improving and had talked of taking a house by the sea.

On Sunday, 4 March he had been at his mother's house from 3.30 until 6 o'clock.[13] He and his sister Grace had gone for tea and to discuss some business arising out of Vera's will, in respect of which he and Grace were co-executors. In response to a question about how he got inside, Tom said that either his mother or Mrs Noakes always let him into the house – he had given back his key after moving out and as far as he was aware, his sister Grace did not have one either.

He went on to explain that on Monday, 5 March, for the first time since Vera's funeral he had not called at his mother's house in the morning, dropping in instead at about 2 p.m. He could not remember who had answered the door, but he thought it could have been Dr Binning – at any rate, he saw Dr Binning as soon as he entered the hall. He had been surprised to find Dr Binning there, as his mother's usual practitioner was Dr Elwell. Binning explained that he had been called because Violet had been taken suddenly ill and he expressed concern about her condition. Tom went upstairs to her bedroom, with Binning following, and there he found his mother in bed, being tended by his sister Grace. 'Soon after I entered the bedroom, my mother suggested that she had been poisoned. I think she mentioned something about her medicine, but I am not sure whether she mentioned the medicine, or Grace mentioned it.' At some stage Violet also told him that the medicine tasted nasty and gritty.

Tom said he then remained in the house, mostly at his mother's bedside, until she died at 7.15. She was suffering from diarrhoea and vomiting, and complaining of stomach pain and a cold, shivery feeling. He only began to fear his mother might die when he heard the doctors discussing her pulse between 4.30 and 5 o'clock. Earlier in the afternoon she had appeared a little better and he assumed she was going to recover and went down to the dining room for a cup of tea. While there he saw the medicine bottle, standing on the dining room table. He had not touched it, but noticed it had a thick sediment all around the inside. Up until then he had never seen this bottle – he believed that when his mother was taking medicine, she generally kept the bottle on the dining room sideboard, but he could not recall seeing this particular bottle on any of his previous visits.

When the two doctors entered the room, he overheard them discussing the contents of the bottle – the name of the medicine was mentioned, but he couldn't remember what it was. Dr Elwell had said there was 'nothing in it to kill a baby.'

Coroner Jackson pressed Tom to try to recall the name of the medicine, but he could not. 'I cannot remember. If they had said arsenic, I should have known it, because it is an acute poison and usually associated with poisoning.'

Arsenic – the word was finally out in the open.

'What made you mention arsenic, just now?' asked Dr Jackson.

'Because it is one of the few poisons I have known to be used in recent years.'

'Criminally, do you mean?' asked the coroner.

'Yes. I would like to add that no thought of criminal poisoning entered my mind at that time.'

Prompted by the coroner, Tom Sidney explained that he assumed his mother had been accidentally poisoned, either by something she had eaten, or perhaps because her medicine had been dispensed in a dirty bottle. Had his mother not specifically mentioned the medicine he would not have been suspicious of it.

After three and a half hours in the witness chair, Tom Sidney was able to stand down. His place was taken by the only other witness of the day, Dr John Binning, who said he was in partnership with Dr Elwell and practised from 1 Birdhurst Road. Dr Binning explained that although he numbered Tom Sidney, his wife and children among his patients, Violet and Vera Sidney were his partner's patients and he had never attended Violet Sidney professionally before 5 March.

At around 1.40 that day Grace Duff had come to his house, asking him to call on her mother. She said, 'Please come at once, she seems very ill.' Binning said he paused only to put on his coat and collect his bag, arriving at the house within three or four minutes; Mrs Duff had gone on ahead of him and let him in. She showed him straight to the dining room, where he found Violet sitting on a dining chair, looking ashy grey, 'in a stricken condition', holding a basin in her lap, into which she had recently vomited. Within minutes of his arrival, she vomited again and suffered an uncontrolled bout of diarrhoea. She told him her symptoms had begun immediately after lunch and she felt that she had been poisoned, mentioning that when she had taken the last dose of her medicine before lunch, it had left a peculiar taste. Although she felt sick after taking the medicine, she had eaten her lunch as usual.

During this discussion, Mrs Sidney had pointed out the medicine bottle, which was then standing on the sideboard, together with a wine glass. Dr Binning picked up the bottle and noticed that there was just enough liquid left to cover the bottom, and sediment on the inside of the bottle, which had the appearance of sago grains. He extracted the cork and sniffed, but there was no peculiar smell. It was a 4oz bottle, labelled 'F.S. Rose, George Street' (a local chemist) but there was no indication of what it had contained. He replaced the bottle on the sideboard and telephoned Mr Rose, who told him the preparation he had supplied was Metatone.

Dr Binning said he had also considered it possible that the patient was suffering from ptomaine poisoning[14] and asked her what she had eaten for lunch. She told him she had had chicken, bread and butter, milk and water and later that evening he had collected samples of all these to be handed on to the coroner's officer.

Within about twenty minutes of his arrival, Mrs Duff put Mrs Sidney to bed, surrounded by hot water bottles. Mrs Duff told him that she had given her mother an emetic[15] of salt and water and Binning himself gave her an emetic of sodium bicarbonate and water. Tom Sidney had arrived at about 2.15 and, obviously surprised to find his general practitioner there, asked, 'What are you doing here?'

Binning said that from the moment he first saw Mrs Sidney, he thought she was going to die, although he had not told her son and daughter this. At about 3.40 he went to fetch Dr Poynton, a specialist, with whom he returned at about 5 o'clock. In answer to further questions he agreed that both Tom Sidney and Grace Duff seemed anxious that everything possible should be done for their mother; and when someone suggested calling in a specialist, Tom Sidney agreed at once. Binning thought it was probably Dr Elwell who had suggested a specialist.

Dr Elwell had arrived at about 3.30, at which time Dr Binning had shown him the medicine bottle on the sideboard. After discussing the contents of the bottle with his colleague, Binning said he replaced the bottle on the sideboard and it was still standing there when he returned downstairs after Mrs Sidney had died. By then it was 7.30; he put the medicine bottle in his pocket and went to the kitchen to collect the food samples. Kathleen Noakes was there, but made no comment on what he was doing. She did say what a great shock the events had been to her. He did not remember seeing the medicine bottle on the dining table at any time, or hearing Tom Sidney say that someone should take care of the medicine bottle.

Dr Binning took the various samples home with him and kept them under lock and key, until he eventually handed them over to Samuel Clarke, the coroner's officer. He had reported Mrs Sidney's death to the coroner at 11 p.m. on the night she died.

At this point the inquest was adjourned until Friday, 12 April. The proceedings were extensively reported, so it was perhaps no surprise when, on Wednesday morning, Dr Jackson found himself confronted with a hand-delivered letter from Cyril Herbert Kirby, a London solicitor, writing on behalf of Frederick Rose, the Croydon chemist who had dispensed Violet Sidney's last medications.[16] The letter was starchy in tone and complained that Tom Sidney's remark at the inquest, that he thought his mother's illness might have been caused by 'a dirty medicine bottle', 'cast aspersions' on Mr Rose and the way he conducted his business. Mr Rose requested the opportunity to deny the suggestion, preferably at the reconvened hearing in two days time. The bearer of the letter had been instructed to wait for Dr Jackson's reply. By this time, Dr Jackson was already facing a whole variety of pressures in connection with the Sidney case and an irate local chemist was probably the least of his worries. No doubt he sent a placatory letter to Mr Rose's solicitor, having added his client's name to the growing list of witnesses who would be called to appear. Mr Rose would have to wait his turn.

When the inquest recommenced on 12 April, Tom Sidney was recalled to the witness chair to answer a series of questions aimed at establishing without doubt the identity of the remains which had been exhumed.[17] By this means the world at large learnt the times at which Violet's coffin had been lifted from the ground, arrived at the mortuary and had its lid unscrewed in Tom Sidney's presence (3.30 a.m., by which time he had been in attendance at these macabre proceedings for more than three hours). Even the name on the coffin plate was subject to enquiry, with Tom confirming that his mother's middle name had been incorrectly engraved as Amelia, rather than Emelia.

He was followed into the witness chair by Sydney Gardiner, an employee of J.B. Shakespeare & Co., whose evidence took Violet's body step by step from her death at Birdhurst Rise to the mortuary, from the mortuary back to the house (where the coffin lid was screwed down), from the house to St Peter's Church and from there to internment in the cemetery. Gardiner had also been present when the body was exhumed and he too confirmed that the body in the coffin was the same woman whose funerary arrangements he had overseen a couple of weeks previously.

The next witness was Detective Inspector Fred Hedges, who stated that he had gone to 29 Birdhurst Rise on 6 March 1929 with his colleague, Detective Inspector Morrish, and the coroner's officer, Mr Clarke.

'We searched the house from top to bottom,' he announced, producing a copy of the list of items he and his colleagues had seen fit to remove. The list was astonishing in its sheer variety, encompassing a wide selection of medications, from eye ointment to Dr Gregory's Stomach Powder, household products such as Jeyes Fluid, Higgins Photo Mounter, an empty eau de cologne bottle and some skin cream prescribed by a veterinary surgeon, presumably for Violet's cat. Their haul included powders, potions and liquids in every hue from browns and reds, through pinks, to 'cloudy white' and yellow.[18]

The trio had then gone to Dr Binning's house at 1 Birdhurst Road and taken possession of the empty medicine bottle and samples of the deceased's vomit and stools. On the following day Hedges had returned to 29 Birdhurst Rise with Inspector Morrish and Tom Sidney and taken possession of a wine glass which he found on the sideboard, and subsequently handed over to Samuel Clarke on 11 March. On 9 March he was back at the house again, commandeering yet more articles of assumed interest, including another of Violet Sidney's many part-used bottles of medicine, one and a half apples and a packet of Symington's Oxtail Soup Powder, after which he returned to Dr Binning's premises to collect the samples of food which the latter had sequestered on the night of Violet's death. By this time these samples, in particular the four-day-old milk, must have been somewhat unsavoury and it is not easy to understand the thought process which had placed a higher priority on ensuring the prompt collection of an empty bottle of eau de cologne. In addition, Samuel Clarke's presence at this 9 March foray begs the question of why Hedges did not hand the wine glass over to him at this point, rather than retaining it for another forty-eight hours; by now the coroner and jury were probably so bemused by this litany of visits to various premises, and the confiscation of miscellaneous household items, that these oddities escaped them.

Nor had the tireless Hedges finished his retrieval of possible clues. He had also been to obtain the original bottle of Metatone from which Rose the chemist had dispensed Violet's tonic, and on 20 March he and Morrish had visited 59 Birdhurst Rise, the home of Grace Duff, where they had searched the premises and taken possession of yet more bottles, boxes and tins. Later the same day he and Morrish paid a visit to Tom Sidney at 6 South Park Hill Road and added to their collection, which now included a tin marked 'weedkiller' and a box marked 'rat poison'.

The tin of weedkiller was produced and handed over to the jury for their inspection, while Hedges informed them that he had received it from Tom Sidney, who had retrieved it from a shelf in an unlocked garden shed.

At this point Tom Sidney interrupted, 'I think that's wrong, Inspector. I had the key.'

Hedges altered ground fractionally. Mr Sidney had preceded him, he admitted, so he could not be sure whether he had opened the shed door with a key or not. In addition to the weedkiller handed over by Mr Sidney, he had obtained a tin of liquid weedkiller from Arthur Lane, Violet Sidney's gardener. Both lots of weedkiller had been sent to Dr Ryffel for analysis. At this point, the coroner interposed to point out that according to his notes, Mr Sidney himself had informed Inspector Hedges of the existence of the weedkiller, several days before it was actually collected by the police.

Hedges now gave way to Samuel Clarke, who confirmed the various dates on which he had officially received all these items from Hedges. He was followed by John Henry Baker, the mortuary attendant who had assisted Dr Bronte at the original post-mortem on Violet's body. Baker stated that Dr Bronte had removed various organs and placed them in three jars, which had been sealed, labelled, and sent for analysis. There had been a piece of heart, a piece of kidney, a piece of liver, the spleen, stomach and contents, intestines and various other body parts. As Baker worked his way through this list, Grace Duff, clearly distressed, rose and said, 'May I go out just a moment. This is too awful.' The coroner immediately acquiesced and she left the room hurriedly. Baker was the last witness before the lunch adjournment.

Violet's relatives had wisely retained the services of a counsel, Mr William Fearnley-Whittingstall, to represent their interests, and when the proceedings resumed, he asked that Tom Sidney might be allowed to return to the witness chair. Prompted by questions from his counsel, Tom Sidney explained that he had returned home one evening to learn from his wife that a detective had called and questioned her as to whether there was any poison kept in the house. She had answered in the negative, having forgotten that they had some Eureka Weed Killer in the shed, probably because it had not been used for some time. He had been using that sort of weedkiller for about fifteen years, but only on an occasional basis, when the weeds got bad. The tin in question had not been used for about eighteen months. At all events, as soon as his wife mentioned the detective's visit, he rang Inspector Hedges to let him know about the weedkiller in his shed. He had used this same brand of weedkiller when he lived with his mother and there had been some empty tins lying about there for years – in fact he had seen one in his mother's tool shed only the day before yesterday.

The coroner wanted to know more about this tin in Violet's shed and although assured by Tom that it was empty aside from a little rust, concluded that its presence on the premises where death had occurred made it a sufficiently important item to merit further examination.

From weedkiller Tom's evidence moved to his sister Vera's will. He explained that his mother had been left £2,000, which would now be split equally between himself and his sister Grace. Vera had left Grace £2,000 in her own right, himself £1,000 and the residue, a sum just in excess of £2,000, was to be divided equally between Vera's five nieces and nephews.

Finally came the evidence the hacks had been awaiting: Dr John Henry Ryffel came to the witness chair and stated his credentials. He was, he said, an official Home Office Analyst, based at Guys Hospital, who had previous experience of analysing human remains for coroners' courts, including several cases of poisoning. He had tested parts of various organs of the late Violet Sidney and found nearly 2½ grains[19] of arsenic in the body in total. He explained that arsenic is a rapidly expelled poison, but the amount remaining in the body was ample to cause death – 3 grains was a fatal dose. In his opinion, the poison had been taken no more than twelve hours before death. He had examined samples of the deceased's hair and fingernails and found no evidence that she had received any previous doses of arsenic.

He then moved to the bottle discovered on the sideboard. When he received it, it had still contained a small amount of liquid and on analysis he discovered that this residual liquid contained 1 grain of arsenic. He had not measured the amount of liquid he managed to extract from the bottle, but estimated it to be less than ¼ of a teaspoonful. From this he calculated that in a dose of 2 teaspoonfuls, there would have been 8 grains of arsenic. The liquid in the bottle had been a deep red colour and he had noticed some slight sediment, which in his opinion looked nothing like sago grains. Dr Ryffel had also received numerous other bottles, jars, tins and so forth from the coroner's officer, but none of them had tested positive for arsenic.

The small amount of sediment found in the wine glass recovered from 29 Birdhurst Rise had also been analysed and was 'rich in arsenic' – although the quantities involved had been too small to measure. Finally he had tested samples of the solid and liquid weedkillers submitted to him and both had contained arsenic (which was hardly surprising, given that arsenic was among their stated ingredients).

It was the sensation the papers had been waiting for. 'Arsenic Found in Both Body and Medicine Bottle', screamed the *Croydon Times & Surrey County Mail*,[20] a headline taken up to a greater or lesser extent by all the London-based dailies and Sundays.

The resumption of the inquest was eagerly awaited, like the next instalment of a lurid serial in a weekly magazine, and five days later the major cast members assembled for the next episode. Clarke and Hedges were briefly recalled to confirm the lists of articles which had been handed over to Dr Ryffel, before a new character was introduced to the proceedings.[21]

Owing to the fact that Arthur Henry Lane was 'very deaf and semi-blind' he was given a seat closer than usual to Dr Jackson, in order to better hear the coroner's questions. He confirmed that he was a jobbing gardener, who had worked half a day per week for Violet Sidney for the past ten years, going to 29 Birdhurst Rise every Saturday morning, summer and winter alike. He had performed a similar service for her daughter Mrs Duff, he said, up until Whitsun the previous year.

'Have you not worked for her since?' asked Dr Jackson.

'Well, I think all last summer. Anyhow till she moved.'

'When did she move?'

'Last October.'

If Lane had been introduced specifically to provide some knockabout comedy, Central Casting could scarcely have found anyone better suited to the role. After another failed attempt to clarify precisely at what point his employment with Mrs Duff had ceased, Dr Jackson asked if Lane had ever used any weedkiller during his decade working at 29 Birdhurst Rise.

'No,' replied Lane.

'Did you hear my question?' asked Dr Jackson.

'I heard it.'

'Did Mrs Sidney keep any weedkiller on the premises?'

'Never.'

The coroner now handed Lane the old Eureka tin (which had been retrieved on the coroner's instructions immediately after the previous hearing) and asked the gardener whether he had ever seen it at Mrs Sidney's house. 'Never,' the witness insisted. When Dr Jackson pursued the point, again showing Lane the tin and repeating the question, the old man made no reply.

'You have got a lot deafer, you know, these last two minutes,' Jackson said, at which Arthur Lane restated a firm denial that he had ever seen the tin.

The coroner tried a different tack, gradually drawing from the witness the reluctant agreement that whenever he worked for Mrs Sidney, he had always used the tools which belonged to her and were kept in the shed, ('was it a big shed, or a small shed?' asked the coroner. 'A medium sized shed,' came the reply); that he had always fetched the tools from the shed and put them back in the shed and was thus in and out of the shed in which the tin of weedkiller had been kept, week in week out, summer and winter, but Lane still insisted he had never seen the tin. Mrs Sidney had used salt for weedkiller, he said. Eventually a kind of compromise was reached, by which Lane conceded that he might not have seen the tin, because it was quite dark in the shed.

From the shed, the coroner moved to the house itself. Had Lane ever been inside, he asked? 'Never.' At this Inspector Hedges leant across and whispered something to the witness.

'Leave him to me, Mr Hedges, he can give his own evidence,' said Dr Jackson. 'I don't want any suggestions.'

After further coaxing from the coroner, Lane reluctantly agreed that he had sometimes taken wood down to the cellar, or entered by the front door and walked through to the back, although he would not admit to having been inside the house since before Christmas. When asked whether he had ever talked with Mrs Noakes, he reluctantly conceded that he had – although never about Mrs Sidney. Dr Jackson was becoming increasingly impatient. He reminded Lane that he was on oath and must tell the truth. Eventually it emerged that after Violet Sidney's death, Mrs Noakes had told him about the episode of the nasty-tasting medicine.

The coroner now showed him yet another tin. This one the old man recognised at once as a tin of Noble's Liquid Weed Killer which he had recently given up to the police. He told the coroner he had had it about six months, having obtained it from Mrs Duff. It had been lying around in her garden and she had asked him to take it away, because of the danger to her children, so he had taken it home and kept it in his own shed ever since. Asked about the condition in which he had received it, Lane told the coroner that the cork had already been taken out and there was a funnel in the neck. He had carried it home in this condition, managing not to spill any of the contents, in spite of the tin being almost full – a feat in which he clearly took some degree of pride.

'Did you not cork the neck of the tin, before you took it home?' asked a presumably incredulous Dr Jackson.

'No.'

'Wasn't that a silly thing to do? You knew it was dangerous stuff?'

'Yes.'

Since acquiring the weedkiller, Lane said he had used only about a teaspoonful, to put on meat to poison some rats in his shed.

The coroner changed tack, enquiring if Mrs Sidney had been in the habit of doing much gardening. Lane said that she had not – he had been responsible for all the digging, weed killing and also for planting the vegetable seeds. The vegetable seeds had been purchased by Tom Sidney, who then handed them over to Lane. The coroner now pointed out a packet of carrot seeds inside the empty weedkiller tin, which the witness had so vehemently denied ever seeing. Lane agreed that the seeds were the ones Tom Sidney had given him. The packet was dated 1927, which, the coroner pointed out, meant that the tin could not have lain unnoticed for years as Lane had tried to suggest. 'You can't say how the packet got there?'

'No, I can't.'

Inspector Hedges was recalled and deposed that he had taken possession of this tin from the shed at 29 Birdhurst Rise, after Tom Sidney had mentioned it in his evidence at the previous sitting. Although it had originally contained weed-killer, it was now empty apart from the packet of carrot seeds and he had not originally attached any importance to it. It is clear from the tone of his evidence that Hedges was irritated by the whole issue of the old Eureka tin – his original haul from the scene had included various empty receptacles of one sort of another, so it is a fair guess that if he had gone into the shed and discovered a tin which had obviously contained poison at some stage, he would have removed it. Thus by inference, Tom Sidney's drawing attention to this object considerably undermined his original extravagant claim to have searched the premises 'from top to bottom'.

The next witness was Kathleen Noakes, who stated that she was now living at 44 Scarbrook Road, Croydon, and was the wife of Robert Henry Noakes, an able seaman in the Royal Navy who had taken divorce proceedings against her. She confirmed that she had been the only servant at 29 Birdhurst Rise, having worked there from August 1928 until the death of Mrs Sidney.

Asked about Violet's reaction to her daughter's death, she agreed that Violet had grieved very deeply for Vera.

'Used she to talk to you about her frequently?'

'No, not a lot.'

'She did say something I suppose?'

'She once said, "I don't know how I'm going to live without her".'

'Did you like your mistress?'

'Very much.'

'And you were happy there?'

'Yes.'

Kathleen Noakes confirmed that Mrs Sidney ran the household herself. There was no charwoman, so Mrs Noakes did everything, although Violet helped when a room was being 'turned out' by doing some dusting, or helping to lay things on a bed or a table. The routine was to turn the dining room out once a fortnight. Mrs Sidney would move things from the sideboard to the table, one of them would do the dusting, then Mrs Noakes would generally put things back. It had last been done the Wednesday before Violet died, at which time Mrs Noakes had not noticed either a medicine bottle or a wine glass. Wine glasses were not normally kept in the dining room, but in the housemaid's pantry on the ground floor, which had a sink with hot and cold running water, which Mrs Sidney used among other things for doing the flowers.

Mrs Noakes was then asked when she first knew that Mrs Sidney was taking a tonic and recalled a morning some time after Vera's funeral, when Dr Elwell had called. After he had gone, Mrs Sidney mentioned that he had prescribed her a tonic, which she remarked would probably not do her much good – the implication, as understood by Kathleen Noakes, being that her main problem was actually constipation. Shortly after the doctor's visit an errand boy arrived with two packages, one small and the other obviously a bottle of medicine. Mrs Noakes straight away put them on a silver tray and took them to her mistress, at which Mrs Sidney said, 'That's my medicine.' Mrs Noakes did not see her unwrap the packages, or see what she did with them afterwards. She was absolutely clear that she never actually saw Mrs Sidney taking any kind of medicine in all the time she worked for her.

The coroner now read aloud the instructions from the medicine bottle: 'Two teaspoons to be taken four times a day before meals, in a wine glass full of water. Did Mrs Sidney have four meals a day?' he asked.

Mrs Noakes said she did. They were all taken in the dining room except afternoon tea. She had no idea whether Mrs Sidney had been in the habit of taking the medicine before or after her meal. She had never been asked to get a wine glass, or water with which to take the medicine, but Mrs Sidney could have got both herself from the housemaid's pantry. The witness agreed that the medicine bottle might have stood on the sideboard without her noticing it, as the sideboard was 'crowded with silver and things', but equally there were numerous other shelves and places in the house where it could have been kept. She agreed that she might have told Inspector Hedges that she dusted the sideboard every day, but in fact she only did it every three or four days. She had once seen Mrs Sidney descending the stairs carrying a wine glass, and on the Saturday before Mrs Sidney died, she had observed her making up a senna mixture in the housemaid's pantry. However, Mrs Noakes thought that if Mrs Sidney had been regularly using a wine glass to take medicine, she would at some point have seen her washing it up.

The coroner then asked Kathleen Noakes about visitors to the house. Mrs Noakes agreed that both Tom Sidney and Grace Duff appeared very attached to their mother; they both visited every day, usually in the morning, when they would sit with their mother in the dining room. Some days Mrs Duff returned in the afternoon. Tom Sidney's wife also came sometimes and Mrs Duff's children came on Saturdays and Sundays. On Sunday, 4 March, Mrs Anderson, the new curate's wife, had come to tea at the same time Mr Sidney was there. In answer to another query, Mrs Noakes confirmed that she had admitted Tom Sidney to the house that afternoon, but couldn't recall which room she had shown him into, or where her mistress was at the time.

Violet Sidney had seemed to Mrs Noakes to be in her usual health throughout Sunday afternoon and evening. She had not heard her mistress moving about during the night and first heard her go to the bathroom the next morning at about 8.30. Mrs Sidney came down to breakfast at about 9 o'clock, when she made her own boiled egg and coffee (there was a gas ring in the dining room) then left her dirty breakfast dishes on a butler's tray outside the dining room door as usual, for Mrs Noakes to wash up. The items on the tray had not included a wine glass. A little later Mrs Sidney brought a slate into the kitchen with her orders for the day, after which she went upstairs to prepare her bedroom for turning out by Mrs Noakes.

During the morning Mrs Duff called in very briefly and when passing the open dining room door, Mrs Noakes overheard Mrs Sidney asking her daughter to bring in some butter and a reel of thread. A few minutes later, Mrs Sidney came up to her bedroom where Mrs Noakes was working. She took something out of a drawer and asked, 'Why have you got that window open?' Mrs Noakes had apologised and closed the offending aperture.

Dr Elwell called just before lunchtime and Mrs Noakes let him in and showed him into the dining room. He only stayed about five or ten minutes, letting himself out. It was then getting on for 1 o'clock and, almost immediately afterwards, Mrs Noakes entered the dining room to lay the table for lunch and found Mrs Sidney pulling awful faces. She was standing by the sideboard, where Mrs Noakes saw her put a glass down next to a medicine bottle. When asked what the matter was, Mrs Sidney said, 'My last dose of medicine tasted so nasty.' Mrs Noakes asked whether she had shaken the bottle, to which her mistress replied that she did not think she had.

Mrs Noakes then served lunch as usual; a leg of roast chicken, cooked the previous week; brown bread and butter; milk and water to drink and a pudding made from rolled oats. Mrs Sidney took about half an hour over her lunch and when Mrs Noakes returned to the room, she found her part-way through eating an apple.

When Violet subsequently said she felt sick but was unable to vomit, Mrs Noakes brought a bowl from the scullery and Mrs Sidney sat with it on her lap. About this time Mrs Duff returned with the reel of thread and the butter and was admitted into the house by Mrs Noakes. She mixed a cup of salt and water for her mother, saying perhaps that would make her sick, and maybe then she would feel better. Mrs Duff telephoned for Dr Elwell, but as Dr Elwell was not at home, she said she would run down for Dr Binning, and ran out at once, saying she wouldn't be long. She was back within a few minutes, saying the doctor would arrive soon. Mrs Noakes stayed with Mrs Sidney all the time from Mrs Duff giving her mother salt water, until the arrival of the doctor. During that time Mrs Sidney was sick twice and also had very bad diarrhoea where she sat. At some point after Mrs Sidney vomited she said, 'I believe I've been poisoned Kate.'

Dr Binning examined Mrs Sidney in the dining room and after that Mrs Duff put her to bed. Tom Sidney arrived while Mrs Sidney was being put to bed, Dr Elwell came later on and then a specialist.

Mrs Noakes also confirmed that Mrs Sidney had not been out of the house since Miss Vera died three weeks before. In answer to further questions, the cook stated that so far as she knew, there had not been any poison in the house – she did not recognise the weedkiller tin, but claimed that she seldom had any cause to enter the woodshed.

At the coroner's request she gave details of her previous employment, as a domestic servant and working in a home for sick children. Although she had been described as a nurse there, she said that she was not a nurse and her duties had never included giving medicine. She had never been dismissed from a post. In October she had originally given Mrs Sidney notice to leave on 29 November, but Miss Vera had persuaded her to stay on until someone else could be found. At this juncture the inquest was adjourned for a further five days.

CHAPTER THREE

SONS AND DAUGHTERS,
CHEMISTS AND DOCTORS

The adjournment of the inquest on Violet Sidney was by no means the end of the Croydon Poisoning drama for that week, because next day the inquest into Vera Sidney's death was resumed.

Grace Duff, who had yet to testify at her mother's inquest, now became one of the first witnesses to appear at her sister's.[1] Before they heard from Mrs Duff, however, the jury were addressed by the coroner, who issued them with a similar warning to the one he had given their counterparts at Violet's inquest, reminding them to disregard anything except the evidence presented at the official proceedings. Their task, said Dr Jackson, was to determine whether Vera Sidney had died from natural causes and if they decided she had not, then to say whether she died by her own hand, accidentally or from some form of homicide. At this stage he would add that death had taken place either just before or just after midnight on 14 February. The deceased had been unwell since the beginning of that week, although on Wednesday 13th she had been well enough to spend some time seeing to her motor car, the radiator of which was frozen. When she returned home that afternoon, she suffered from some diarrhoea and vomiting; her illness worsened and although attended by her own doctor, a second doctor and a specialist, she died.

Grace Duff's evidence began with a rehearsal of the relationships and addresses of various family members. She explained that she had been in the habit of visiting her mother and Vera and they her, 'every other day or so.' Her brother Tom had also been a frequent visitor to his mother's home.

She described Vera as having been a generally healthy woman, fond of outdoor sports (particularly golf) and mentioning that she kept a motor car which she drove herself. She was normally of a cheerful temperament, had not suffered from mental illness or depression and had no worries, except that Grace felt she had recently been getting worried about her health, because lately she 'could not do so much', and in Grace's view had been 'overdoing it' for some time. She had never threatened to take her own life.

'Did you ever think she would be likely to do so?' asked the coroner.

'No.'

'Do you think now that she has done so?'

'No.'

'Was she very attached to your mother?'

'Yes.'

'And was your mother passionately fond of her?'

'Yes.'

At this point, Grace broke down and wept. The coroner gave her a moment or two to recover, before continuing the interrogation. His questions now moved to the period leading up to Vera's death, starting with Sunday, 10 February, when Grace had seen Vera during the evening at their mother's house. She was 'fairly all right,' Grace said, although she had not been feeling well for some days, having had a cold and cough and being bothered by the rheumatism in her shoulders which had been troubling her for a couple of years. Grace was uncertain whether or not she had seen her sister on Monday, but she had been in her company twice on Tuesday. The first time was during the early afternoon, when Grace had popped in for about fifteen minutes to find Vera in bed. She had seemed very poorly, complaining that her eyes could hardly bear the light and she had been sick all night. She also mentioned that both the cook and the cat had been sick. When Grace asked what they had all eaten, Vera said she had had some soup at suppertime on Monday, but that Kate Noakes had been sick before having the soup. Since Grace assumed that the cat would not have been given soup, she thought there might be gastric flu in the house, although her mother had not suffered from any sickness.

Grace returned to her mother's house later the same evening, offering to go and empty the radiator in Vera's car as she knew Vera was worried about it, but Vera declined, saying that Grace didn't know enough about cars. By then Vera appeared a little better and had been up for a while.

When Grace telephoned her mother's house the next morning, Kate Noakes answered the phone and informed her that Vera had gone out to 'see after her car'. Grace said she was 'horrified' to hear this. A little later her mother had called Grace to ask her if she would meet her aunt, Mrs Greenwell, from the station. Mrs Greenwell (the late Thomas Sidney's sister) was expected for lunch and Vera had originally been going to meet her, but Violet thought she wouldn't be up to it. Grace recalled that Violet seemed to be very worried about Vera – who was still out – and expressed the view that she ought not to have gone out in the cold, having been ill in bed the day before.

Grace met her aunt at South Croydon station as requested and escorted her to no.29. They arrived at about 1 p.m. and were shown into the drawing room, where Vera and Violet were sitting. Vera did not look well and when Grace asked how she was, replied that she felt rotten. She said she had been turning the handle of her car, but felt so bad that she had to stop. Grace stayed about five minutes, leaving before the others sat down to lunch.

It had been arranged that Vera and Mrs Greenwell would go to Grace's for tea, but Vera phoned part-way through the afternoon to say that she felt too unwell to come round, mentioning that she had been dreadfully sick again. Grace was not sure, but thought Vera also said that Mrs Greenwell had been sick. She went straight round to her mother's house, arriving at about 3 p.m. Kate Noakes opened the door and Grace said, 'Whatever's the matter with the family?' To which Kate Noakes replied something to the effect of: 'It's that veal I expect.'

Grace found Vera and Mrs Greenwell in the drawing room, both of them looking miserable and cold. Violet suggested that castor oil might help and began to hunt about for some. When she could not immediately find any, Grace offered to fetch a bottle from home, but was no longer able to recall whether she fetched it before or after seeing Mrs Greenwell back to the station. By the time she returned from the station, Vera was in bed and vomiting again, which she continued to do on and off throughout the evening, although she appeared to become a little better later. By this time Violet had given Vera both castor oil and some brandy and Dr Elwell had been summoned.

When Grace arrived at the house the next morning, she discovered that her sister was still in bed and Violet had sat up with her all night, not even bothering to get undressed. Grace was now also worried about her mother, who appeared worn out. At that stage, Vera was not complaining of stomach pain, but did say she felt dreadfully weak, as if she had no strength.

Grace was in and out of her mother's house several times that morning and in the afternoon she called in briefly on her brother Tom, who was also unwell, having had a cold for a while – she couldn't remember for exactly how long. His children had been ill too. Tom had appeared very concerned about Vera, saying, 'It's this awful gastric flu which is going round.'

Grace returned to her mother's again that evening and learned that a specialist had been to see Vera. The specialist had told Violet that Vera was 'critically ill'. No one discussed a specific diagnosis with Grace, but she had heard one of the doctors mention gastric influenza and say that Vera was dehydrated. During the day Vera had been complaining of pains in her legs and she was now in great pain, restless and 'only half and half' conscious. Grace went home to get her things, preparatory to staying overnight and sharing the nursing with her mother, but by the time she got back, the services of a professional nurse had been obtained. A second nurse arrived to relieve the first, just before Vera died, and between them Dr Binning or Dr Elwell had been in attendance the whole afternoon and evening. The doctors had eventually persuaded Violet to leave the bedside, so she and Grace were downstairs when Vera died and Dr Elwell came down to break the news. They went upstairs with him immediately and, as they entered the room, Grace thought she heard the clock strike midnight.

On this grim note, the inquest adjourned for lunch. After the interval, Grace was recalled to the witness chair, and the coroner asked whether she had entertained any suspicions about the cause of Vera's death. Grace said she had wondered about the soup and veal – but when she asked Dr Elwell whether there would need to be an inquest, he said, 'No. There is no question about it.'

Asked about the domestic routine at no.29, Grace said she personally had never had anything to do with food preparation and very rarely entered the kitchen. The last time she had been in there was Christmas 1928, when she went in to wish Kate Noakes a Happy Christmas.

So far as she knew, her sister's life was not insured, but she had been aware that her sister had made a will and although she had not known the terms, she had thought it very likely she would be a beneficiary. Asked by the coroner if she had known how much her sister was worth at the time of her death, Grace said she thought probably £4,000–£5,000.

Those who had been following the two cases closely were by now aware that only one major participant had yet to sit in the witness chair. This was Dr Elwell, and during the afternoon he became the second witness to give evidence about Vera Sidney's death. Dr Elwell told the court he practised at 14 Addiscombe Road, Croydon. He had attended Violet and Vera Sidney since 1920, but prior to her final illness, he had not seen Vera Sidney professionally since February 1928, when she had been in bed with influenza. During that illness he had called on her about six times, but there had been no vomiting involved on that occasion.

On the evening of Wednesday, 13 February he returned home to find that a message had been left, asking him to call on Vera Sidney. He arrived at 29 Birdhurst Rise at about 9 p.m. and found Vera suffering from vomiting and diarrhoea. She had a temperature of 108 and no detectable pulse. She was given champagne and bicarbonate, both of which she brought back up, then an injection of morphia. At around 1 o'clock she complained of pain in her right leg. When he left at about 2 o'clock the next morning, she seemed generally improved and more comfortable. However, when he returned at 9 o'clock on Thursday, she was still in a very collapsed condition. Her temperature was 100, she was very restless and complained of pain in her legs and a catch in her throat – but not of any feelings of suffocation or burning.

Dr Elwell consulted with his partner Dr Binning and they agreed that an expert should be called in – Dr Charles Bolton, who specialised in gastritis and intestinal diseases. Dr Bolton attended at about 3 o'clock and gave the opinion that Miss Sidney was suffering from gastro-intestinal influenza, aggravated by dilation of the heart, brought on by violent exercise (with the car starting handle) on Wednesday morning.

Dr Elwell stayed with the patient almost continuously until she died at about 12.30 on 15 February. When he first arrived on Wednesday evening, Mrs Duff and Mrs Sidney had been in the house, but he could not remember whether Mrs Duff was still there when he left in the early hours of Thursday morning. Both women had been very anxious and wanted to do everything they could for Vera. Mrs Sidney and her daughters had always seemed very attached to one another. He confirmed that he had known Vera Sidney quite well – she had sometimes taken massage cases for him. In his opinion she was not the sort of person to have taken her own life.

According to Dr Elwell, Vera had not mentioned anything to him about suspecting that her illness was due to something she had eaten; the question of food poisoning had never entered his mind and there were no symptoms of chronic arsenical poisoning.

At this point, Inspector Hedges had a swift consultation with the coroner, who then asked, 'Were all the symptoms you observed consistent with acute arsenical poisoning?'

'Not all. In the first place there was the temperature, which was enormous for a poisoning case.' Pressed by the coroner, he admitted that he did not think he had ever seen a case of acute arsenical poisoning, but added that dilation of the heart was not a symptom of poisoning either.

At this stage the inquest was adjourned until 27 April, some five days after the inquest on Violet was due to resume. This was to become the pattern throughout the spring and early summer, with sittings alternating between one case and the other, averaging one a week, keeping the story in the news.

On 22 April Grace Duff and Dr Elwell were under the spotlight again, but this time the coroner was enquiring into Violet Sidney's death.[2] Much of Grace's evidence merely confirmed what had gone before: her mother had spent mornings in the dining room and afternoons in the drawing room, she had been extremely attached to Vera and, after her death, said she did not know how she could go on without her. When the coroner asked whether Grace herself had been very much attached to both her mother and sister, she could only nod, with tears in her eyes. She agreed that her mother had been unwell with a cold and had not been out of the house since Vera's death.

Asked about Violet's mental state, Grace told the coroner that her mother had never suffered delusions or mental illness, or threatened to take her own life, and the idea that she might do so had never occurred to Grace, except perhaps on the night Vera died, when her mother was '…beside herself and locked her door. We were terrified outside, but except for that, I am perfectly sure she would never have done such a thing.' Indeed she had heard her mother say that suicide was wrong and cowardly – 'she …was too good and religious to do it.' In the days immediately before she died, Violet had appeared to be getting better and on the morning of her death she had mentioned something about going to stay by the sea for a while.

At this point the coroner was informed that Mr Rose the chemist had arrived, so Grace Duff stood down while he gave his evidence. Mr Rose – clearly taking no chances with his professional reputation – was being represented by a barrister. Answering questions posed by his own counsel, the coroner, and Mr Fearnley-Whittingstall on behalf of the relatives, he provided the fullest possible background on the now infamous bottle of medicine.

He firstly explained that Metatone was a patent medicine manufactured by Messrs Park, Davies & Co., so dispensing it was merely a question of pouring the prescribed quantity from a large bottle in the dispensary into a small bottle for the patient. Dr Elwell had prescribed Metatone for Mrs Sidney on 25 February and

Rose had dispensed the prescription himself. It was for 4fl oz – sixteen doses, to be taken four times a day – thus if the medicine was still being taken on 5 March, it had evidently only been taken in sporadic doses. Metatone contained ⅟25 grain of strychnine, but no arsenic. He did keep arsenic in the dispensary in both solid and liquid forms, but had never dispensed anything for Mrs Sidney which contained arsenic and it would have been absolutely impossible for any arsenic to find its way into Mrs Sidney's Metatone.

When the pills and medicine Dr Elwell had ordered were ready, they were wrapped in white paper, sealed at each end with sealing wax and then delivered to Mrs Sidney's home by one of the four delivery boys employed by Mr Rose – after this length of time he was unable to establish which of them had undertaken this particular delivery. Rose was confident that the bottle used for Violet Sidney's medicine had been absolutely clean. Medicine bottles were always held up to the light in the dispensary before filling, to make doubly sure that they had been properly washed. The bottle from which he had obtained the Metatone had been nearly full on 25 February and he had subsequently dispensed large quantities from it, without anyone else suffering any ill effects. He himself had tasted Metatone and it would never be described as tasting gritty, nor had he ever observed any sediment in it.

Mr Rose's contribution was followed by the brief appearance of William Stafford Sidney, Violet's brother-in-law, who, together with Vera, had been appointed executor of Violet's will. Her last will had been made on 13 June 1927, he said, and although it was not proved yet, she had left probably in the region of £9,000–£10,000. The will provided for one or two personal and household effects to go to Vera, her jewellery to be split equally between her two daughters and the remainder of her estate to be divided equally between all three children.

Grace Duff was then recalled. The coroner first asked whether her mother had been comfortably off financially, which, given the evidence of William Sidney, was surely somewhat academic – by 1929 standards, assets of £10,000 represented a small fortune to most people.[3] Not surprisingly, Grace answered in the affirmative.

The coroner returned to the medicine. Had Grace been aware that Dr Elwell had prescribed something for her mother? She said she had; her mother had mentioned it, probably the day after the doctor's visit. She had never actually seen her mother taking the medicine or noticed the bottle anywhere, although she could not say on oath that it had not been on the sideboard. Nor was she altogether sure where her mother kept medicines – a small cupboard in the sideboard was a possibility, or perhaps her bedroom. Since enquiries had been afoot, her son John had mentioned seeing a bottle of medicine on the chest of drawers in his grandmother's bedroom a few days before she died, although whether or not this had been the Metatone he could not say. The first time she had definitely seen the Metatone bottle herself was in the dining room, when her attention was drawn to it by her mother and the maid, on the day of her mother's death.

Nor had she noticed a wine glass about the place; her mother would not normally have a wine glass on the table unless there was a party, nor would she have one in her bedroom. She was sure Kathleen Noakes had never been involved in administering medicine to her mother and she herself had never given or prepared medicine for her mother either. 'Mother was rather reserved and old-fashioned and would have preferred to take her medicine alone.' The only exception to this had been the night of Vera's death, when Grace helped the nurse persuade her mother to take a sleeping draught.

When the coroner asked whether she had recently eaten any meals in her mother's house, Grace said she had not – although she might have had a cup of tea there. She had definitely not been to her mother's house for tea the day before she died. (This question was prompted by Tom Sidney's previous evidence that he and Grace had both been to tea with his mother on 4 March – a statement he subsequently recalled to be incorrect.)

This brought them to the day of Violet's death itself and here Grace's account both added to and slightly contradicted the versions already offered by other witnesses. According to Grace, she called in just after 10 a.m., staying no more than a few minutes as she had a busy day ahead. Her impression was that her mother looked somewhat better than she had done recently. While she was there, Violet told her that Tom had been to tea the day before. She also mentioned that the curate's wife had called on her and there had been a visit from a plumber.

As her daughter was going to the shops, Violet asked Grace to bring in some butter and thread and also to call at the registry to enquire about a replacement for Kathleen Noakes, who had given notice to leave on 14 March. Grace did not recall her mother going upstairs while she was there, but said it was hard to remember, one way or the other. Similarly, she thought her mother saw her out as far as the hall, but could not be sure. She was sure that her mother had not given her any money for the shopping, the intention being to settle up later.

After this Grace returned home to bath the baby, then went out shopping. On her way back to her mother's house at between 1.15 and 1.30 she encountered her brother Tom, with one of his children, coming down the road from the direction of their mother's house, but he told her that he hadn't gone in, as it was lunchtime and the child would annoy her.

When Grace arrived at the house, Kathleen Noakes answered the front door and Grace asked if her mother was still eating lunch, to which Mrs Noakes replied that she had finished lunch, mentioning nothing at all about Violet feeling unwell. Grace found her mother in the dining room. 'She was sitting in a chair, with a handkerchief to her mouth. I thought she was dead, her head and her face were deathly white. She looked up at me and she said, "I have had some poison".'

Having heard from Violet about the unpleasant taste of the medicine, Grace briefly examined the bottle on the sideboard, which she uncorked and sniffed, deciding it smelt funny. She first asked Kate Noakes to get salt water from the kitchen, then rang Dr Elwell; finding him out, she ran down the road for Dr Binning, asking him to come at once. (In 1929 many people who owned a telephone would refrain from routinely using it over short distances – not only were calls relatively expensive, but there was often a slight delay while calls were connected via the exchange. Grace's instinct to go for the doctor on foot was thus not all that remarkable.)

After alerting Dr Binning, Grace ran straight back to her mother's house without waiting for him, but he arrived only two or three minutes behind her. He examined Violet and then Grace helped her to bed. Her brother arrived just after this and she heard her mother telling him about the medicine and saying she thought she had been poisoned. No one mentioned arsenic and according to Grace the possibility of criminal poisoning never occurred to her at all.

After the coroner had taken her through the events of the evening, which she remembered much as the previous witnesses had done, he returned to financial matters. How much had Grace Duff known about her mother's will? Grace said she was aware that her mother had made a will, but she didn't know the contents – it had never been discussed. She did not know exactly how much money her mother had, nor whether her mother's life was insured. She agreed that her mother had been helping her financially for some time, making her an allowance of £50 per year and occasionally settling bills for her.

Grace was then shown the tin of liquid weedkiller which the police had confiscated from Arthur Lane. Grace explained that it had been purchased by her husband before he died, then been put in the cellar of her previous house and forgotten about. After the move to 59 Birdhurst Rise, she and Vera had discovered the tin and put it out in the garden until Mr Lane next called, when she asked him to take it away. She had never taken any of the weedkiller out of the tin herself. Shown the tin of weedkiller taken from Tom's garden shed, she said she had not known he had it.

Dr Elwell was the last witness that day. He told the court how he had called to see Mrs Sidney on 15 February (the day of Vera's death) and found her very distressed. He called again several times and on 25 February he prescribed Metatone tonic and some tablets. When he visited on 27 February Mrs Sidney mentioned that the tonic had arrived, but said she had not started taking it. On 5 March he called between 12.45 and 1 p.m., staying only for about seven minutes. He found Mrs Sidney somewhat better; her blood pressure and pulse had improved, but she was complaining of a loss of appetite. When he asked her about the tonic, she admitted that she had 'not been very regular with it recently.' He told her it would not do her much good if she did not take it. He did not notice a medicine bottle or a wine glass while he was there.

Later that afternoon he returned home to find a message asking him to attend Mrs Sidney, which he did, arriving at about 3.20, when he found her in a collapsed state, with a temperature of less than 97. (His thermometer did not go any lower.) A specialist, Dr Poynton, was called in and suggested various possibilities, including a metallic poisoning of some kind: both copper and arsenic were mentioned. He and Dr Binning had done their best for the patient, but she died at around 7.30. He considered that all the symptoms observed on 5 March could be accounted for by acute arsenical poisoning.

By now the number of column inches devoted to the case was increasing. Pictures of Vera and Violet were starting to appear in the national Sunday papers.[4]

Strangers came to Birdhurst Rise with the express purpose of staring up at the house in which Violet and Vera had lived and died, and photographers snapped Tom Sidney and Grace Duff as they entered and left the coroner's hearings.

On 27 April the court's attentions returned to the death of Vera Sidney. The first witness of the day was Sydney Gardiner,[5] and presumably mindful of Grace Duff's distress during the description of her mother's exhumation and post-mortem, Dr Jackson offered both herself and her brother the opportunity of leaving the room while this part of the evidence was given. Grace took advantage of this suggestion, but Tom stayed put while the undertaker's man gave his evidence, mentioning at one point that the plate on Vera's coffin gave her date of death as 14 February – 'Bear that carefully in mind, gentleman,' Dr Jackson cautioned the jury. 'You have had evidence from the doctor that death took place on 15th.' One can well imagine the exasperation of some of those present at this point: Violet's coffin plate had contained a minor error too, but given that in normal circumstances, once buried, coffin plates never saw the light of day again and in any case were no kind of evidence or official record, this surely scarcely mattered?

After Gardiner, Tom Sidney gave evidence confirming that he had identified his sister's body and he was followed by Inspector Hedges, who repeated all the evidence he had previously given at Violet Sidney's inquest, stating what articles had been removed from various premises on what dates, and to whom they had been communicated for analysis. In addition to the long list he had presented at the previous hearing, Hedges now added two items specific to the investigation into Vera's death – a soup tureen and a kitchen hearth rug. The hearth rug was the one on which the cat had been sick a few days before Vera died. He had also received two sealed packets from Tom Sidney, which the latter had handed over to him on 16 April, saying he had found them at his mother's house.

One can imagine the inhabitants of the public benches, several of whom had become regulars at every session, sighing impatiently through Hedges' evidence while they awaited a new star turn. Eventually Sir Bernard Spilsbury took the place of the man from the Met and read from what the *Croydon Advertiser* described as 'a long and carefully prepared report … [some of it] of a most gruesome detail.' According to Spilsbury, death was due to syncope[6] consequent upon fatty degeneration of the heart and kidneys. There was no disease to account for those changes, but there were signs of a gastro-intestinal irritant. The lack of post-mortem degeneration was remarkable in a body which had been buried for five weeks. At this Mr Fearnley-Whittingstall asked Sir Bernard whether he had noticed that some hyacinths in Vera's coffin showed almost no sign of having withered.

'They were withered to a certain extent,' the pathologist replied.

'I am suggesting that the air-tightness of the coffin kept them fresh,' pursued counsel.

'Yes, I think that is so. It would keep them from dying.'

Surely, Fearnley-Whittingstall suggested, this would equally hold good for the body. Sir Bernard agreed that the air-tightness would affect the preservation of the remains. The significance of this state of preservation was not spelled out in court that day, but it sent out a clear message to all those present at the inquest, or reading their newspaper accounts in the following days: there had been several high profile arsenic cases in the recent past and arsenic was known to impair decomposition.

Spilsbury was followed by the second expert of the day, Dr Ryffel, the Home Office Analyst, who explained that he had received samples of Vera's organs and body parts – eighteen jars in all – which he had subjected to analysis. Altogether he had discovered 1.48 grains of arsenic – not in itself a poisonous dose, Ryffel explained, but taking into account that Vera had survived for thirty-six hours after the 'fatal dose' and therefore that a large amount of arsenic must have been eliminated from her body by vomiting during that time, he calculated that the original dose must have been at least 5 grains – which was a poisonous dose.

Ryffel had also analysed a great many other items, including the soup tureen and the hearth rug, neither of which had tested positive for arsenic, which negative result he assumed was due to the fact that they had been thoroughly washed before he received them. The packets of unknown substances provided by Tom Sidney had proved equally innocuous. The Eureka Weed Killer had of course tested positive and he found that it contained 291 grains of arsenic to each fluid ounce. He had tested rust from inside the empty Eureka tin found in Violet Sidney's woodshed and his analysis had shown that the rust contained a small quantity of arsenic.

After Dr Ryffel, it was the turn of Tom Sidney to face the coroner's questions again. The session began well enough, with Tom yet again called upon to run through the litany of who was who in the Sidney family; restating his opinion that his sisters had been on very affectionate terms – the whole family were interested in each others' affairs and concerned for one another's welfare – 'a happy, united family' in fact.

The first hiccup came when the coroner tried to establish how long Tom had lived at his present address in South Croydon. Tom casually answered four or five years, later deciding it was nearer six, but pointing out that this had not been continuous, as he had spent some time in America. The dialogue between himself and the coroner was clearly not a meeting of minds – Coroner Jackson wanted to establish matters with exactitude – Tom Sidney suffered from a slightly hazy memory and obviously failed to see what possible significance his various travels could have had upon the death of his sister. They eventually settled on the fact that Tom had not been abroad since summer 1927. Then there was the question of a key to no. 29. Tom said he did not have a key to the house from the time he moved out until the day after Violet died. He was probably irritated when Dr Jackson followed up this response with, 'You are sure that you have not had a key before?'

'Yes, I'm quite sure,' came the firm reply.

'Were you ill, when Vera died?'

Tom said yes, he had been suffering from 'suppressed influenza', with a high temperature and a bad cough. The coroner now tried to establish when this illness had begun, agreeing that Tom should consult his diary, as it was difficult to remember after such a long period of time. After checking the diary, Tom said it had started on 8 February, when he was in Edinburgh. He had returned home the following day by train. The coroner asked whether he had called Dr Binning out that night and Tom said he did not think he had seen him until the next day. At this, Dr Jackson said Dr Binning had informed him that a consultation had taken place on 9 February. 'Well it might have been the 9th,' the witness was getting exasperated. 'I don't remember.'

On Sunday, 10 February he was sure he had stayed in bed all day, but on Monday he went for a long walk: at least two hours. After the walk he had gone back to bed for a couple of hours. That night he had attempted to give a performance at The Connaught Rooms, London, but was taken ill during the performance; his voice had given way and he had to go home. After that he stayed in bed until Wednesday, 13 February, when he got up for a while, but did not get dressed.

Next the coroner wanted to know when he had first heard that Vera was ill. Tom said that would have been Thursday, 14 February, when Grace called in. When had he last seen Vera, asked Coroner Jackson? That had been on Wednesday. Vera had called in for a few minutes and Tom had expressed surprise at seeing her because he had heard she was ill. This of course contradicted what he had said moments earlier. The coroner asked again when he had first heard that Vera was ill. Tom decided it had been either on Monday or Tuesday.

'From whom had you heard that?'

'I am afraid I don't know. One of the members of the family I suppose.'

Dr Jackson pressed the point, but Tom was unable to clarify the matter and did no better when it came to recalling exactly when he had last seen Vera before her brief visit on Wednesday. Eventually Tom Sidney's original witness statement was produced. According to the witness statement Tom had greeted Vera with surprise on Wednesday, as he heard that she had been ill, but Vera had replied, 'I'm all right again now, but I have got to go and see to my car. The radiator is frozen.'

Dr Jackson wanted to know whether Tom was quite clear on the point that Vera had said she was better, but Tom was not at all clear. He thought that Vera had said 'she was well enough to go out … or something of the kind.' She had definitely mentioned the car radiator was frozen. It had been a very short conversation, with Vera staying no more than two or three minutes at most.

At this point the proceedings ran out of time and were adjourned until 1 May.

CHAPTER FOUR

'TO THE BEST OF MY RECOLLECTION...'

The long cold winter of 1928/9 was at last giving way to summer, but for the remnants of Violet Sidney's family, it must have seemed all but impossible to move forward. On the first day of May, while school children in rural districts danced around the maypole, Tom Sidney found himself back in the witness chair, vainly attempting to recall the events leading up to his sister Vera's death in February.[1] What day of the week, the coroner wanted to know, had he first heard that Vera was suffering from vomiting?

'I cannot quite remember.'

'She called on you herself, on Wednesday morning, and you knew then that she had been ill?'

'Yes.'

'Now what I am asking you is when you first heard of the vomiting?'

Tom Sidney undoubtedly knew perfectly well what the coroner was asking him. Any lack of understanding seems rather to have lain with Dr Jackson, and his apparent failure to comprehend that here was a family which habitually popped in and out of one another's homes, engaging in a perpetual round of trivial chit-chat, chiefly concerned with what various members of their clan were doing. Confronted with family tittle-tattle on that level, it must have been all but impossible – even after a comparatively brief interval – to remember with any certainty who had said what to whom and precisely when. However, Dr Jackson continued to press for the information, while Tom answered that he might have heard of Vera's illness from his wife – or possibly his mother – on Tuesday, although he knew she had actually been ill on Monday. He knew she had been ill on Monday, he added, because he had read it in Vera's diary. Here too a graphic illustration of the inherent danger in pressing a witness for 'memories' long after the event: by now Tom had read Vera's diary and doubtless discussed the events in question many times with his wife and sister – all of which would have coloured whatever genuine recollections he might have had.

The obvious fact that Vera's death must have been discussed between the family was underlined a few moments later, when the coroner asked whether Tom had heard any suggestions as to the cause of Vera's fatal illness. Tom said that he had. On the day of Vera's funeral he had stayed back at the house with his mother, and it was then that his mother had mentioned Vera's suspicions about the soup. According to Violet, when the soup was brought in for lunch on Wednesday, 13 February, Vera had said, 'Here's that wretched soup that made me so ill on Monday.'

How about Mrs Duff, the coroner wanted to know: had she made any suggestion about Vera's illness when she called in on Thursday? Tom said he could not remember. Had not Tom himself said it was gastric flu, the coroner persisted?

'I might have done. That was the general impression we all had at the time.'

The coroner then produced the statement Tom Sidney had made on 7 March. While Tom agreed that he had made the statement, he said it contained some misrepresentations.

'Was the statement made by you on 7 March and signed by you on 9 March?'

'Yes.'

'Before you signed it, had you satisfied yourself that it was a correct record of the statement that you had made to Inspector Hedges?'

'Yes – but there's a slight –'

'Just a moment. The second statement, made by you on 9 March and signed by you on 12 March, was that read over to you?'

'Yes.'

'Before you signed it, you satisfied yourself that it was a correct record of a statement made by you to Inspector Hedges?'

'Yes, but…'

Waiving aside these attempted protestations, the coroner drew Tom's attention to part of the 7 March statement in which he said he 'had had a week in bed with influenza' immediately before his sister Vera died. In evidence at the previous hearing, Tom had already admitted that was not the case – on the Monday of that week he had been for a two hour walk and later attempted to perform at the Connaught Rooms. The coroner now wanted to know why Tom told the police he had been in bed for a week, when that was not so.

'I made that statement in a haphazard way. I did not know then that they were going to exhume my sister and find arsenic in her body.'

'But you say "I had had" – that's as plain as anything could be.'

'I feel sure, sir, that we are straining at a gnat. I was speaking back about a fortnight.'

When Dr Jackson continued to question why Tom Sidney had previously claimed to be laid up in bed for the whole period, Tom was eventually moved to appeal to his counsel, Mr Fearnley-Whittingstall, who told him that the coroner was entitled to ask whatever questions he liked. The exchange went on and on, with Tom repeating that he had answered Hedges' questions in a loose, conversational way. Again it became apparent that the coroner and the witness were on entirely different tracks. To Dr Jackson, Tom Sidney had made a carefully considered statement to the police, but according to Tom Sidney, when Inspector Hedges called on 7 March he had not realised that he was 'making a statement' and had not expected to be asked to sign it. According to Tom, Hedges had asked him a series of questions and his answers had been taken down in short-hand – Inspector Hedges had told him it was just normal police procedure to do so – he had not even realised the police were making enquiries into Vera's death at that stage.

'Then what did you think Inspector Hedges had called on you about?'

'About my mother's death.'

'Then why did you say, "First I wish to talk about Vera"?'

'Inspector Hedges put that statement into my mouth. I did not wish to speak about her. The whole point is that I did not think that my statement would be brought up before a jury. I did not dream that the information I was giving might possibly be used in an attempt to incriminate myself.'

At this point Mr Fearnley-Whittingstall suggested that it might be pertinent to call Inspector Hedges, as a great deal appeared to turn on the circumstances of these statements, but the coroner declined. He was only concerned, he said, with the information given in the statement.

'I was making this statement a month later,' protested Tom. 'There's this terrible tragedy of my mother and my sister and my whole life's upset.'

'What it comes down to is that on account of these facts, you may not have been quite accurate as to dates?' Finally Dr Jackson and Tom Sidney's differing perceptions appeared to converge.

The sequence of events now established was that Tom had indeed gone for a long walk on Monday – something he said he habitually did in order to get himself in condition for a performance the same night. He could not remember where his walk had taken him, but he was sure he had not gone anywhere near his mother's house, as she would not have approved of him visiting while in an infected condition.

Was he *absolutely sure* he had not gone in, the coroner asked?

It was the final straw. 'As things are going now, I would rather say I went in and stayed for several hours,' Tom burst out. 'You are trying to prove or disprove that I had something to do with this poisoning!'

The coroner tried to pour oil on troubled waters. 'Unfortunately we have got to go into all the circumstances. It is only necessary for you to say what you know. I don't want to press you on anything you don't remember clearly. I only want you to say what you are sure of.' This may have been Dr Jackson's perception, but the current and previous hearings would have been foreshortened by several hours if, every time Tom Sidney had admitted that he had no clear recollection, the coroner had accepted his answer without further probing.

Then came more questions about Vera's will, following which the whole saga of the collection of the tin of Eureka Weed Killer from Tom's shed had to be gone over again for the benefit of this particular jury. On the matter of the empty weedkiller tin found in his mother's shed, Tom said that he personally attached more importance to it than Inspector Hedges appeared to: 'There was a small amount in the bottom and that residue has now been found to contain arsenic. We have learned that it only takes a small quantity of arsenic to kill a person. Why make so much about a tin found at my premises and ignore a tin found at my mother's?' 'At this point he handed the coroner another 'exhibit' – a paper packet which contained what appeared to be 'a mixture of chalk and sugar', which he said he had found in his mother's shed.

At the conclusion of this mammoth session, the coroner read over Tom's evidence. When he reached the sentence 'I did not know at the time I made the statement to the police that it would be used in an attempt to incriminate me', Tom Sidney gave a loud 'Hear, hear.'

Then Arthur Lane, the gardener, was called and gave much the same evidence as he had done for the benefit of Violet's inquest, with little new emerging except that he felt Mrs Sidney's woodshed might not seem so dark to people who did not have his sight problems. Asked what Mrs Noakes had told him about Vera Sidney's illness, he said that Mrs Noakes told him Miss Vera had died of pneumonia.

After Lane's evidence, Vera's inquest was adjourned for just over a week, but in the meantime, the next instalment of Violet's inquest was due to take place on 6 May. It was the tenth occasion Tom Sidney had been required to attend before the coroner and at all but three of these hearings he had been called upon to give evidence, sometimes for several hours at a time. Even if it had not occurred to him any sooner, by 1 May he had come to realise that he was being treated as a suspect and on 6 May this became more obvious still.

After the formal resumption of the proceedings, Dr Jackson recalled Tom Sidney first asking him about his financial position prior to his mother's death, to which Tom responded that it was normal: he was solvent and not in any financial difficulties.[2] The coroner then reverted back to the matter of door keys. He was not quite clear, he said, exactly when Tom came into possession of a key to his mother's house. Tom replied that this had been on the night of 5 March, after his mother died.

'Had you a key before that?'

'Not after I left home.'

'You are quite clear about that?'

Tom repeated the fact that he had not held a key to his mother's house since shortly after his marriage, presumably wondering why it was necessary to return to this aspect of his evidence yet again. The coroner now asked him to recall the morning of the 5 March, when he had been seen in Birdhurst Rise, with his little boy.

Tom corrected this – it had been his little girl. 'She is a very noisy little girl and got on my mother's nerves a lot. That was why I did not go into the house that morning.' (Here is yet another instance of Tom's dubious powers of recall: in a statement given to the police on 4 April, Tom clearly stated that it was his son who had accompanied him – neither the police, nor the generally pernickety Dr Jackson, appear to have picked up on or questioned the discrepancy.)[3]

'You have told us that you arrived at 12.55 and did not go in … you did not even go into the hall?'

'Not even into the garden.'

'You are quite certain of that?'

'Quite certain.'

'Your memory is not very good in general, is it, Mr Sidney? Do you think you did go inside the hall and that you have forgotten it?'

'Oh no, sir, that is not possible.'

The coroner then asked instead about the Sunday afternoon immediately before his mother's death. Tom agreed that while he was there, the curate's wife had called on his mother and was in the house from around 4.30 to 5.30. She had been shown into the drawing room within seconds of knocking at the door and he had seen her out when she left. She had never been alone during that time and could not possibly have touched his mother's medicine.

After this, the coroner produced a letter, dated 5 March, which he read aloud:

My dear Amy,

It is very kind of you to ask me to pay you a little visit and thank you very much for your kind thought, but it is really impossible for me to leave home at present. I have been very unwell and have not been out of the house for three weeks and could not undertake even the shortest journey now. The doctor tells me to keep very quiet and is giving me a tonic, but my cold is very bad; I feel very weak and even speaking to anyone for a little while brings on neuralgia. The worst of it is that my maid, who was to have gone at Christmas, leaves me in ten days. I have been unable to find another yet. The pipes have been a great worry, four of them have burst and there was other trouble, but I hope nothing more will happen and the men will finish up the repairs this morning. I am sorry that you have had pipe trouble and that your cook is still queer. It has been a terrible winter. Thank you for your previous letter and the comfort you tried to give me. My faith, thank God, is sure and I know life is not put out by death, and that the earthly body is only laid aside as an outworn garment. But to grieve is very selfish – oh how I miss my darling Vera!

Thank you for your kind invitation and sympathy.

Yours with love

Violet Emelia Sidney.

Tom Sidney confirmed that the letter was in his mother's hand. Amy was Miss Amy Sidney, one of his mother's sisters-in-law. He had noticed the letter lying on the hall table at about 4 p.m. and posted it himself, having first scribbled a note on the back of the envelope, saying that his mother was very ill. (Yet more evidence of Tom's amnesia when it came to details. The letter had clearly been posted between Tom's finding it at 4 o'clock and Violet's death some three hours later, but Tom had previously stated on several occasions that between arriving at his mother's house in the early afternoon and her death that same evening, he never left the premises. Again neither police nor coroner appear to have noticed the contradiction.)

'I thought you ought to hear that letter, gentlemen,' the coroner addressed the jury, 'as showing her state of mind on the day she died.'

After a few questions regarding Violet's will and whether Tom had known her monetary worth, the coroner released him and recalled Kathleen Noakes. The coroner's renewed interest in Tom's activities on the morning of his mother's death became clear when Mrs Noakes was asked to state at what time she had first seen Mr Sidney on the day Violet Sidney died.

'To the best of my recollection, I fancy I saw him in the hall that morning.'

'I don't want you to fancy,' said the coroner. 'I must impress upon you that this is a serious matter and if you have any doubt, you must not say it.'

Mrs Noakes rephrased her answer slightly, still saying that she 'fancied' she saw him in the hall. He had one of his children with him, she said, but she wasn't sure if it was the boy or the girl. He had spoken to her, saying, 'I won't go in to see mother, because it's nearly 1 o'clock.' After that he left via the front door.

'Are you quite sure of that?'

'Yes.'

'Did you say anything to him?'

'No, I didn't speak.'

Mrs Noakes said she particularly recalled the incident because she had been surprised to see him, and wondered how he had got inside without her opening the door. However, when the coroner asked again if she could be completely certain of the day, she backtracked, saying that she could not be absolutely sure that this encounter had taken place on the day Violet died. The coroner then produced a statement Kate Noakes had given to Inspector Hedges on 27 April, in which she stated that this encounter had definitely taken place on 5 March, just after Dr Elwell left and prior to Mrs Sidney taking her medicine: at this Mrs Noakes changed her mind again and said she was quite sure the statement was correct.

Dr Jackson tried again – how could she be sure of the date? Mrs Noakes shifted ground: although she had said it was definitely that day in the statement, it might have been a mistake. Dr Jackson pointed out that this particular statement had been made some six weeks after the event. He asked again how she could be sure that Mr Sidney's visit had been the same day as Dr Elwell's? Kate Noakes replied that she was sure when she saw Tom Sidney it was just after Dr Elwell had left, but that this was not necessarily the same day as Violet Sidney had died. Moreover, she now thought that what she had said in the statement (that she saw Tom Sidney when she was taking things in to lay the table for lunch) was wrong – the encounter had taken place before she laid for lunch, as she was coming down the stairs. She agreed that since Vera died, Tom Sidney had been calling in every day – however, he did not usually have one of his children with him. Prompted by the coroner, she agreed that he could have got in through the back door, which she was in the habit of leaving ajar for the greater part of each day, propped open with the doormat.

Mr Fearnley-Whittingstall was allowed to examine the witness and he went straight to the heart of the matter. Was it not the case that she had already made at least three statements to the police prior to this one on 27 April? How was it that she had never so much as mentioned this incident up until then?

'Because I have been thinking about different things, about different incidents all the time.'

When asked in what circumstances she had come to make this statement, Mrs Noakes claimed that she had done so of her own volition on the evening of 27 April after the adjournment of one of the hearings. She initially claimed that the statement was all her own words and not a series of responses to questions put by Inspector Hedges, but later conceded that 'certain passages' might have been in response to Hedges' questions. How often, Fearnley-Whittingstall wanted to know, had Inspector Hedges asked her whether Tom Sidney had called on the morning of his mother's death?

'Each time he's taken a statement, I think.'

'How many conversations has Inspector Hedges had with you, since this inquest opened?'

'Every day – but not always about this case.'

'How many times has he been to your house?'

'Several.'

'What about?'

'This case.'

'When did he last go?'

'About Tuesday week.'

'That was after the last inquest hearing on Mrs Sidney and before the one on Miss Sidney. What did you talk about then? Did he ask you anything about Tom Sidney coming to the house?'

'I don't think so.'

'What questions did he ask?'

'I don't know.'

'Then let me suggest to you that it is very possible he may have asked you about Tom Sidney.'

'It may have been.'

'He must have asked you dozens of times whether Tom Sidney had been to the house on that day – March 5?'

'Yes.'

'And all he could get you to say at the end of six weeks is "I fancy so"?'

'I told them I wasn't sure.'

'You told him on April 27 that you weren't sure?'

'Yes.'

'And that's the best Hedges can do, after six weeks of questions and badgering?'

Hedges interrupted at this point, to say he strongly objected to the use of the word badgering. Fearnley-Whittingstall retorted that as counsel, he could use whatever words he chose. 'If she says "dozens of times" I am entitled to interpret that as badgering.'

The coroner asked Mrs Noakes to clarify whether Inspector Hedges had questioned her about any one person more than another. When she denied this, Hedges broke in again to state that he had not singled any one person out.

After the coroner had questioned the frequency and location of her conversations with the police, Hedges was allowed to ask whether it was not the case that the witness had also had conversations with others involved, including Mrs Duff. Kate Noakes said she had talked with Mrs Duff, but only once. Hedges also persuaded her to agree that many of their conversations had simply been 'asking how you are and so on' and that she had at no time been badgered or threatened by himself or Inspector Morrish.

The coroner got proceedings back on track, with questions to the witness reverting to the events of 5 March. Kate Noakes told the court that apart from the one occasion when she had encountered Tom Sidney in the hall, she had never come across anyone in the house who she had not admitted herself. Mrs Sidney had sometimes let visitors in during the summer, but not in winter, as she was afraid of draughts. She was sure that Mrs Sidney had not left the dining room to go upstairs in between Dr Elwell leaving and herself laying the lunch and therefore Tom Sidney could not have entered the dining room without his mother seeing him. She was equally sure that if he had gone in to see his mother, Mrs Sidney would have mentioned it when she went in to lay for lunch.

After brief appearances from Hedges and Clarke, detailing yet more objects handed over to Dr Ryffel for analysis, Ryffel himself was recalled to give evidence. The analyst firstly dealt with the substances discovered and handed over by Tom Sidney, which he had found to be harmless. It was a very different story when he moved to Violet's organs, which had tested positive for arsenic, as had her hair, fingernails and toenails. The organs had been surprisingly well preserved, with post-mortem changes barely noticeable. In total Ryffel claimed to have found 3.48 grains of arsenic – ample to cause death. From his analysis of the hair and nails, he found no evidence that the deceased had taken previous doses of arsenic.

Ryffel had also conducted some experiments with the Metatone and the weedkiller. Metatone was a rich red colour and Eureka Weed Killer a shade similar to lilac. Mixing the two together resulted in a brownish colour, which did not correspond to the liquid in the medicine bottle which Ryffel had received from the police. When the Metatone and Eureka mixture had been allowed to stand, a sediment formed, which, according to Ryffel, was similar to that which he had observed in the medicine bottle, but not identical, because the original mixture had been thicker – as if more solid had been added. He had also made up a mixture of Noble's Liquid Weed Killer and Metatone, but that had the effect of thinning the medicine and left no sediment.

He had calculated that there was 1 grain of arsenic in the ¼ teaspoonful of liquid left in the bottom of the bottle and therefore before Mrs Sidney took her dose there must have been 2 ¼ teaspoonfuls in the bottle, containing 9 grains in all. As the Eureka Weed Killer was not 100 per cent arsenic, 14 grains of weedkiller would have had to have been added to the tonic in order to yield 9 grains of arsenic. At Mr Fearnley-Whittingstall's request, Dr Ryffel set up what some of the papers referred to as 'a chemistry experiment in court', weighing out 14 grains of weedkiller and adding this to a bottle containing 2 ¼ teaspoons of Metatone.

The jury and some of the witnesses gathered round to watch, while Dr Jackson was heard to remark to Mr Fearnley-Whittingstall, 'We don't know exactly what was done and we have to assume things.'

Questioned by Mr Fearnley-Whittingstall, Dr Ryffel admitted that the resulting concoction did not greatly resemble the original exhibit he had received from the police. (As Dr Ryffel's test had used the original exhibit in its entirety, all the witnesses were obliged to fall back on memory.) The mixture of Eureka and Metatone made up in court had purple splashes in it and a complete absence of the white sediment which had been observed in the original bottle. Dr Binning was invited to look at the various bottles Ryffel had produced in court and in his laboratory and he too remarked on the fact that even when left to stand for several days, the mixtures of Eureka and Metatone had distinct purple or violet elements which had not been a feature of the bottle he had seen on 5 March.

Dr Robert Bronte was the next witness called and deposed that in his opinion, which was principally based on the analysis provided by Dr Ryffel, Violet Sidney's death had been due to acute arsenical poisoning. The brown atrophy he had observed in her heart and kidneys, however, were not due to acute arsenical poisoning and must have been the result of some chronic condition. When asked what he thought the cause could have been, Bronte answered candidly that he did not know.

It was a bumper week for the local newshounds. In normal run-of-the-mill times, their papers were often reduced to leading with stories about an appeal to rebuild the hospital – in generally law-abiding Croydon, where even a story about a local ten-year-old cutting his foot on some broken glass[4] rated a mention, headlines such as 'The Poison Drama'[5] and 'Croydon Arsenic Mystery'[6] must have seemed heaven sent. On the second weekend in May the Saturday editions had two stories to cover – Violet's inquest on Monday, with its suggestive allegations and chemistry demonstrations and then Thursday's inquest on Vera – a labyrinthine affair, which would be principally concerned with oxtail soup.[7]

The first witness on Thursday 9 May was Kathleen Noakes, who, perhaps mindful of the rough ride she had had at the beginning of the week, informed the coroner, 'I don't feel very well. I will give answers to the best of my ability, but I won't be bullied.'

'It is not a question of being bullied,' the coroner replied. 'You may have to be cross-examined. Every witness has to.'

Dr Jackson began gently enough. He took Kate Noakes through her employment history, ending with her most recent position with Mrs Sidney, asking whether she had been happy there, before attempting to draw her out on the subject of the late Vera Sidney. According to Mrs Noakes, Miss Vera had been generally healthy, but had complained a lot lately about the cold and had been feeling very tired. Echoing Grace Duff, she opined that Vera did lead quite a strenuous life, playing a lot of golf and having late nights. She had never known Miss Vera to suffer from vomiting before Monday 11 February. At this the coroner produced Vera's diary, pointing out that according to an entry on 25 January, Vera had suffered from vomiting then. Did Mrs Noakes know anything about that?

'No – she used to like rich cakes.'

Dr Jackson ignored this possible diversion into confectionery and asked about Vera's general appetite, which Mrs Noakes agreed had been poor during the last two weeks of her life. She had also been suffering from painful chilblains in her feet, but apart from that Mrs Noakes had been unaware of any aches and pains.

Dr Jackson asked about visits from the family. Mrs Duff had called round pretty much every day, said Mrs Noakes. Mrs Margaret Sidney would drop in perhaps a couple of afternoons a week; she and Mr Sidney would often bring their children round for tea on Sunday afternoons. As Sunday was her afternoon off, she never saw them arrive herself – she left the house at 3 o'clock and returned about 10 o'clock – but Mrs Sidney would tell her if the family had been. They seldom stayed for supper – if they had, she would know, because Mrs Sidney or Miss Vera would probably tell her and anyway she would have missed some food. Before Miss Vera's death Tom Sidney had not been in the habit of visiting the house so much on his own. Neither he, his wife nor Mrs Duff had ever come into the kitchen, or had anything to do with preparing food; although on Christmas afternoon, Mrs Duff had come into the kitchen, while she was doing the washing up, and given her half a crown.

The coroner now took her through the events leading to Vera Sidney's death. On Sunday, 10 February, Mrs Noakes said that Vera had come down to breakfast complaining of a head cold, then stayed indoors all day, which was unusual for her. When Kate Noakes returned to the house at 10 o'clock it was Vera who let her in. Vera then had a runny nose and watery eyes, and said she felt seedy. She did not say anything about being sick. On Monday, 11 February Vera had gone out to lunch in Oxted. She was at home for tea and supper with her mother, partaking of her usual supper of soup, fish, potatoes, pudding and fruit, with which she would have drunk water. She didn't drink wine or spirits – only occasionally stout – and did not take coffee after a meal, unless there were visitors.

The coroner asked who had made the soup and Kathleen Noakes confirmed that she had. Cautioning her to think very carefully, Dr Jackson asked whether Vera had been ill after eating the soup on Monday?

'I'm not sure whether it was the Monday or the Tuesday. To the best of my recollection it was Tuesday.'

Dr Jackson reminded the witness that both Dr Elwell and Grace Duff had already testified that Vera had told them she had been ill after drinking the soup on Monday evening: 'I want you to try and think and get it straight in your mind whether it was Monday or Tuesday, because it is not much use our going into how the soup was made on Monday if she was ill on Tuesday, or vice versa. Did she have a whole day between the first vomiting and the second vomiting coming on?'

'I don't know.'

'The evening that she vomited, did you vomit too?'

'Yes, I had had the soup as well.'

When the coroner asked if they had both eaten all the same things, Kate Noakes claimed that on the evening in question she had nothing but half a cup of soup – drinking it out of a breakfast cup and giving what was left to the cat, who, on drinking it, was immediately very sick. She had begun to 'feel funny' straight away and had vomited about fifteen minutes later. The soup given to the cat had been the very last of the batch, although she couldn't remember if the cat's soup had come out of the saucepan, or was the leftovers in her own cup.

Questioned further, she said that she started to feel sick while doing the washing up, so she went upstairs to get herself an orange. She met Vera on the stairs, with her hand to her mouth, and they both commented on feeling unwell. After eating her orange she was very sick and continued to be sick into the early hours. When she came down the next morning, she found the cat had been sick on the oilcloth, the sight of which made her sick again. Knowing that she was unwell, Mrs Sidney had told her not to bother completely turning out the dining room and drawing room and to just dust them.

Asked about the making of the soup, she said that she normally made enough for two days. She could not say for sure that she made soup on Sunday, but on Tuesday she had made a fresh batch, using some cooked veal left over from the previous Thursday. The soup made on Tuesday was in preparation for a visitor who was coming to lunch on Wednesday, but Vera would have had some of this soup for her supper on Tuesday evening. Mrs Noakes denied that she had immediately suspected a problem with the soup, saying that she had initially ascribed her nausea to some cake she had eaten.

'But that would not account for Miss Vera and the cat?'

'No,' Mrs Noakes agreed.

The coroner wanted to know more about this suspect cake, so Mrs Noakes explained that on Sunday she had been present at a celebration for a friend's son who had turned twenty-one. She had eaten a piece of rich iced fruitcake at suppertime and it was to this that she was referring. Dr Jackson pointed out that she would not expect something to make her ill forty-eight hours after she had eaten it – might it not have been Monday night, rather than Tuesday night, when she was sick? Mrs Noakes agreed that it probably was on Monday and admitted that she had originally told Miss Vera that she suspected it was the cake she had eaten on Sunday which had made her feel ill. Miss Vera had not expressed any opinion on what might have caused her own symptoms.

Mrs Noakes was then allowed to stand down for a time, while Dr Binning gave evidence. He explained that he did not normally attend Vera Sidney, but had been called in by his partner, Dr Elwell, on Thursday, 14 February. When he arrived between 4 and 5 o'clock in the afternoon, a specialist, Dr Bolton, had already seen Vera and diagnosed gastric influenza.

Binning said that on arrival, he found the patient acutely ill and in a collapsed state, her pulse was rapid and feeble, her hands and feet cold, her colour greyish, and her heart dilated. He was with the patient almost continuously until she died at 12.20 that night. He did not observe any vomiting or diarrhoea, although Dr Elwell told him there had been vomiting the previous evening. Vera had not made any statements to him concerning her illness. No one had prescribed any arsenic to her at any time. He had not entertained any suspicions that it was anything but death due to natural causes and Dr Elwell had signed the death certificate.

Having had a break and some lunch, Kathleen Noakes was recalled and the focus of the enquiry returned to soup. Via a series of questions and answers the court learnt that under normal circumstances Vera Sidney was the only member of the household who ate soup – Mrs Sidney never ate it and Kathleen Noakes was not supposed to. (Mrs Sidney forbade it on the grounds that she did not believe her servants needed a three-course meal.) The routine was to make suffi-cient soup to last for two days. After initial cooking, it was put through a wooden strainer into a basin, which was then carried down to stand in the pantry until the soup was required.

The coroner was very interested in the location of the pantry, so Mrs Noakes explained that it was one of three cellars below the house. These were accessed down some stairs, through a door which led off the rear passage, and this door was opposite the back door, just a few feet away. And wasn't Mrs Noakes in the habit of leaving the back door ajar all day, asked the coroner – this was after all what she had told the court only on Monday? Now she changed her tune – she 'might leave the door open, if it was a nice morning and we wanted a breath of fresh air.' But surely, the coroner asked, the proximity of the back door to the door of the cellar stairs meant that anyone could get in and be down to the pantry in seconds? Again Mrs Noakes hesitated – not if she was in the kitchen or scullery, she thought, though she agreed that it would be possible, providing she was else-where in the house.

Back they went to the mechanics of the soup. Mrs Noakes explained that once the batch was made, it would be brought back upstairs and reheated in its entirety, each time a portion was required. She could not remember anything about the making of the soup on Sunday, 10 February, but she must have made it on Sunday, because the soup that she and the cat had on Monday was the last of a batch. She would therefore have made some more on Tuesday – and this she did recall clearly: the ingredients had been tap water, carrot, onion, turnip, Symington's Oxtail Soup Powder and the remains of the veal from Friday or Saturday.

'You are quite sure that when you made the soup on Tuesday you had already been sick?'

'Oh yes. I can swear to that,' declared Mrs Noakes, having apparently forgotten her uncertainty on the point only that morning.

She did not believe that Vera had eaten any of this soup on Tuesday, because she had been ill in bed. At this point Vera's diary was consulted in an attempt to clarify the issue. On Tuesday, 12 February she had written: *Felt rotten, stayed in bed. Grace came and I made an effort and went downstairs, did not do any eating during the day, only tea and Oxo.* The entry for Monday made reference to returning home at about 7 o'clock: *Feeling rotten. After dinner I was awfully sick, again and again.*

Mrs Noakes said that her own suspicions only turned to the soup after Vera had come into the kitchen on Wednesday, to see if the saucepan used for heating it was clean.

On that morning Vera had begun the day with a boiled egg for breakfast. Afterwards she rang the garage about her car then came into the kitchen to leave a message if her sister called, saying she wouldn't be gone long. When Mrs Duff rang later, and was given the message, she expressed surprise on hearing that Miss Vera had gone out after being so ill.

Vera returned home at around midday, and Grace arrived with Mrs Greenwell at just on 1 o'clock. Mrs Noakes had shown them into the drawing room and soon afterwards sounded the dining room gong; she confirmed that Mrs Duff only stayed a few minutes and was gone before they went into lunch. After sounding the gong, she went straight back to the kitchen, where she poured the soup from the saucepan into the soup tureen. She had not eaten any of the soup, but she had tasted it for flavour as she always did. She carried the tureen into the dining room and put it on the table, not staying to serve the soup, but going straight back to the kitchen to see to the white sauce. The next course was boiled chicken with parsley sauce, potatoes and Brussels sprouts.

At this point Dr Jackson enquired whether she had left the kitchen much that morning; for example, when had she got changed to serve lunch – was this before or after Mrs Greenwell arrived? Kathleen Noakes said she could not remember. 'In that case, you can't remember all the other details you have told us either,' he retorted.

Mrs Noakes hastily decided that she had changed before Mrs Greenwell arrived. Dr Jackson let it go and the witness continued with the story of the lunch party. When the diners were finished with the soup, a bell summoned her to collect the dishes and tureen. According to Mrs Noakes, Violet Sidney's soup plate was unused, there was a little soup left in Vera's plate and rather more in Mrs Greenwell's. Having cleared away the first course, she brought in the second. She recalled Mrs Greenwell saying she would not have any chicken as it was Ash Wednesday, but the other women each took a small portion.

At this point, before Mrs Noakes could describe the serving of the baked custard pudding and tinned fruit, the inquest was adjourned until 1 June.

On Monday, 13 May the regular cast reassembled for another instalment of the enquiry into Violet's death.[8] John Baker, the Mayday Hospital mortuary attendant, was the first witness, testifying that he had handed over various jars containing samples from Violet's body to the two witnesses who followed. The first of these was Dr Herbert Southgate, the Croydon Borough pathologist, who testified that after taking sections of various organs and subjecting them to bacteriological examination, he had found nothing abnormal.

The second witness was Dr Robert Bronte, the Harley Street pathologist, whose earlier testimony had closed the previous session. Bronte agreed with the other medical witnesses that his findings were consistent with Violet Sidney having died as a result of ingesting arsenic at about 1 o'clock on the day of her death, but he differed from Dr Ryffel's conclusions in one significant respect: Bronte was insistent that this could not have been Violet's first encounter with arsenic, because Ryffel had discovered arsenic in the dead woman's hair, finger-nails and toenails, which indicated that she must have taken some arsenic at least five days before her death.

'You are certain of that?' asked Dr Jackson.

'I am quite certain.'

'Do you think it was more than five days?'

'Probably, but I am prepared to say at least five days.'

Dr Jackson reminded the witness that Dr Ryffel had said most definitely that his findings did not indicate an earlier dose, but Bronte stuck to his guns, explaining that arsenic could only enter the hair and nails through the growing ends, via the bloodstream, and this would take considerably longer than the six hours Violet had survived after the onset of her illness. 'No arsenic could be found in the hair or nails if one single fatal dose had been taken and no other arsenic taken.'

'That is correct?'

'That is an established fact.'

Bronte went on to say that the amounts in the nails and hair were very small, indicating non-toxic doses, such as occurred in medicinal use. Dr Jackson reminded him that Mrs Sidney had not been prescribed any arsenic, but Bronte refused to be shaken. He also cast doubt on the suggestion that enough arsenic for a fatal dose could have been incorporated in a 2 teaspoon dose of Metatone, as arsenic tended to be insoluble.

At this point, one of the jury asked how Mrs Sidney had been in the habit of measuring out the dose, since there were no measurements marked on the side of the bottle. Tom Sidney explained that his mother had utilised a silver teaspoon, which had in fact been left lying on the sideboard, alongside the bottle and wine glass – he had washed it up himself, only the other day. The coroner remarked that this was the first he had heard about this teaspoon – no doubt he was wondering why the item in question had not been produced as a material exhibit long ere now.

The next witness was announced as Mr Rupert Fortnum, the manager of Barclays Bank, South Croydon branch. Aware that Fortnum had been called to give evidence about his clients' financial affairs, Mr Fearnley-Whittingstall appealed to the coroner to take the evidence in camera: 'It's hardly fair to broadcast their private affairs so that everyone from the charwoman to the office boy knows them.'

The coroner agreed to examine the statements and other documents Mr Fortnum had provided over lunch. In spite of this, the bank manager did answer some questions in public and thus the wider world was able to glean the information that while both accounts had been with the bank for several years and had always been satisfactory, Mrs Duff's account had occasionally been overdrawn by as much as £12 – although the bank had never had to press her for payment.

The inquest was then adjourned until 12 June, with the coroner reassuring the jury that he did not think there would be much more evidence to hear. He explained that the length of the present adjournment was principally due to the availability of William Fearnley-Whittingstall, who was contesting a seat in the forthcoming general election.[9] This long adjournment must have been something of a disappointment to the journalists for whom the weekly inquests had been providing such good copy, but in the event they did not have to wait long for the next sensation: within five days the Croydon Arsenic Mystery was making bigger headlines than ever.

CHAPTER FIVE

'NEW TURN IN ARSENIC DRAMA'

Back in March, when the Croydon Mystery first hit the headlines, there had been speculation in the press that the Home Office was about to order three exhumations,[1] but when only two coffins were raised, rumours about a third mysterious death had swiftly been forgotten – until Saturday, 18 May, when the body of Grace Duff's late husband, Edmund Creighton Duff, was disinterred. This latest twist in the tale made the front page of the *People* under a banner headline 'New Turn in Arsenic Drama'.[2] 'New Exhumation Sensation', screamed the *Sunday Express.*[3]

Permission to carry out the exhumation had only been received from the Home Office the previous day.[4] Unlike the disinterment of Violet and Vera, there was no attempt at secrecy, the business being carried out in broad daylight, with no effort made to exclude either press or public from the cemetery. The gravediggers began at 7.30 a.m. and it took them several hours to dig down as far as the coffin, which lay at a depth of 7ft. As well as reporters and passers-by, the proceedings were observed by a gaggle of police officers, including Superintendent Brown of Scotland Yard, Detective Inspector Hedges and half a dozen others. Dr Binning was also present, along with Sir Bernard Spilsbury, Sir William Willcox (described in some papers as 'the poison expert') and finally, Tom Sidney.

Getting the coffin to the surface was no easy task. It had been buried for just over a year and a strong suction had set up between the base of the coffin and the clay soil in which it lay. After a considerable struggle, the undertaker's men managed to get the straps underneath and the coffin was raised to the surface at 11 o'clock: 'a gruesome object', the *Croydon Advertiser* said, with soil adhering all over it. The name plate was wiped clean and Sir Bernard Spilsbury carefully copied the details into his notebook before the coffin was loaded into the undertaker's van and taken to the mortuary. The van was followed on foot by Tom Sidney and three of the police officers, with five cars coming after carrying other officers, medical men and officials. As the procession made its way out of the cemetery and along Queen's Road, groups of passers-by stopped to stare at this latest act in the drama.

At the mortuary Sydney Gardiner and Tom Sidney were confronted with the task of identifying the remains in the coffin, before Spilsbury undertook a post-mortem examination. In a grim re-enactment of the earlier visits to the Mayday mortuary, various samples were extracted to be sent for analysis, after which the body was returned to the undertakers for the reburial, which took place without ceremony at around 2.30 that afternoon.

On Saturday evening, Dr Jackson told reporters who called at his home that he had no information as to whether another inquest would be held. 'One inquest has already been held by me, and unless I have any further instructions from the Home Office, there will not be another.'

At the original inquest in 1928, Dr Bronte had given evidence that Edmund Duff's was a natural death, due to myocarditis,[5] and a verdict of natural causes had been brought in. However, the Coroners' (Amendment) Act of 1926 allowed that a second inquest could be ordered in certain circumstances[6] – and the public were left in no doubt as to what sort of circumstances anyone had in mind. By 1 June the papers were able to report that the Home Office Analyst, Dr Roche Lynch, had already presented a preliminary report to the authorities, on receipt of which Superintendent Brown had been in conference with Sir Archibald Bodkin, Director of Public Prosecutions. News that Edmund Duff's body had been found in a good state of preservation, with marked absence of decomposition, had already found its way into the public domain.

What in the meantime of Edmund's widow? The *Croydon Times & Surrey County Mail* had managed to get a quote. Mentioning what a tragic figure Mrs Duff had presented at the inquests into her mother and sister, and reminding its readers that she had already undergone hours of interrogation at the hands of the coroner and detectives, they reported her saying:

> It is my dearest wish that this dreadful mystery should be cleared up as soon as possible. I want everything to be done that can to throw daylight on the horrible things which have happened to our family. It was dreadful for me to have the body of my husband exhumed. It seemed such desecration – worse than his first burial. But I am glad they did it, if it will help them discover the truth.[7]

In the meantime, the legal process ground relentlessly onward. On Saturday, 1 June the enquiry into Vera's death continued.[8] The first witness was Gwendoline Mary Stafford Greenwell, one of Violet Sidney's numerous sisters-in-law, who was fifty-nine years old and married to Herbert Greenwell, a retired Lieutenant Colonel of the 4th Durham Light Infantry. The Greenwells lived in Newcastle-upon-Tyne, but while on a trip to London, Mrs Greenwell had written to Violet, suggesting that she come for lunch and Wednesday, 13 February had been agreed a suitable date. Now Mrs Greenwell recalled this visit for the benefit of the court, starting with her arrival at South Croydon station, where she was met by her niece, Grace. They had walked to Violet's house together, Mrs Greenwell carrying a fresh pineapple, which she had brought as a gift for her sister-in-law.

She insisted that she had been feeling perfectly well that day, although she agreed that *en route* from the station she had probably told Grace about a bad cough which had troubled her about a week before.

Mrs Greenwell was uncertain whether Grace had come into the house with her, saying that if she did, she had come no further than the hall. Violet had come into the hall to meet her guest and they went into the drawing room together. (This was of course not the exact sequence of events as either Grace Duff or Kathleen Noakes had previously recalled them.) They were only in the drawing room about five minutes before going in to lunch. According to Mrs Greenwell's recollection, the soup tureen was already on the table when they entered and, noticing there were only two soup plates, she asked Violet if she was not going to have any soup, to which Violet replied that she never did. (This of course contradicted Kathleen Noakes' account of clearing away three soup plates.)

When Violet was about to serve, Vera said she did not want any soup, because it had made her sick – Mrs Greenwell said she thought Vera said 'yesterday', but she might have said 'Monday'. Violet had dismissed this as nonsense, saying the soup could not possibly do her any harm. It was thick brown soup, Mrs Greenwell recalled, and although it did not taste funny, after half a dozen spoonfuls she felt that she did not want any more. She noticed that Vera also left a good deal in her plate. The next course had been chicken, with potatoes and sprouts, of which Mrs Greenwell had taken only some potatoes, although her companions both had a portion of everything. There had been several sweets, including stewed pears, baked custard and something else she couldn't remember. She had some baked custard, as did Vera – she was unable to recall what Violet ate. No one had wanted coffee after the meal.

Immediately after lunch she and Vera both suffered from vomiting and diarrhoea, although Violet was unaffected. When Violet left the two women alone in the drawing room for a few minutes, they compared notes and Vera told her aunt that she had been sick before – she was anxious in case she had 'given … [their visitor] … a germ', but Mrs Greenwell reassured her that was quite impossible, as she had not been in the house long enough. During this exchange Vera mentioned that the cook had also been sick, but said nothing about the cat. Again Mrs Greenwell had the impression that Vera said the cook's sickness had occurred 'yesterday', rather than Monday, but she could not be sure. Vera was just asking her aunt if she thought the problem could be the soup when they heard Violet approaching, at which Mrs Greenwell begged her not to say anything more about it 'as it might upset your mother.'

Vera had telephoned Grace during the afternoon, and when Grace returned to her mother's there had been some talk of cod liver oil. At about 4 o'clock Grace walked her aunt back to the station, and on the way she suggested Mrs Greenwell might prefer to stay the night with her, as she did not seem well enough to go back to her hotel, but Mrs Greenwell declined, saying she would much rather go back. They had not discussed what might have caused her own or Vera's illness. After returning to the hotel, her illness had continued for six days. She had been attended several times by a Dr Caithness. He had not said what was wrong with her, but she told him she had had some soup which disagreed with her.

During the course of this interrogation came what the *Croydon Advertiser* described as 'a dramatic incident'. When the coroner asked Mrs Greenwell if she thought she had had something which had poisoned her, the witness paused for some time before replying, toying with an ebony-rimmed lorgnette she had in her lap. Eventually she said, 'Yes, I was quite certain of that.'

Finally the coroner asked about the relationships between her nieces and nephew, which the witness said she believed to be perfectly friendly although, as she pointed out, she very seldom saw any of them.

The second witness was another newcomer to the proceedings, Mrs Dorothy Winifred Gent, who had been employed by Tom and Margaret Sidney as a general servant since June 1928. Mrs Gent said she could remember Mr Sidney coming home early from Scotland in February, because he was unwell, and that Miss Vera Sidney had called on him that Wednesday and stayed only a few minutes.

Attention then turned to an episode the previous summer, when Mrs Gent had encountered her employer in the scullery, attempting to get the lid off a small round tin, the same size and shape as a tin of boot polish. When he was unsuccessful, she tried to remove it, and while she was doing so, Mr Sidney told her it was rat poison, which he intended to put down near the dustbin. Asked to describe the contents of the tin, Mrs Gent said she could not remember, at which Tom Sidney interrupted to say that it was an off-white powder.

It was when Mr Fearnley-Whittingstall began to cross-examine the witness, however, that the fireworks began. He wanted to know about the circumstances in which Inspector Hedges had extracted the information about the rat poison, and although the words badgering and bullying were not used, the implication of the questions was obvious and eventually brought Hedges to his feet, protesting strongly about the line which was being taken. 'They are most improper questions,' he said.

'I shall ask you to be quiet,' said Fearnley-Whittingstall. 'You have no right to interrupt.'

'You are making improper suggestions, sir,' said Hedges.

'Unless you keep silent, I shall ask that you be removed from court,' retorted the barrister.

At this point the coroner intervened to say that he thought Mr Fearnley-Whittingstall might be going too far and reminded him that he must not put words into the witness's mouth. Resuming his interrogation, the family's counsel drew from Mrs Gent the information that it had taken nearly an hour for Mr Hedges to take her statement, during which time, 'I felt that my first answer had not been satisfactory, as I was asked so many more questions…'

When Fearnley-Whittingstall had finished, Inspector Hedges was allowed to cross-examine the witness. To a large extent, his efforts to undermine what had gone before became an exercise in shooting himself in the foot, particularly when he asked the witness whether she had not volunteered the information about the incident in the scullery. 'No,' said Mrs Gent, 'you asked me first.'

Before the proceedings closed for the day, Tom Sidney made a brief reappearance in the witness chair, where he confirmed the episode of the rat poison. It had been Rodine rat poison, he said. He had spread some on pieces of bread and put them in the yard, but later removed them, as he was afraid they might be eaten by his children or cats.

Thursday, 6 June was the seventh time the jury had assembled to hear evidence relating to the death of Vera Sidney, and the fourteenth occasion on which the relatives had been required to attend the coroner's court. Kathleen Noakes, whose evidence had been ongoing when the hearing was adjourned on 9 May, was back in the witness chair.[9] First of all, the coroner wanted to know what she would normally have for her evening meal at Mrs Sidney's. Mrs Noakes said it would usually be fish and pudding. Why then, the coroner wanted to know, had she only eaten soup on the night when she and Vera became ill with vomiting?

'I did not feel well enough to eat anything else.'

'Had you already been sick before you had the soup?'

'No, sir.'

'In what way were you feeling unwell?'

Mrs Noakes said she had a cold and it was very cold weather, so she had fancied soup. She had not wanted anything to eat.

'Perhaps you had not much appetite, before you sat down to the soup?'

'Well we'll say that.'

'Don't say "well we'll say that",' said the coroner. 'You must give a definite answer. You're here on oath, you know, and must tell the truth.'

The coroner got no further on the subject however, and when questioned about Vera Sidney's previous sickness, Mrs Noakes continued with the line that she was unaware of Vera having been ill on any previous occasions. Even when Dr Jackson read out Vera's diary entry for 25 January: *Had rotten night. Feeling very sick for ages and then was sick at 4.15 a.m.* it failed to jog her memory. The dairy then provided a further challenge to her recall, when the coroner read out the entry for Monday, 11 February: *I went for a brisk walk up to the golf links and then across the links. Then played bridge. Got back about seven o'clock, feeling rotten. After dinner I was sick again and again, even as late as 11.30.*

At a previous hearing, Kate Noakes had testified that Vera went to lunch at Oxted on 11 February, but now she made haste to correct herself: she remembered that everything had happened as the diary said. She had already told the detectives — here Dr Jackson cut in to say he was not interested in what she had told the detectives, 'What we're worrying about is what you told me on oath.'

Returning to the meal on Monday evening, Mrs Noakes said she could state on oath that in addition to the soup, Miss Vera had eaten fish, fried potatoes and pudding.

How often had Mrs Noakes taken soup before at Mrs Sidney's, the coroner asked?

'Never.'

'You had been in her service since the preceding August and you had never taken soup before?'

Kate Noakes insisted that this was so – she only had some that night because she had a cold. Neither herself nor the cat had been sick prior to consuming the soup.

'Then it is only a coincidence that on the only night out of 180 nights that you take soup, you are sick after it?'

'Yes sir.'

The coroner wanted to know more about the soup pan. The witness told him that it was a heavy iron saucepan, not enamelled. After lunch on Wednesday, although not generally in the habit of coming into the kitchen to check the saucepans, Vera had visited the kitchen to examine the soup pan, thinking that it might not have been properly cleaned before use. She had run her finger round the inside, then said, 'That's all right, Kate.' After that she made a comment about 'those old saucepans'.

Asked about the rest of the soup, Mrs Noakes said it had been thrown away on Mrs Sidney's orders. She now also remembered that there had been water, cider and crusty rolls on the table when Mrs Greenwell came to lunch. The soup tureen was an old one which had been mended with a rivet across the bottom.

Dr Jackson then asked about Grace Duff's arrival on the afternoon of the lunch party. Mrs Noakes agreed that when she let Mrs Duff in, she had told her that Miss Vera and Mrs Greenwell had both been sick and opined that it was on account of the veal.

'Did you think it was the veal?'

'Well veal's funny stuff – '

'Did you think it was the veal?'

'Yes.'

The coroner reminded Mrs Noakes that in an earlier statement she had attributed the sickness to using old saucepans, at which Mrs Noakes said she did not know what to think, but on that Wednesday afternoon she had thought it was the veal.

Thursday had been her half-day and she had been out from 3 o'clock until 10 o'clock. She claimed that she had offered to forgo it, as Vera was so ill, but Mrs Sidney 'would not hear of it'.

'Did you give notice, when you came in that night?' asked the coroner. Kate Noakes denied it, claiming that what she had told Mrs Sidney was that she did not feel well and that if she did not get better, she would have to go away for a few days.

'So my mother's a liar then!' Tom Sidney burst out.

When the coroner warned him that he must not interrupt and any further interruptions would see him removed, Tom stood up and walked out of the room of his own volition. A few minutes later he returned and apologised to the coroner, before resuming his seat.

In the meantime Mrs Noakes had explained that the first time she knew Vera was dead was when she came downstairs the following morning and heard the news from the night nurse, who said Vera had died of pneumonia.

Finally Kate Noakes was asked about an incident which she alleged had taken place at 29 Birdhurst Rise on the day after Violet's death. According to Mrs Noakes, Mr Clarke, the coroner's officer, had been to the house to ask her some questions about Vera and when Tom Sidney came round later, he appeared to be annoyed, saying that there ought to be a member of the family present when any enquiries were being made, 'as the dead can't speak, but they can make it very uncomfortable for those who are still living.' The coroner wanted to know in what way Tom Sidney had seemed upset – had he told her she ought not to have told the coroner's officer anything about Vera? Kate Noakes admitted that he had not, he just 'seemed rather cross' and had pushed the cat off the kitchen table. The coroner remarked that he did not think this indicative of being cross, as the table was not a proper place for a cat.

'It wasn't ever used for food,' said Mrs Noakes.

Dr Ryffel was the next witness. He presented the report of his analysis, in which he had concluded that there was a total of 1.48 grains of arsenic in Vera Sidney's body. As this was essentially the same evidence which had been presented at the hearing on 27 May, some participants might have been forgiven for feeling that things were now going round in circles. And when, at the conclusion of Dr Ryffel's evidence, the coroner informed the jury that there was a likelihood of another long adjournment before the next hearing could take place, Tom Sidney jumped to his feet, saying, 'May I formally protest against these long adjournments, sir?'

'I am afraid we are bound to have another long adjournment,' said Dr Jackson. 'Even if I could get through all the evidence – which I don't think is possible – there are reasons which I cannot go into at this stage why there must be another long adjournment.'

Detective Inspector Morrish was next under the spotlight. He had been assisting Inspector Hedges since the outset of the enquiry and on the night of the double exhumation he had travelled by car with Tom Sidney to the cemetery. By then Tom had been made aware of the results of the original post-mortem, which indicated that his mother had died of arsenical poisoning. Morrish claimed that during this journey, Tom Sidney said, 'If they have found arsenic in Mother, there is no reason why they should not find it in Vera,' later adding, 'Thank God I was indoors for a week with flu at that time.'

Tom was recalled and asked to explain what he meant. He said he did not remember the exact words of the conversation, but it may well have happened as Morrish told it. He had been 'highly strung up at the time' and was 'not used to getting up in the middle of the night to see my mother's body exhumed.' What Tom Sidney did not add in court, but did mention in a police statement, was that he had also understandably fortified himself with 'a few whiskies' prior to setting out. [10]

The coroner wanted to know when arsenic had first been mentioned in connection with his sister's death. Tom said that on the day after his sister died, Dr Binning had called at his house and remarked that if he had not known the family, he would have suspected arsenical poisoning in Vera's case. Asked when he had himself first suspected that arsenic had been the cause of Vera's death, Tom said it was in the mortuary, when the coffin was opened and the body appeared so well preserved. He had read somewhere that this was a sign of arsenic poisoning. In addition, someone in the mortuary had mentioned arsenic. When the coroner asked who, Tom declined to name names, saying that it had been whispered all around.

What about his remark thanking God that he had been in bed the week before? Tom said that 'with respect' he considered the statements attributed to him by the police inspectors 'highly coloured' to fit in with their own theories. Personally, he was surprised the policemen had been able to hear anything he said at all, considering the noise their car was making – an observation which provoked laughter in the court. As to saying 'thank God', it was an expression he would use many times in a day; he would, for example, say 'thank God if this inquest were over'.

'You won't be alone in that,' agreed the coroner, to the sound of renewed laughter.

As the day's proceedings drew to a close, the coroner again referred to the need for a lengthy adjournment, due to factors about which he could presently say no more. Attempting to fix a date for the next sitting, Dr Jackson noted that the holidays of two members of the jury were liable to be affected, saying that he did not want to cause unnecessary inconvenience. Dates in June were being suggested, at which Grace Duff said, 'I would like to be away on 24 and 25 June.'

'I doubt very much if that will be possible, Mrs Duff,' the coroner replied, before setting a date of Saturday, 22 June. The inconvenience or otherwise of Mrs Duff was apparently not a high priority.

It hardly took a crystal ball to work out that the factors upon which Dr Jackson was so reticent involved the exhumation of Edmund Duff, and confirmation was not slow in coming. On 12 June the *Croydon Times & Surrey County Mail* ran a story explaining that, owing to the result of the latest exhumation, the coroner was postponing the resumption of the inquest on Violet Sidney (which should have taken place that day) until 27 June, adding that police were now making enquiries into the death of 'an elderly lady who died in 1927 and is buried in Queen's Road Cemetery.' By the Saturday editions, the name of the elderly lady was given: Miss Maria Kelvey, a 'family friend' of the Duffs and Sidneys, who had died in 1927 at the age of seventy-six. In response to this press speculation, Scotland Yard issued a statement to the effect that although enquiries had been instigated three weeks ago in connection with the death, the case had now been closed and 'no further exhumations are contemplated.'

Although no formal announcement had been made to indicate that a second inquest on Edmund Duff was planned, the papers managed to get hold of the fact that Inspector Hedges had travelled down to Fordingbridge, Hampshire, to interview Mr and Mrs Edwardes, the friends with whom Edmund Duff had stayed the weekend before his death. Ever well informed, the *Croydon Advertiser* was able to state that Undercastle, the home of the Edwardes, was in an isolated spot on the borders of the New Forest and that although Mr Duff had been 'bounding with health' when he left home for his fishing trip, he had complained to the Edwardes of feeling a bit off-colour before he set out on the journey home.[11]

With no fresh inquest to report, many papers took the opportunity to give a full résumé of the mystery so far, explaining that Violet Sidney had undoubtedly taken a fatal dose of arsenic in her Metatone tonic, while Vera had succumbed to arsenic-laced soup.

'The arsenic mystery has focussed the attention of the world on Croydon,' declared the *Croydon Advertiser*. 'Never has there been a case so bizarre and bewildering.'[12]

Deprived of regular glimpses of Mrs Duff at the inquests, reporters took to door-stepping her at her home. On 16 June the *Sunday People* published an exclusive interview with her, asking about the soon-to-be denied rumours that another two bodies might be exhumed.

'I am bewildered,' Grace is alleged to have said. 'There seems no end to these exhumations. It is just one awful shock after another. The strain is terrible. It seems like some horrible, ghastly nightmare...' Naturally she added that no one was keener than she was to get at the truth and insisted that the police were only doing their duty – 'they have been so kind and straightforward.' She refused to discuss Miss Kelvey, beyond saying that she had known her very well and was shocked at reports of any investigation.

In an attempt to escape the tensions of the case, Grace Duff travelled down to Somerset, but there was no evading the press. On 16 June the *Sunday Express* ran the headline: 'Tragic Croydon Widow's Secret Holiday', thereby ensuring that any element of secrecy was short-lived. In an apparent game of spot-the-venue, the copy was provided by an *Express* reporter 'somewhere in Somerset', who wrote of Grace as 'a lonely widow in black ... in the shadow of the great weathered cathedral ... her only wish to be alone.' It was not a wish the newshound was about to grant and after evidently observing her for over an hour, he approached her for a quote. Grace, whose eyes were 'red with tears', said:

> It is too, too terrible ... people coming to see me, knocking at my door, the police calling and all these terrible inquests, with their ghastly, gruesome details, months and months of it ... there seems to be no release ... There are only my children now, they are all I have.

Grace's escape was cut short the following day, when she hurried home to Croydon on receiving news that her daughter, Mary, was unwell with a temperature.[13] Even more unwelcome news was about to come her way; although there had still been no official announcement about a fresh inquest, by the following weekend someone had leaked to journalists the news that Home Office Analyst Dr Roche Lynch had discovered arsenic in her late husband's remains.[14]

In the shadow of this latest news, the inquest into Vera Sidney's death was resumed on 22 June. By now the papers were devoting double-page spreads to the case, with the *Sunday Express* including an inset crib: 'Who's Who in the Poison Mystery'[15] and headline writers outdoing one another in producing a phrase to arrest the eye. 'Whispering Man in Poison Drama' was perhaps the most imaginative and irrelevant,[16] a phrase which referred to the fact that by the time proceedings re-opened, Tom Sidney had lost his voice. In order to overcome the difficulties this presented, he was given a seat immediately beside the coroner, who sometimes had to repeat his replies for the benefit of the jury.[17]

The coroner wanted to know exactly when Tom had first entertained suspicions that his sister's death might be due to arsenic. After some thought, Tom said that Dr Binning had first put the idea into his mind, the day after Vera died. After this the coroner moved to the question of Vera's diary, reading some extracts aloud:

1 January 1929 *Very tired tonight.*

2 January 1929 *Feeling very tired after a bad night.*

5 January 1929 *Had a bad night after a dance so did not have breakfast until 10.00. Got home at 11.20 and slept badly again.*

6 January 1929 *Very tired.*

13 January 1929 *Feel extraordinarily tired still. I seem always tired now.*

25 January 1929 *Some people came for bridge and stayed till 6.15. Had a rotten night. Feeling sick for ages and was very ill at 4.15.*

In answer to the coroner, Tom said he had not been aware, until he read the diary, that his sister had been sick on 25 January and nor had he been aware that Vera had left a note requesting that her diaries be burned, until Grace had told him about it. Grace Duff interposed at this point to say that she had found a note to this effect with Vera's will.

The coroner wanted to know more about Mrs Noakes' claim that Tom Sidney had been annoyed when he found out she had been talking to the coroner's officer about Vera's death without a member of the family being present. Tom agreed that he had been cross, believing that the proper procedure would have been for the coroner's officer to speak with a member of the family, prior to entering into discussion with a servant. Regarding the comment that the dead could make it difficult for the living, he did not think he had used those exact words.

'Did you wish for an investigation into Vera's death, to clear up the doubt?'

'I did not.'

'At this time on 6 March, did you think your mother had been poisoned?'

'I did not think that she had been criminally poisoned … I thought it was probably that she had been poisoned by her medicine and I was anxious that there should be the fullest possible investigation.'

'If that is so, why did you not want a similar investigation into your sister's death?'

'I did not want an exhumation, unless I had stronger doubt than I actually did as to the cause of her death.'

Had Tom been aware that Mrs Greenwell was coming to lunch on 13 February, Dr Jackson asked. Tom said he only heard about it on the same morning, when Vera popped in on her way to deal with her car. Had he been aware that Vera was taking any kind of medication before her death? 'Only something for piles,' Tom said.

At this point Dr Elwell was briefly recalled to state that he had never prescribed medicine containing arsenic for Vera, before Tom's interrogation was resumed. The police had managed to get hold of a letter Tom had written, in November 1928, resigning from The Savage Club,[18] which the coroner proceeded to read out in court. In the letter Tom had explained his desire to resign in terms of it being 'sometime before I can look my creditors in the face' and hoping that he would be able to rejoin the club in the future. Questioned about the letter, Tom said that he had no creditors – he had invented this supposed sudden financial embarrassment as an excuse to withdraw, when he realised after a month's probationary membership that it was going to cost him far more than he had anticipated to maintain a membership there.

Dr Jackson clearly could not fathom why anyone might have wished to suggest they had creditors when they did not, but Tom insisted it had merely been an invention to stave off embarrassment at resigning so soon. The statement had simply been untrue.

Finally Dr Jackson returned to arsenic. Had Tom any idea how it might have got into his sister's soup? Had there ever been an intimation that his mother had any arsenic in the house? Tom replied that he thought there might have been at one time, because during the war his mother had been very nervous and had said she would take poison if the Germans came.

After this it was Grace Duff's turn to give evidence. She too was subjected to more personal questions about her finances, admitting that she had been overdrawn by almost £10 at the bank when Vera died, but denying that she was in difficulties, or being pressed by her creditors. At the time she had recently purchased her current house outright, using the proceeds of her husband's life insurance policy, and was negotiating to let out the ground floor flat at a rate of £3 per week. Her aggregate income had been about £460 a year.

She confirmed her earlier remarks about Vera's diaries – there had been about twenty of them in all, and Vera had left a note asking that in the event of her death, they be burned unread.[19] When the coroner asked about the entry in the diary on 25 January, Grace said she had not been aware of her sister's illness that night, although Vera had mentioned that she 'had not been herself' at some point after Christmas.

Another diary entry related to Sunday, 10 February: *Grace came in this evening and stayed until 8.00.* Did that mean Grace had eaten supper there that night?

Grace said she seldom ate supper at her mother's house, although she had done so occasionally – possibly on 3 February – when she had some soup.

'Can you remember what sort of soup it was?'

'I remember that I did not like it at all,' the witness replied, with a hint of a smile.

She had not seen Vera or Violet have any supper while she was there on 10 February and they had spent the whole time in the drawing room. She had no idea how arsenic could have got into the soup and between Christmas and the day of Vera's death she had not been into either the kitchen or pantry of her mother's home. She was unaware that Kathleen Noakes habitually left the back door ajar. She had first heard that her aunt would be coming to lunch a couple of days before the visit took place, but she could not recall exactly when.

'When did you first have any suspicion that Vera's death was not a natural one?'

'Well I don't know. I thought she died of influenza, but I felt it was accelerated by the soup. I never felt quite easy about that soup. I felt the veal bones had probably been kept too long and gone bad.'

Sir Bernard Spilsbury appeared next. Speaking in a calm, deliberate voice, he stated that the cause of death was syncope due to acute arsenical poisoning. The analysis showed this and the symptoms were consistent with it. The empty condition of the stomach and intestines and the unusual state of preservation of the body were also characteristic of arsenical poisoning. He was of the view that Vera had taken a first dose of arsenic on Monday, when it had also made the cook and the cat sick. This dose had weakened Vera, damaging her heart and other organs. The second fatal dose had been taken on Wednesday, probably around lunchtime, in liquid rather than solid form. This pointed to arsenic having been present in the soup.

The coroner wound up proceedings for the day by announcing another lengthy adjournment, 'for reasons I cannot go into today.'

There was no chance of the story going cold however, because the next chapter in Violet Sidney's inquest was designated for 27 June. The hearing opened with a further appearance by Home Office Analyst Dr Ryffel,[20] who had been recalled because the coroner said he wished Dr Ryffel to make more plain the issues surrounding the arsenic found in the bottle of Metatone. He led Ryffel through this evidence again, starting with the fact that when the analyst first received the Metatone bottle, it had visibly contained a small amount of red liquid and a white sediment. The coroner was particularly interested in the white sediment, but Ryffel could not say whether the white sediment had specifically contained arsenic, because he had made no attempt to separate it before he added water to rinse out the contents of the bottle – and once water was added, the sediment had dissolved. He had then identified arsenic in the resultant solution.

The coroner moved on to the wine glass. Ryffel said this had contained a small amount of sticky liquid, which had a few small specks of sediment in it. He had identified a considerable quantity of arsenic in the content of the glass – too much to be accounted for by the small amount of sediment.

Mr Fearnley-Whittingstall weighed in with some questions of his own. Could Dr Ryffel say exactly how much arsenic he found in the wine glass? Ryffel said he had not measured the quantity, the method he used was 'a perfunctory' one. He had 'formed an impression'. His conclusions were based on the assumption that some liquid must have evaporated from the wine glass, but of course he was unable to calculate exactly how much. Pressed by counsel he admitted that he had not attempted to ascertain precisely how much liquid or solid material remained in the wine glass, or exactly how much arsenic was present. Was it not the case, asked the family's counsel, that it was difficult to find a mineral substance that was entirely free of arsenic and indeed that science did not know all there was to know about arsenic? Ryffel agreed, but said that as far as arsenic in ordinary, everyday substances were concerned, 'science knew all about them.' In spite of this confident assertion, as the cross-examination proceeded the imponderables inherent in Ryffel's report became obvious.

The coroner wanted to know whether the addition of Eureka or Noble's Liquid Weed Killers would produce sediment in Metatone, or give it a gritty taste. Ryffel had undertaken some experiments with Noble's Liquid Weed Killer, and established that it would produce sediment when mixed with Metatone, but only if it was allowed to stand for at least a week. According to Ryffel, adding either Noble's or Eureka Weed Killer to Metatone 'might' make it taste gritty – as would various other forms of arsenic available on the market. He still insisted that his analysis of the finger and toe nails proved that the arsenic had been ingested as one single dose – six hours was ample time for arsenic to be absorbed into the skin, and the skin had still been attached to the nails when he had done his tests.

When Dr Ryffel was released, Inspector Hedges briefly took the stand to state that Tom Sidney had purchased a tin of Eureka Weed Killer at a Croydon chemist's on 26 September 1927, signing the poisons register with his own name and address.

The next witness was Clara Collett, who had been Kathleen Noakes' predecessor at 29 Birdhurst Rise, working there from May 1927 until August 1928. She told the court that Violet's had been a happy, affectionate family and she could not recall any quarrels. Violet and Vera had been in good health and she had never thought her mistress eccentric or mentally unstable. In the fifteen months she had worked there, she could only recall Mrs Duff entering the kitchen once and that had been in order to break the news to her that Mr Duff had died. She had never seen Mr Tom Sidney in the kitchen and nor could she recall Lane the gardener ever entering the house. Neither Mr Sidney nor Mrs Duff had keys to the house. Mrs Sidney had not been in the habit of leaving medicine bottles on the sideboard; she thought medicine would have been kept in a small cupboard in the sideboard, or else in the pantry cupboard. She had never been aware of any arsenic on the premises.

Dr Bronte was recalled and asked for his opinion on Ryffel's testimony about the arsenic found in the Metatone bottle – was it possible that it could have been introduced into the medicine well before the last dose was reached, but concentrated as sediment in the bottom of the bottle, so that there were no poisonous effects until the last dose was taken? Bronte explained that this could only have occurred if arsenic was particularly slow to dissolve in Metatone – otherwise some of it must have been ingested each time the patient took a dose and this would have brought on symptoms of poisoning. However, in the light of hearing that Dr Ryffel tested the fingernails while they were still attached to the skin, he did withdraw his contention that there must have been a previous dose of arsenic.

Mr Fearnley-Whittingstall then posed one of the most convoluted, if not face-tious, questions ever put by counsel in a coroner's court: 'If an unknown amount of water was added to an unknown amount of medicine, containing an unknown amount of sediment which contains an unknown amount of arsenic, of which an unknown amount was dissolved and an unknown amount left, would you consider that sufficient data on which to form a theory such as Dr Ryffel has formed?'

'I am afraid I cannot follow the question,' replied Dr Bronte. 'My answer must therefore remain unknown.'

Frederick Rose, the local chemist, was recalled and it transpired that he too had turned detective, carrying out some experiments of his own with Metatone and a variety of arsenic-based substances. He had tried dissolving arsenic in both Metatone and water, observing that although arsenic dissolved more easily in water than in Metatone, there was not really much difference between the two.

Then came Ivy Walker, who had been employed as Grace Duff's 'daily' since the beginning of the year. She deposed that she first heard Mrs Greenwell was expected on the day itself, when Grace asked her to prepare extra food as Mrs Greenwell would be coming round for tea.

She also recalled the day of Mrs Sidney's final illness. Mrs Duff had come home during the afternoon and described how she found her mother in the dining room, looking as if she had suffered a stroke. When Mrs Walker arrived for work the following day, she learned from Mrs Duff that Mrs Sidney had died. Mrs Duff had appeared very upset and said she could not understand it, but had not expressed any suspicions about the cause. Afterwards she had cried a great deal.

Grace herself was the next witness called, and for the second time in recent days, she was required to go over her financial position for the benefit of another jury.

Tom Sidney followed her in the witness chair, because Dr Jackson wanted to revisit the alleged discovery of the dirty teaspoon on the sideboard. Why had Tom not mentioned finding it until some weeks after the event? Tom said he had not thought it important. He had not noticed it until some time after Inspector Hedges had taken away the wine glass. The coroner wanted to know why he and Hedges had missed the spoon when Hedges took away the glass, but Tom was unable to say.

Returning to financial matters, the coroner went into the whole business of the resignation letter to The Savage Club again, with Tom repeating that he was not in financial trouble and had not been receiving money from his mother or any other relatives. He confirmed that on the day before she died, he had been talking to his mother about some investments in connection with Vera's estate, but it had been a perfectly amicable discussion.

With regard to Kathleen Noakes' claim to have seen him in the hall on the morning of his mother's death, Tom was adamant that the incident described by Mrs Noakes had 'never occurred'. There had never been an occasion at any time when he had entered his mother's house with one of his children, but not gone in to see his mother.

A juryman wanted to return to the question of the spoon: surely Mr Sidney must have realised before he washed it up that it was evidence? Tom said he had not thought it important, because the police already had the medicine bottle and the glass. Inspector Hedges, ever anxious to defend any possible question of his own competence, also chipped in. Was it not possible that Tom Sidney had collected the spoon from some other part of the household, then left it on the sideboard and forgotten it? Tom agreed that it was possible.

'If my eyesight was sufficiently good to see the wine glass, would it not be sufficiently good enough to see the spoon beside it?'

Tom might well have retorted that Hedges had failed to spot the dirty wine glass until forty-eight hours after his original 'top to bottom' search of Violet's house and had in fact missed numerous other 'suspicious' items, including the old Eureka tin in the shed, but he merely shook his head and laughed.

Kathleen Noakes was the last witness of the day and was asked to confirm yet again that she had never seen any arsenic at 29 Birdhurst Rise. The proceedings were then adjourned until the end of July.

CHAPTER SIX

'LIKE SOME HORRIBLE, GHASTLY NIGHTMARE...'

The rumour mills were still churning as June turned into July. A suggestion that there might need to be a second exhumation involving the body of Edmund Duff provoked an angry letter from his widow, which was published in *The Times* on 2 July and swiftly reprinted by many of its competitors.

Describing Edmund as a 'loving and faithful husband', Grace claimed that she had not objected to the first exhumation because if the previous post-mortem had been 'in any sense perfunctory' then it was only right to hold a second. However, she stated that, since the exhumation had taken place:

> I have not been told one word officially about what was or was not discovered in my husband and when I naturally expected an immediate second inquest to clear the matter up, I was told I had no right to demand one. Now through the public medium of the Press I learn that 'a second exhumation of Mr E.C. Duff is being considered'. Surely as his widow and the mother of his children, I have the right to ask that before a further disturbance of his grave takes place, a public inquest should be held to see if such a course is truly necessary?
>
> I know this is a dreadful and difficult case, and I do not want to make any difficulties, but I do consider that the second examination should have been absolutely thorough; and that it should not be possible in a Christian country that the body of a good and decent citizen should be treated in such a cruel and casual way, because two or three Home Office experts disagree, presumably about the decimal quantities of the drugs found in him, a year after his death. Even savages respect their dead.

Grace closed by saying that any wife who had cared for her husband would understand her feelings.

Scotland Yard were swift to refute the idea that they were contemplating a second exhumation of Mr Duff's body. On the same day the letter was published, Grace got her wish, when the Attorney General appeared before the Chief Justice to apply for a second inquest – a step which entailed the formal quashing of the original verdict. By Friday, 5 July these legal formalities had been completed and Dr Jackson opened a second inquest into the death of Edmund Creighton Duff, just over thirteen months after he had closed the first.[1]

Having sworn in a jury, Dr Jackson began by outlining the story of Edmund Duff's last days: how he had gone to stay with friends for a few days fishing, come home complaining of feeling unwell, become ill and died the next day – a story with which, unless they had been living on another planet for the previous four months, the jury members must have already been extremely familiar, as versions had been appearing in the local and national newspapers for several weeks.[2]

The process of taking evidence began with coroner's officer Samuel Clarke, who described how he had visited the Duffs' home twice in the days after Edmund Duff's death. Mrs Duff had given him every assistance, he said, pointing out a tin of Noble's Weed Killer in the cellar when he asked whether any poisons were kept in the house. He had taken a sample of the weedkiller, using a funnel to pour it out of the tin. Clarke said he could not be sure whether the tin had been opened previously, but it had appeared pretty full and he had great difficulty getting the cork out of the neck. At this point, anyone whose memory stretched back to Arthur Lane's original evidence might have been moved to consider whether the coroner's officer was just as careless with poisonous weedkiller as was the old gardener – the uncorked tin having been discovered, still with a funnel in it, when Grace Duff asked Lane to remove it from her property several months later.

Mrs Duff obtained the coroner's permission to leave the court while John Baker, a mortuary attendant, gave evidence about the original 1928 post-mortem, firstly listing which organs had been extracted and put into jars for analysis on that occasion. Baker told the court that Dr Bronte had conducted two post-mortems at the Mayday Hospital on the day in question: Edmund Duff's and that of an eighty-four-year-old woman called Rose Walker, but no organs had been extracted from Rose Walker's body. The Duff post-mortem had been undertaken first and the organs placed in sealed jars – it would have been impossible for any organs other than Edmund Duff's to have got into the jars labelled with his name.

The third witness was another regular member of the Croydon Mystery cast, undertakers' man Sydney Gardiner, who deposed to identifying the remains in the Mayday Hospital – a service he had now performed in respect of all three members of the family.

Dr Elwell followed Gardiner. He stated that he had been attending the Duff family since about December 1920, but prior to the end of April 1928 he had only treated Edmund Duff about five times, always for minor ailments. He had never prescribed him any arsenic. His first intimation of Edmund Duff's final illness had been a telephone call from Mrs Duff, at about 7 o'clock on the evening of 26 April 1928, asking him to call as her husband was unwell. When he arrived about twenty minutes later, he found Edmund Duff sitting in the drawing room. The patient had a temperature of 99, was complaining that his throat was bad and said he thought he was in for a dose of malaria. Elwell had given him aspirin and quinine and advised him to go to bed.

The following day another message had been left for him to see Mr Duff, but as he was unavailable Dr Binning had attended instead. Binning subsequently told him that the patient was suffering from vomiting and diarrhoea and that he had found nothing to account for these symptoms. Later that night Mrs Duff telephoned again and asked him to come to the house urgently, which he did; Dr Binning had arrived shortly after he did. On arrival he found Edmund breathing very badly. Asked about Grace Duff, Dr Elwell said she had appeared very anxious and had asked, 'He's not going to die is he?' She attempted to give her husband a cup of tea, but although he tried to take a mouthful, his lower jaw dropped and the tea fell out of his mouth: 'he gave three or four gasps and was gone.'

Although Edmund was obviously dead, he and Binning had performed artificial respiration for about twenty minutes, in an attempt to lessen the shock for Mrs Duff. When he explained to her that he could not issue a death certificate, she had raised no objection and indeed she appeared keen to find out what had caused her husband's death. He himself had been puzzled by the illness, which he had initially conjectured might be some form of food poisoning.

After Dr Elwell's evidence, the inquest was adjourned until the following Thursday, when Dr Jackson opened proceedings with the announcement that Dr Roche Lynch, the analyst who had performed various tests on Edmund Duff's organs, was unable to attend. He had, however, submitted a written report. Roche Lynch had calculated that there was 0.815, 'or about ⅘ grain – a considerable quantity', of arsenic in the body.[3] This announcement presumably caused less of a sensation among the public than it would have done had the papers not broken the news that arsenic had been found in Edmund Duff's remains more than three weeks previously. Not that this prevented the *Croydon Times* from running a front-page headline 'Sensational Evidence in Croydon Poison Drama – Analyst's Report Made Public'. The layout of the *Croydon Times* was unusual in that it tended to put unrelated photographs on the front page beneath its main news headline, leading to incongruous juxtapositions of bridal groups or smiling lady tennis players, who at first glance appeared to be somehow implicated in the arsenic case – thus beneath the 'Sensational Evidence' headline were depicted the entrants in the local bonny babies contest.

The first witness to testify in person on 11 July was Colonel Charles De Vertus Duff, a retired army officer turned tennis coach, who lived in Earls Court. He explained that he was Edmund Duff's youngest brother and they had five other siblings who all lived abroad.[4] According to Charles Duff, he had been in the habit of meeting up with his brother about half a dozen times a year, sometimes at the Duffs' home in Croydon, sometimes elsewhere. He said Edmund had appeared very happy in his home life and very fond of his wife. He had never known the couple to quarrel or complain about one another.

'Would you say your brother was a jealous man?' asked Dr Jackson.

'I daresay he was.'

'Did his wife ever give him cause for jealousy?'

'None whatever.'

When the coroner asked about Edmund's health, Colonel Duff replied that Edmund had suffered from malaria in both India and Africa, but he could not say whether he had had any attacks since returning permanently to England. Recently he had appeared a thoroughly healthy man and only a month or so before his death, Charles Duff had observed his brother vault over a sofa to sit beside his wife. He had learned of his brother's death from Mrs Duff, who telephoned him immediately after it happened. Until he heard of the exhumation he had never thought his brother's death to be other than from natural causes or ptomaine poisoning, and in fact he had thought the exhumation unnecessary.

The coroner asked whether he had ever known his brother to take arsenic. Charles Duff said he had not, but that anyone who had spent a long time abroad would be in the habit of doctoring themselves, and arsenic was sometimes taken for malaria. He had been aware that his brother took Calomel,[5] which was a 'favourite medicine'.

On the subject of Edmund's drinking habits, Charles said his brother had been a moderate drinker, who usually had a bottle of beer with his evening meal. He had never known Grace to drink beer.

Dr Elwell was recalled and agreed that Duff had always appeared a healthy, robust man. He was aware that his patient had suffered from malaria while abroad and was afraid of the disease recurring. In fact, he and Edmund had sometimes discussed tropical diseases; they had been on friendly terms, the doctor said – if he called about one of the children and Edmund Duff was at home 'we had a yarn together'.

Moving on to his house call on the night of Edmund's return from Hampshire, Dr Elwell said he was vague about the times, but now thought he had arrived at the Duffs' house by car at about 8 o'clock. The front door was open and he had gone straight in. Mr and Mrs Duff were in the sitting room and he had not been aware of a maid or anyone else in the house. He had not thought Edmund Duff seriously ill when he first visited on 26 April, but his condition had worsened the following day. He had not seen any food on that first visit, or any sign of a meal having recently been eaten. He had been puzzled by the symptoms and, after Mr Duff died, he had reported the death to the coroner. He agreed that he had told Mrs Duff he suspected ptomaine poisoning. Asked if the symptoms were consistent with arsenical poisoning, Elwell replied, 'In the later stages, certainly.' Dr Elwell was then called upon to describe the moments immediately before and after Edmund's death. When Mrs Duff realised her husband had died, Elwell said, 'she was frightfully distressed and grieved. She knelt by his side and kissed him.' As Elwell outlined the scene Grace was observed to be wiping tears from her eyes.

Mr Fearnley-Whittingstall wanted to know whether Edmund had ever suggested to Dr Elwell that he had been doctoring himself. Elwell replied that he could not say whether the deceased had been in the habit of this, but in his experience, when patients did self medicate, the last person in the world they would tell was their own doctor.

It had been another long interrogation. At the commencement of the Edmund Duff inquest, the Metropolitan Police had also engaged the services of a barrister – Mr Roome – and now he too cross-examined witnesses, so that the proceedings became even longer, more than ever taking on the appearance of a trial, even if no one had been openly accused.

After the lunch break, Tom Sidney was back in the chair. As usual the formalities had to be gone through and when Tom had identified himself and given his address, Dr Jackson prompted: 'You are an entertainer?'

'I was.'

'But it is still your occupation, isn't it?'

'I may return to it, if these inquests end before my old age,' said Tom, with what the *Croydon Advertiser* described as 'some show of irritation in his tone'.

As usual the coroner initially concentrated on establishing background and relationships. According to Tom Sidney, he first met Edmund Duff in 1911 and they had always been good friends. Edmund and Grace had lived happily together and been mutually fond of each other, and Grace had been a very good wife to him. He had never known them have a serious quarrel, although he had once seen Edmund become angry with her.

The coroner was most interested in this and Tom was required to elaborate. He claimed that the episode had occurred while he was in the sitting room at Grace's house, two or three days before Edmund went on his fishing trip – his wife had asked him to fetch something and Edmund 'jumped up in a frightful temper' and left the room, although when he returned a minute or two later he was perfectly placid. Questioned further, Tom said he could not be sure whether the anger had been directed at Grace or himself, but when Dr Jackson asked if this might have been an isolated incident, Tom said he did not think it was, as his mother once told him that Edmund had been quick-tempered. The coroner said he could not put that in the deposition, as it was hearsay.

'I daresay Mrs Duff will bear me out,' said Tom.

'Certainly not,' Grace interposed. 'He was a very good-tempered man.'

Tom confirmed Charles Duff's contention that Edmund was a moderate drinker, in the habit of taking a bottle of beer with his evening meal and also a heavy smoker. He did not think Grace drank at all, except a glass of champagne at Christmas.

The last witness of the day was Amy Clarke, who testified that she had been the Duffs' domestic servant for about three months by the time Edmund died and had continued with Mrs Duff until August 1928. Her hours had been 7.30 in the morning to 7.30 at night, although she sometimes stayed on up to an hour later. In her experience the Duffs had been a happy couple; she had never heard them quarrel and he had seemed a cheerful, healthy man. She confirmed that Edmund was the only beer drinker in the house and liked to have a bottle of Bass every evening with his supper.

On the evening Mr Duff returned from his fishing trip, she had prepared his supper and taken it into the sitting room on a tray; the whole family were in there, Mr and Mrs Duff and their three children. The supper tray had comprised roast chicken, potatoes, cheese and a bottle of beer. She had not poured the beer out, but had removed the paper seal and the stopper. When she took the tray in, Mrs Duff said to her, 'Don't you think Mr Duff looks well?' and she had replied in the affirmative. She left the room before Mr Duff started eating.

At this point the inquest had to be adjourned, but after months of plodding the proceedings seemed to gain a new mood of urgency. Instead of a lengthy adjournment, the coroner reconvened the following morning for another all-day session, commencing with Amy Clarke back in the witness chair.[6]

The coroner began by asking her about the day of Edmund's death. Amy Clarke said she had arrived for work as usual and learned from Mrs Duff that Edmund was ill in bed. She had prepared no food or drink for him that day except a cup of Bovril, but she did not think he had drunk it. Mrs Duff had not discussed the symptoms with her, but she did say that her husband had been 'seedy' in the night and 'looked very queer'. Mrs Duff had spent a good deal of the day with her husband, while the older children had played in the garden.

The coroner took her back to the evening before, when Edmund Duff returned from Hampshire. Amy Clarke confirmed that Mrs Duff went to meet her husband from the station and she heard them enter the house together and go into the sitting room. About twenty minutes later she had taken Mr Duff's supper in. He always had his supper on a tray in the sitting room at about 7.10. Mrs Duff and the children ate their main meal at lunchtime, then had tea in the afternoon, and thus on a working day the only meal Mr Duff took with the rest of the family was breakfast. Other details of the Duffs' domestic life emerged, including the fact that Mr and Mrs Duff had separate bedrooms – she sleeping in the large front bedroom and he in a smaller adjoining room. Amy Clarke had never seen any arsenic or Calomel in the house, but she did know that Mr Duff had often taken Eno's Fruit Salts. Mr Duff's beer had been delivered to the house, six bottles at a time; these were kept in their crate in the larder, which was close to the side door of the house. She agreed that as the side door was not locked during the day, it would have been easy for anyone to get in without being seen.

After Mr Duff's death, Mrs Duff had been much more careful about her expenditure and Amy Clarke left her service when Mrs Duff could no longer afford to employ a maid for a full day and wanted someone to work part time hours.

Tom Sidney – without whose participation no session appeared to be complete – was recalled and asked about the Duffs' financial position. His brother-in-law had never confided in him about financial matters, he said, so he had no idea how much he earned – nor had either man ever borrowed money from the other. It was common knowledge in the family that about five years before he died, Edmund had invested and lost a greater part of the £5,000 legacy Grace had received on her father's death, although Tom believed some of that money had been used to buy a house.

He had first heard of Edmund's illness on the day after Edmund returned from Hampshire. He couldn't recall whether it had first been mentioned by Vera or his wife Margaret. On the Friday, Vera had said something to the effect that there was nothing much wrong with Edmund, who was making a big fuss over nothing, but next morning she had come round at about 7 o'clock to break the news that Edmund was dead. Tom agreed that there had been some discussion in the family about Edmund's last illness, with speculation about tropical diseases and also what he might have eaten while away from home. He had not attended the original inquest, but Vera had gone with Grace and later 'told us all about it'. He denied that he had ever wondered whether Edmund died of arsenical poisoning before his body was exhumed, or that he had been puzzled by Vera's death. Nor had it occurred to him that there was anything suspicious about his mother's death until arsenic was found in her body. He did not think he had repeated to anyone Dr Binning's remark after Vera died – about suspecting arsenic if he had not known the family.

Although pressed by Mr Roome, Tom denied that the similarity in the symptoms of all three of his relatives had struck him as suspicious. He said that his own theory about Edmund's death was food poisoning from eating bad fish and he hotly denied entertaining some other theory which he would prefer not to speak aloud. Pointing a finger at the witness, Mr Roome asked if he was trying to shield someone, to which Tom replied angrily, 'Certainly not.'

When asked again who had first put the idea of arsenical poisoning into his head, he said, 'I might bring in the name of Inspector Hedges...' – at which the coroner rebuked him for being flippant.

The hearing was adjourned to the following day, and when it recommenced at 1 p.m., many of those required to attend must have felt they would prefer to be otherwise engaged. It was a hot sunny Saturday, the Gentleman versus Players match was in full swing at The Oval, while down at Grangewood Park a different kind of bowler could cast his woods to the distant strains of popular tunes from the bandstand, and residents tending their back gardens in Birdhurst Rise could hear the sound of tennis balls being thwacked at the nearby Birdhurst Tennis Club. In spite of these multiple opportunities for recreation, the room was packed, with all the press and public seating claimed by the time proceedings began.[7]

Tom Sidney returned to the witness chair for another gruelling cross-examination by Mr Roome, who wanted to know all about the tin of weedkiller in his shed. Tom agreed that anyone who went into the garden could go into the shed and see the tin standing on the shelf, but pointed out that not many people did walk about in his garden and when asked specifically about Grace, he said that he did not think his sister was even aware that he kept any weedkiller.

When Mr Roome returned to the 'quarrel' observed by Tom Sidney a few days before Edmund Duff went on holiday, Tom pointed out that it was not a quarrel – in fact, on reflection he thought Edmund had been annoyed with him, rather than Grace. He had been in the habit of going round to play his latest compositions for Grace, but unfortunately Edmund always loathed Tom's music, so it had probably been his own impromptu performance on the piano which provoked his brother-in-law's irritation.

One of the jury asked what terms Edmund Duff had been on with his wife's family.

'My sister Vera liked him – they were great pals. My sister Grace loved him dearly. I can frankly say that my mother didn't like him, although he was fond of her.'

Asked to elaborate further about his mother, Tom explained that Violet blamed Edmund for the loss of Grace's inheritance and also felt that Edmund had been wrong to give up his well-paid job in Nigeria.

'My mother liked the good things in life. She liked people to have money and they had lost their money.' She had also blamed Edmund for the fact that the Duffs had what Violet considered to be too many children, as every addition to the family 'caused worry'.

Throughout most of this evidence Grace Duff had been visibly struggling with her emotions and when the next witness began to talk about her husband, she took out her handkerchief and wept openly. Harold Edwardes had been one of Edmund Duff's oldest friends; first meeting him when they were stationed together in Nigeria, more than twenty years before. When Edwardes was transferred elsewhere the two men had stayed in touch by letter and in 1914, when Edwardes returned to Ilorin, serving as Duff's second in command for four months, they had become 'great friends'. When Edwardes retired from the colonial service in 1925, he and his wife had once stayed overnight with the Duffs and there was a longstanding reciprocal invitation to stay at the Edwardes' home near Fordingbridge.

It had eventually been arranged that Edmund should come for a few days fishing and he had arrived on Monday, 23 April 1928, by the 3.30 train. He brought with him photographs of Grace and the children and spoke about them in affectionate terms. On Tuesday he spent the whole day fishing. It had been a very hot day, Mr Edwardes recalled, and Edmund had not worn a hat. He had not said anything about feeling unwell on Tuesday, but on Wednesday morning, after strolling out to get a paper, he said he had a touch of fever, which his friend took to mean malaria. On account of his feeling unwell they had not gone fishing that day, although Edmund did have 'a knock at tennis' for a while. Next morning he read in the library and after lunch his hosts took him to the station. He had appeared cheerful and talked about coming down again, so when Mrs Duff telephoned to tell them that Edmund was dead the Edwardes had been 'astounded'. Grace had asked whether any member of their household had been unwell, but no one had had any illness at all and Edmund had eaten nothing which they had not eaten themselves.

Asked whether he had any arsenic on his premises, Edwardes said he did not – except of course some Eureka Weed Killer in his workshop. The workshop was not kept locked, but he had no idea whether Edmund had gone in there during his visit. He knew that Edmund had used arsenic in Nigeria to treat horses for tsetse fly, but was unable to say whether he had also used it for his personal medicinal needs, although Mr Edwardes himself had often taken arsenic in the form of Easton's Syrup, which was 'a favourite tonic in the tropics'.

As the rest of the hearing was devoted to further medical evidence, Grace Duff obtained the coroner's permission to absent herself, and went to sit under the trees outside; everyone else remained in the stuffy overcrowded room, waiting to hear what the doctors had to say.

Sir Bernard Spilsbury was first. He explained that, on opening the body, he found a number of organs were missing, because of the earlier post-mortem. He carefully listed the absent items, making particular mention that the whole of the trachea[8] was still *in situ*, before laying great stress on the good state of preservation in which he found the body. With so many organs missing, he said, it would be impossible to state what had been the cause of death from a post-mortem alone, but he based his conclusions on the preservation of the body and the analyst's report.

Instead of Dr Ryffel, who had handled the analysis and appeared as a witness at Violet's and Vera's inquests, the Home Office had appointed Dr Gerard Roche Lynch, whose report, the coroner noted, contained a curious error – it dated the exhumation and post-mortem as having taken place on 17, rather than 18 May – as did Sir Bernard Spilsbury's.

While heads nodded in the heat, Dr Lynch read out his long complex report, which incorporated a series of mathematical calculations by which he had arrived at the conclusion that Edmund Duff's body contained 0.815 grain of arsenic. From this result he was confident that Edmund Duff's death had been the result of a large dose of arsenic, taken within a day or two of his death. Had the missing organs been available for testing, he had no doubt they would have yielded up more arsenic.

Mr Fearnley-Whittingstall wanted to know if that was not a rather dangerous assumption – had a case of death by arsenical poisoning ever been diagnosed before on the basis of finding just 0.815 grain in the remains? Lynch responded that the amount of arsenic was low because the victim had survived for some length of time after consuming the fatal dose, a great deal of which would therefore have been expelled by vomiting. Since no one knew when or how Edmund Duff had consumed a dose of arsenic, this was clearly conjecture and Fearnley-Whittingstall went so far as to suggest that Dr Lynch had worked on a premise of assuming what he wanted to prove was correct, then setting out to prove it. The analyst stuck to his guns, however, saying he had no doubt that a fatal dose of arsenic, taken several hours before Duff's demise, had been the cause of death.

The next witness was Dr Bronte, the pathologist who had performed the first post-mortem in April 1928. Referring to his original notes, Bronte said that when he had examined Edmund Duff, he found the stomach wall was normal and showed no evidence of poison. He had removed various body parts and organs for testing and these had been placed in jars which he had sealed himself. The organs were listed in the mortuary post-mortem book (which was produced) and he had instructed the mortuary assistant to lock the jars containing the samples in the cupboard as usual, until they were handed over to the district analyst. His notes included: '? As', which meant that the tests undertaken should include arsenic.

Earlier the same day he had carried out a post-mortem on the body of Rose Walker. It had been conducted on a separate table, no organs had been removed and that examination had been completed before the examination on Edmund Duff began. He had not put a section of trachea into any of the jars.

He had subsequently been present on 18 May 1929 when Sir Bernard Spilsbury had undertaken a second post-mortem, and was now of the opinion that death had been due to acute arsenical poisoning. Asked what had changed his mind, he said, 'The analysis of Dr Lynch and the report of Sir Bernard Spilsbury.'

The final witness of the session was Hugh Candy, the chemistry lecturer at the London Hospital Medical School, who had performed the original analysis on the organs sent to him by Dr Bronte, which had produced a negative for arsenic. Candy was questioned closely about exactly what had been in the jars he received. In the notebook he had used to record the contents of each jar as he opened them, he had written 'lung and trachea'. Spilsbury's insistence on mentioning that Edmund Duff's trachea remained intact now became clear: there was an underlying suggestion afoot that the organs in the jars sent to Candy had not come from Edmund Duff, but had somehow been confused with those of Rose Walker, although Candy somewhat undermined this by pointing out that although he wrote 'trachea', the sample attached to the lung might have been a piece of bronchus.[9] It was rather more difficult for him to explain how he could have missed the presence of arsenic when he was specifically testing for it. Candy's only explanation was that he had been testing for a whole variety of poisons and while it was true that the single organ he had tested for arsenic had shown an absolute negative, perhaps he would have found it if he had tested other organs. Perhaps the organ he had chosen to test had been 'poorer in arsenic' than all the others, he suggested.

It had been a long day in a hot, airless room. As the hours ticked by, the public began to drift away and by the time the inquest closed at 9 o'clock that night, the jury might have been forgiven for completely losing track of which organ had been extracted at which post-mortem and had tested positive for what – and moreover their respite from this oral bombardment was to be short lived as the inquest was adjourned to resume in less than forty-eight hours time on Tuesday, 16 July.

On Tuesday morning, spectators were present in even greater numbers than before, with more than 100 people, mostly women, packing into the seats designated for the public.[10] Interest in the proceedings had intensified even further with the rumour that two more exhumations were being contemplated, although, like the stories about Maria Kelvey, this proved to be false, with Scotland Yard issuing a formal denial by Thursday – alas not soon enough to prevent the *Croydon Times* going to press with its 20 July edition containing a report that 'application may be made in the next few days to order exhumations on Kathleen Duff who died age 7 on 20 September 1919 and Suzanne Duff who died age 2 on 16 March 1924.' As if this kind of thing were not bad enough, the family were also being plagued with anonymous letters at the rate of several a day from all over the country, some offering suggestions about the mystery, but many of an abusive or threatening nature.[11]

The first witness on Tuesday morning was Dr Binning, whose performance in the witness chair was a mass of half-remembered contradictions – perhaps not altogether surprising in view of the fact that he was being asked to recall, in detail, an episode which had taken place some fifteen months previously. He said that he had first become involved in the case when he called at Dr Elwell's house on the morning of 27 April and picked up a message from Mrs Duff, asking for a house call. He made the visit himself, arriving between 11 a.m. and midday, when he was told by Mrs Duff that her husband had suffered some vomiting and diarrhoea. Dr Jackson said this was an important point and he wanted to know whether Dr Binning was sure he had been told this on the first visit. Binning said he was sure, although he couldn't recall whether Mrs Duff or her husband had told him.

He had made a fairly cursory examination of the patient, because he had not thought him very ill; 'he was always a man to make the most of small things,' and Binning assumed him to be making a fuss about nothing. He decided it was a bad case of colic 'due to some indiscretion in diet' and prescribed a dose of Calomel. He was not in the house for more than ten minutes.

In response to another call from Mrs Duff, he visited again between 6 p.m. and 8 p.m. and found Edmund Duff much worse. He was now complaining of pains in his legs and abdomen, had a rapid pulse and his colour was grey. During this visit Edmund had attempted to get to the toilet and collapsed on the floor, where he had an attack of diarrhoea. This was the only vomiting or diarrhoea Binning had observed and he said that up until then 'it had been my impression that diarrhoea had not been a feature of the case' – the exact opposite of his earlier certainty that he had been told about problems with sickness and diarrhoea during the morning visit. A few minutes later, Binning would contradict himself yet again on this point, by claiming that he thought Mr Duff had told him he had suffered from two or three loose motions during the afternoon.

At this second visit, Binning said he had begun to consider the possibility of food poisoning, asking Edmund what he had eaten the evening before. Edmund told him chicken, potatoes and two bottles of beer, but that he had been feeling unwell before he arrived home and indeed had returned home early, to avoid being ill in someone else's home. Dr Jackson asked if Edmund had also been drinking whisky and sodas throughout the afternoon and Binning agreed that he might have been and that he would have endorsed this as a good treatment. During this second visit, the patient was in so much pain that he and Mrs Duff had applied turpentine stupes[12] to Duff's abdomen in an attempt to alleviate it. It was during this visit that Binning formed the impression that the case was very serious and that Edmund might die. The patient himself was extremely fearful about his condition – he knew that he was seriously ill and 'his terror was marked'.

Binning had done his best to make the patient comfortable before returning home, from whence he rang Dr Elwell and informed him about the grave state of the case. He had only just put the phone down when Mrs Duff rang him again – no more than ten minutes could have elapsed since his leaving her. She said her husband was much worse, but was asking for a cup of tea – could she give him one? He agreed to the tea and returned straight away to the house, where Dr Elwell had already arrived. It was then about 10.30 and Edmund Duff was in a collapsed condition. Binning tried injections of digitalin, followed by strychnine and later pituitrin, but there was no reaction to any of them and Duff died some time between 11 p.m. and midnight.

Dr Jackson now moved to the question of Binning's alleged suspicions about the subsequent deaths. The doctor denied that he had entertained any suspicions about Vera's death until after Violet's, or that he had made the comment to Tom Sidney about suspecting arsenical poisoning if he had not known the family better. He agreed that he had been assured that he had made the remark, but could only think he had said it after Violet's death, rather than Vera's. He also denied telling any member of the family on the day of Edmund's death that the patient was making a fuss about nothing, claiming that he could not remember meeting any members of the family that day – at which Mr Fearnley-Whittingstall interjected that he had been instructed that both Violet and Vera Sidney had visited the Duffs' house in the afternoon of the day that Edmund died. Finally there were more questions about Edmund's symptoms, with Binning saying that they had not been compatible with acute arsenical poisoning in the early stages, but were in the later stages.

According to some reports, when the next witness was called an expectant hush fell across the room. Grace Duff was forty-two in 1929 and contemporary photographs show that she was still an attractive woman, slim and elegantly dressed. People who met her recalled her striking 'lake-blue eyes'.[13] Dr Jackson embarked on his usual scene-setting exercise, guiding Grace through her husband's career, employment and earnings, all the addresses in which they had resided during their long marriage, and the names and ages of all their children. Asked about their life together, Grace predictably stated that they had been happily married and were mutually fond of one another.

The interrogation eventually reached Monday, 23 April 1928, when Grace had seen her husband off at the station for his trip to Hampshire. He had been well and happy, she said, very much looking forward to a few days fishing. She next heard from him on Tuesday evening, when he telephoned her on the night of his fifty-ninth birthday. He had sounded cheerful, telling her what fish he had caught that day. He had not mentioned being unwell, but did say that he had decided he would come home on Thursday. On Thursday morning she received a postcard giving the time of his train[14] – there had been no other message on the card.

That evening she walked down the road to meet him, taking the baby with her, and they met at the end of South Park Hill Road. As soon as she saw him, Grace commented that he looked sunburned and well, but her husband replied, 'It's not wellness, it's fever,' and explained that he had a sore throat and felt he had 'something coming on'.

When they reached the house, Edmund and their son John went into the garden to pick up his luggage. (Number 16 South Park Hill Road backed onto South Croydon station, and the porter was in the habit of lifting the Duffs' luggage over the fence so they would not have to carry it all the way round by road.) No sooner had father and son gone into the garden than John ran back inside to say that as his father bent down to pick up the luggage, he had suddenly trembled all over. Grace went out and helped Edmund inside, while John took care of the bags. She had immediately telephoned for Dr Elwell, but he was out.

The whole family sat in the drawing room and Edmund's supper was brought in as usual. According to Grace, Edmund opened the bottle of beer himself. She said she did not notice whether the paper seal was broken, but was sure Edmund would have remarked on it if it had been. He drank his beer, but did not eat much of the chicken and potatoes. She had no recollection of his drinking a second bottle of beer, but agreed that it was entirely possible he had it without her noticing.

Dr Elwell eventually arrived at about 8 o'clock and examined Edmund. He prescribed some quinine, but later Edmund mentioned that he was also going to take some opening medicine. The first time he actually complained of feeling sick was as they were going upstairs to bed, when he 'came over queer again and went a greenish colour'. He had gone into the bathroom but she did not know whether he had been sick. She retired to her own bedroom, but later she was aware of Edmund moving about a great deal during the night and moaning, although when she asked him what was wrong, he told her to go back to bed. He was sick several times the next morning, firstly at about 7 o'clock, when he said he intended to take another dose of opening medicine. She telephoned for another visit from Dr Elwell, but Dr Binning had come instead, arriving around midday.

As the day progressed Edmund complained of pain in his feet, then in his abdomen and he came out in a cold sweat. They piled blankets on top of him and put hot water bottles in the bed; with Dr Binning's permission she had ordered a bottle of whisky for Edmund, from which he had several whisky and sodas during the afternoon, but nothing to eat. Grace recalled how, as his condition worsened, Edmund became increasingly anxious. The two doctors had not been the only visitors to the house: her mother had called in twice and Vera several times. Margaret Sidney had popped in once, but Tom had not been round that day. None of the family had gone into the bedroom.

Dr Binning returned during the evening, by which time Edmund was 'terrified about himself'. At about 9 o'clock she and Binning were downstairs when they heard Edmund fall. They rushed upstairs to find he was on the bedroom floor and had suffered an attack of diarrhoea – the only instance of diarrhoea in the whole duration of his illness. That was also the only time Edmund had attempted to get out of bed all day.

Dr Elwell had given Grace a sleeping cachet for Edmund, to be given as soon as he stopped being sick for half an hour or more. Sometime between 11 p.m. and midnight she had called Dr Binning to ask if she might give him this with a cup of tea. While she was making the tea, Edmund called out that he couldn't speak or breathe and that something had gone wrong with his throat. She rang Dr Binning and asked him to come immediately.

At this point the inquest was adjourned until Saturday – no doubt much to the irritation of any member of the jury who had other plans.[15] To add to their frustration, the weekend weather again turned out hot and sunny.

The first witness on 20 July was Dr Ryffel, who plodded through his usual list of bottles, jars and tins acquired by Inspector Hedges from various family homes, which Ryffel had already told two inquest juries were harmless except for the various weedkillers, which included arsenic among their known ingredients.[16] Towards the end of this evidence Tom Sidney jumped to his feet and said, 'The agents who are letting my mother's house tell me they have found thirty or forty articles, mostly medicine bottles, which are now locked in a cupboard there.'

'But the police searched the house after your mother's death,' said Dr Jackson.

'Yes, but all the medicine bottles have not been taken away.'

Ryffel attempted to continue with his evidence, getting as far as saying that he had received thirty-one medicine bottles from the coroner's officer, before Tom interrupted again: 'My point is that everything should be tested. I don't want it thrown up later on that I have thrown something away which ought to have been tested.'

The coroner managed to get proceedings back on track by saying that Inspector Hedges would have to go into the matter later, and Ryffel was allowed to finish his evidence without further interruption, after which Grace Duff was recalled. By now the heat in the room was building to an oppressive level, leading a number of reporters to remove their jackets. Eventually even Tom Sidney and his counsel were sitting in their shirt sleeves – an exceptional circumstance for any kind of official public proceedings. That anyone troubled to report this is an indication of the formality of the times, as is the additional information that this was also the first occasion on which Grace Duff had appeared out of full mourning.

Grace was asked all about the layout of 16 South Park Hill Road, with particular attention being paid to the location of the larder where the beer had been stored and whether the external doors were left unlocked. The coroner wanted to know what had happened to the rest of the beer and whisky after her husband's death? Grace said that people had drunk it – she could not specifically say who and when – most people who called at the house were offered a whisky and soda.

Then the coroner wanted to know about the Noble's Weed Killer – did she recall her husband buying two tins of it? Grace did not remember the actual purchase, but she had noticed one tin lying on its side in the yard at some stage and told her husband to put it away, because of the children. She also recalled an episode when a family cat had died, its death being ascribed at the time to suspected consumption of some weedkiller it found in the garden. Was it not the case that a lot of small animals had died? the coroner prompted. Grace said 'there had been frequent funerals' when pet rabbits and similar small animals died, but that had been nothing to do with the weedkiller – the dog had killed one of them.

Returning to the two tins of weedkiller, she said her husband had used the first up completely and thrown the empty tin in the dustbin, but she did not think the second tin had been opened until the coroner's officer came and took a sample of it, the day after her husband died. At a previous hearing Amy Clarke had been asked whether she had seen Edmund Duff using weedkiller in the garden the day before he went down to Hampshire, which she had not. Grace was now led down the same track, but she too denied that Edmund had been using weedkiller, saying that she thought he had been digging for worms to take with him for fishing.

When the coroner asked about her family's relationship with her husband, she said they had all got on well, although Edmund would 'bubble with annoyance' when Tom played his compositions while Edmund was trying to write his articles,[17] and she reluctantly agreed that her mother had not liked Edmund. Pressed specifically about her mother's reasons, Grace replied that many mothers-in-law do not like their sons-in-law. Her mother had considered Edmund extravagant and he had been an 'out-of-doors man' who had little in common with Violet; even so, there had never been a violent quarrel or anything of that sort – they had been on cordial terms.

Mr Roome wanted to know whether Edmund had any enemies. Grace said she knew of none, but added with tears in her eyes that he must have had an enemy if someone had killed him.

'So if he had an enemy, it must have been a secret one,' said Mr Roome, thereby prompting headlines next day full of variations on the 'Secret Enemy' theme.[18]

'Did anyone stand to gain by his death?' Mr Roome continued.

Grace said not, but Mr Roome then asked whether she had not received a payout on some life assurance policies, which she agreed was so. The widow was then subjected to a lengthy cross-examination about her current financial position, none of which had the remotest bearing on how Edmund Duff had met his death – the one question which the inquest had been convened to elucidate. By building up a picture of Grace's financial position, the fact that she had received a small pension from the Colonial Service, and the life insurance which had enabled her to buy a house (part of which was let to tenants), then asking about various allowances which sympathetic relatives had made over to her since Edmund's death, Mr Roome clearly contrived to paint a picture in which Grace had lost very little by Edmund's demise. However, when asked to compare her position before and after her husband's death, Grace retorted indignantly that she had lost everything: 'In one case I was absolutely without responsibility. My husband was keeping me. In the other, the whole burden fell upon myself. I should say it was the difference between being a happy woman and a miserable widow, with no one to look after me.'

When Roome began to ask how much Grace had gained from Vera's will, the coroner finally interrupted to say, 'I am doubtful how far we ought to go into this.'

'Very well, sir,' replied Roome, moving seamlessly back to ask a few more questions about the weedkiller, none of which added anything useful to the sum of known information.

Sir Bernard Spilsbury was the last witness of the day. His evidence was lengthy and complex, but it quickly emerged that in his opinion the most likely vehicle for the fatal dose of arsenic had been Edmund's suppertime beer. Mr Fearnley-Whittingstall was clearly dubious and asked how it was possible that having imbibed arsenic at about 7 p.m., Edmund Duff had not suffered from any vomiting until 7 o'clock the next morning. Spilsbury responded that symptoms of arsenical poisoning varied considerably from one individual to another, and thus delayed vomiting was entirely possible. Beer would disguise the taste of arsenic, he added. Pressed by Fearnley-Whittingstall, Sir Bernard agreed that just about every other drink would disguise it equally well, but continued to insist that the most likely hypothesis was that the arsenic had been in the beer.

Given the delayed vomiting and a variety of other issues, including 'a great deal of conjecture' involved in Spilsbury's theory, Fearnley-Whittingstall wanted to know whether the possibility existed that Duff had taken arsenic before he returned home on 26 April? Spilsbury agreed that he could not absolutely rule it out. The family's counsel now raised the point that Edmund Duff had taken a small travelling flask of whisky on his holiday – could this have been contaminated in some way? Sir Bernard agreed that it was possible.

The coroner wanted to know what explanation Dr Spilsbury could offer as to why the initial analysis had failed to show the presence of arsenic in Edmund Duff's body: was this not very odd, he asked? In one sense it was, the pathologist agreed, but the answer could be that 'only an aqueous extract of the organs was tested and in the organs the arsenic is changed into a comparatively insoluble form.' What the jury made of that is not recorded, although they presumably understood Sir Bernard's emphatic denial when the coroner enquired whether, if arsenic-based weedkiller was used in the cemetery, it might conceivably cause a positive test in an exhumed body.

The proceedings had lasted for more than eight hours. In spite of the endurance test they represented, there had been no shortage of people eager to gain a place in the overcrowded hall. A queue had begun to form at breakfast time and by the time the doors were due to open, such a crowd had gathered that uniformed police had to be called in to help stem the rush and deal with disgruntled late-comers who were unable to obtain a seat. It was not just that the Sunday papers were devoting double-page spreads to the case – that had been going on for many weeks – now there was undoubtedly an added sense of matters building to a crescendo. The conclusion of the inquests on Violet and Vera Sidney had been postponed until such time as all the evidence on Edmund had been given, and this evidence was surely almost at an end? Each session was anticipated as potentially the last; the final sitting in respect of Edmund Duff, which would culminate in the jury giving their verdict – perhaps not just of murder by person or persons unknown, but by a named individual, who would be taken away to stand trial and perhaps face the ultimate penalty ... but the inquest on 20 July ended in another adjournment.

There was another unseemly scramble for the public seats when the doors were opened on Friday, 26 July. Grace Duff and her son John sat beside Tom and Margaret Sidney, with the family observed to exchange affectionate embraces on arrival.[19] Fifteen-year-old John Duff was the first witness.[20] He confirmed his mother's account of Edmund's return home from Hampshire and the obvious signs of illness his father had exhibited when they went to retrieve the luggage from the bottom of the garden. John also remembered that when he and his sister Mary went up to bed that evening, Edmund had instructed the children not to kiss him, as he might have something infectious. Their normal bedtime was 7 p.m. but they had stayed up later that night, although he couldn't recall any details about his father eating supper. Apart from popping into the sick room to see his father for a few minutes between 10 and 11 the next morning, John had never seen him alive again. Asked about this final conversation, John replied that his father had not said much – just that he wasn't feeling well.

Grace was asked to return to the witness box to answer yet more questions about the layout of the house and who might have access to the larder where the beer was kept. She agreed that in theory anyone might walk in, but in practice only members of the family and the children's friends were likely to go in the kitchen.

After this, the flask of whisky Edmund took to Hampshire came under scrutiny. Grace explained that she had noticed it among her husband's things when he was getting ready to go away and she asked where it had come from – had a friend given it to him? Edmund had only smiled and said, 'Aha,' at which Grace suggested, 'Perhaps you have bought it for yourself?' and Edmund laughed. At the time Grace had been amused, simply assuming that he had treated himself, but more recently she had begun to wonder about its origins. She was unable to say exactly when Edmund had finished the contents of the flask, or what had happened to it after he died, but she believed it had been thrown away.

The third witness of the day was Margaret Sidney. As usual the coroner dwelt a long time on establishing background, enquiring when Margaret had first met various members of the Sidney family, where they had lived and so on. Margaret claimed she had always got on well with all her husband's family and had been a frequent visitor at the Duffs' house, although there had been no regular pattern to this – she and the children might be there two or three days in a row and then there could be a ten day gap before she was there again; she had seen Violet and Vera even more frequently than Grace.

Asked for her impression of her sister-in-law's household she said, 'Mr and Mrs Duff and their children always seemed to me to be a very happy family indeed: one of the happiest I have ever known.'

On the night of Edmund's death she had been to the theatre with Vera and, as they walked home together between 10.30 and 11 p.m., they saw Dr Binning's car parked outside Grace's house, at which Vera said she would just pop in and see how Edmund was – the presence of the doctor's car signifying that he might have taken a turn for the worse. When Vera emerged a few minutes later she had appeared puzzled, telling Margaret that although Grace was downstairs, extremely worried, when she had gone upstairs she found Dr Binning quite cheerful. He had assured Vera that there was nothing to worry about and Edmund was making a fuss about nothing. Questioned by the coroner, Margaret agreed that this could have been no more than Dr Binning's tactful way of getting rid of Vera.

Next morning, Margaret had awakened to find Vera sitting on her bed, come to tell her that Edmund had died. In the immediate aftermath of his death, Margaret and Grace had numerous discussions about what might have caused him to die. Malaria, sunstroke and eating bad fish had all been mentioned, but she did not think Grace had favoured any one explanation over another. Margaret had engaged in similar conversations with Vera, who had apparently been particularly interested in the question. Old Mrs Sidney, on the other hand, had been very upset at the idea of an inquest, and 'very much annoyed with the doctors...' who she thought ought to have prevented it.

Margaret was asked about Grace's finances and said she personally thought that Edmund and Grace had managed well, although it was the family's collective opinion that Grace was not good with money, and Violet had worried about Grace, because whereas the old lady was always 'very careful' herself, she considered that her elder daughter did not know how to economise.

Three minor characters in the drama concluded matters for the day. Lane the gardener reprised his story about never using any weedkiller, knowing where any weedkiller had been stored etc, etc. Sam Noble deposed that he had sold two tins of Noble's Weed Killer to Edmund Duff in 1927, and finally Percy Warren testified that he had provided the Duff household with their beer and that there had been no problems with any bottled beer supplied to any of his customers.

It was the end of another long day. Dr Jackson announced that he would adjourn until 6 August – by which time he anticipated that the proceedings in respect of Vera and Violet Sidney would be completed.

CHAPTER SEVEN

'I CANNOT SAY
I AM GLAD IT IS OVER'

With the verdicts fast approaching, interest in the Croydon case reached fever pitch. The attentions of the poison pen brigade extended to Dr Jackson, whose wife became a target of threats that 'she would soon be a widow'. One man even tried to force himself into the house while the coroner was away from home, leading to a police guard being posted at the premises.[1]

It was in this fraught atmosphere that Dr Jackson opened the final session of the inquest into Vera Sidney's death, on the morning of 29 July.[2] Inspector Hedges was called to the witness chair and asked to confirm a series of points arising from testimony given at the respective inquests on Edmund Duff and Violet Sidney. This essentially amounted to the fact that the medical evidence in each case indicated that death had resulted from acute arsenical poisoning.

At 11.17 the coroner began to sum up the evidence which had been given about Vera's death. If certain aspects of the way Dr Jackson had handled proceedings were questionable, few could doubt that his performance now was scrupulously fair. The detailed handwritten notes he prepared for this address to the jury survive in Croydon's archives, a meticulous attempt to draw the salient points from a tangled web of testimony running to some 50,000 words in respect of Vera alone, the result of eight sittings stretching back over a period of more than three months. He reminded the jury that some witnesses had suffered from uncertain memories and that every fact was not known; for example, the court was not aware of what Vera had drunk with her lunch on the crucial day, and so forth. He stressed that they must not draw inferences from the fact that he had allowed witnesses to be closely questioned – this did not indicate the involvement or guilt of any one person.

'It has been proved,' Jackson said, 'that the deceased died at 12.20 in the morning of 15 February and that her death was due to acute arsenical poisoning...'

There were six 'curious points' in the case:

1. All three deaths occurred in the same family within a year.
2. All were from the same poison.
3. In each case the victim already appeared to be suffering from a slight illness.

4. In each case the victim was the only member of the household to exhibit symptoms of poisoning.

5. In each case the poison was apparently administered in something destined to be consumed by that particular member of the family alone.

6. The deaths occurred in two different houses, but in each case, the side door was left unlocked and the pantry easily accessible from it.

The jury would have to consider, the coroner said, whether it was possible that arsenic had coincidentally found its way into all the victims' food and drink by accident. If it was not an accident, they had to consider the various possible suspects in the case. He then took the jury through a series of names, in a manner reminiscent of Hercule Poirot summing up a case before the solution is revealed on the final page. Mrs Noakes, he suggested, had little motive, Margaret Sidney apparently even less. When it came to Grace Duff, he had more to say than on anyone else. They had seen her giving evidence and knew her to be an emotional woman, but otherwise an apparently truthful witness and a sane one. Of course, 'You cannot go into the mind of a human being. There are people, apparently sane, who have been known to take a delight in killing others…', but, Dr Jackson reminded them, 'there is not a tittle of evidence' that Grace Duff administered poison to her sister – moreover had she wished to murder Vera, there would probably have been much better opportunities than the day Mrs Greenwell came to lunch. She had been on affectionate terms with all the victims and had no obvious motive for killing any of them.

Finally he came to Tom Sidney. 'He is at times a person who has not seemed to appreciate the gravity of these proceedings' – at this Tom was observed to smile – but in Tom's case too the coroner conceded that both evidence and motive appeared to be lacking.

The coroner then returned to the most curious point of all: 'All the circumstances suggest the probability of the poisoner having been a member of the household or someone intimately acquainted with its ways,' – how else would they have known that only Vera would be harmed by the soup, that only Edmund drank beer and that the Metatone was being taken by Violet? And yet, there was no real evidence to indicate any one person.

Dropping his voice and looking gravely at the jury, Jackson said, 'Unless you are satisfied in your own minds that a particular individual is responsible, and that rests on sworn testimony, you ought not to name any person…'

He went on to remind them again that they could bring in a verdict of murder by person or persons unknown and finished with the words, '…if I were in your box, I should be unable, on the evidence, to name any culprit. You are of course, perfectly entitled to reject any view that I have expressed.'

Dr Jackson had spoken for forty-two minutes. The jury were out for just seventeen before they returned with a unanimous verdict that Vera Sidney was murdered, by arsenic wilfully administered by person or persons unknown.

Two days later all the main players were back to see Violet's inquest brought to its conclusion. Inspector Hedges was again asked to formally confirm some of the medical evidence given at the other two inquests, before Coroner Jackson embarked on another long speech, similar in character to that which he had delivered barely forty-eight hours previously.[3] He reminded the jury that there was no hard evidence that anyone apart from Violet herself had handled the bottle of medicine between its arrival in the house and her death, and that since she had evidently been taking the contents on a somewhat sporadic basis, if someone had added arsenic to the mixture, they could have done so up to three or four days before Violet actually took it.

As he had done at Vera's inquest, he ran through a possible list of suspects, this time even making brief reference to Dr Elwell and Mrs Anderson, the curate's wife, who had visited the day before Violet's death. Again, he said that he could not find any hard evidence against any of them. He also touched on the question of Violet committing suicide, saying that while the family insisted she never would have done so, he knew of plenty of suicides in which the family's reaction had been exactly that. Just as he had done with the previous jury, he repeatedly emphasised the need to be sure before naming any one individual, as such a verdict 'would have the effect that that person would go to be tried in a court of law.'

This time the jury took a full half hour to arrive at a decision, eventually emerging with a somewhat different conclusion – death due to arsenical poisoning, but with insufficient evidence to show whether Violet Sidney had killed herself, or was murdered by some person or persons unknown.

Less than a week later, it was the turn of the jury in the Edmund Duff inquest to make the headlines, but in this case, there were still two witnesses from whom the coroner wished to hear more.[4] The first of these was Grace Duff, who had been invited to read the statements she made at the original inquest in 1928, prior to giving her evidence. Even having read them, Grace said she had some difficult in recalling details, but felt that her original statements would be the more accurate, having been made much nearer to the events described. She did remember that on the night Edmund arrived home from Hampshire, he had little appetite for his supper and toyed with the food, saying he felt 'a little sicky', and that later, on their way to bed, he had said he felt as sick as a dog. She agreed that he had endured a restless night and had said next morning that he feared he had some kind of dreadful illness coming on, but she could not remember whether he mentioned being sick, or suffering diarrhoea, during the night.

Nor could she add anything about the flask of whisky which had accompanied her husband to Hampshire. She never looked at it closely and had not noticed any label on it, but said it was like the sort sold in railway stations. When her husband got back from Hampshire his things had not been properly unpacked until after his death, and she did not specifically recall seeing the whisky flask among them – it was therefore entirely possible that he had drunk the contents during his holiday, she really did not know.

Sir Bernard Spilsbury was recalled and asked whether, given Edmund's feelings of nausea when confronted with his supper, he might have had some poison before he arrived home. Spilsbury gave a firm negative on this, saying that it was much more likely that Edmund had consumed arsenic in his beer – if he had the arsenic earlier, then consuming food and drink at suppertime would have caused him to vomit. Mr Fearnley-Whittingstall wanted to know how such a conclusion could be reached, not least because Sir Bernard did not know at what time Edmund had started to vomit, but Spilsbury replied that the deceased started to vomit soon after going to bed, which indicated that he had taken the arsenic between his arriving home and going to bed.

The famous pathologist then embarked on a lengthy peroration, saying that arsenic did not cause instantaneous vomiting and that the symptoms could be delayed for up to six hours after ingestion. Fearnley-Whittingstall pursued the inherent contradiction in this – if symptoms could be delayed so long, did that not indicate that the poison could have been taken prior to arriving home after all? Spilsbury emphatically denied it – returning to his stance that attempting to consume food at suppertime would have provoked vomiting and not just a 'sicky' feeling. The beer, he insisted, was the most likely vehicle for the poison, although the chicken and potatoes were a possibility. At this Mr Purchase, who was acting for the police in place of Mr Roome, pointed out that it had been established that the rest of the chicken and potatoes had been eaten by Mrs Duff and the children the following day, with no ill effect whatever.[5]

When Sir Bernard finally stood down, Inspector Hedges was again called upon to attest to the evidence of poisoning in the other two cases, before the coroner began to sum up. On this occasion he spent even longer than before – an hour of solemn, dispassionate speech, during which the spectators (some of whom had queued two hours in the rain for admission) hung on every word. Just as before, Dr Jackson emphasised the need to draw conclusions only from the evidence placed before the court and to hold back from naming any one individual, unless the jury were absolutely certain that person had been responsible. As he touched on the suspects one by one, Grace Duff was observed to be weeping silently, the more so when the coroner observed that there was no reason why fifteen-year-old John or thirteen-year-old Mary would have doctored their father's food and drink, while Mrs Duff herself was markedly worse off thanks to her husband's death and that 'the one outstanding factor of this family is their mutual affection'. Mr Duff's mother-in-law had not liked him, the coroner said, but 'God knows why she should have poisoned him and there is no evidence that she did so...' Vera and Tom had no obvious motive either.

The jury retired at 3.31 and returned twenty minutes later, their verdict echoing the one given in respect of Vera Sidney: acute arsenical poisoning, wilfully administered by person or persons unknown. The coroner took down the verdict, adding it to the 300 pages of foolscap notes he had already amassed in respect of the Edmund Duff inquest alone, and only on looking up again did he realise the foreman of the jury was still on his feet.

'Have you anything to add?' he asked.

'Yes sir. We wish to add a rider. We think that the chemical analysis of the organs at the first Home Office examination was not conducted with sufficient care.'

Dr Jackson demurred, pointing out that there was no evidence to prove that a mistake had been made during the first analysis, but the foreman and his colleagues were not easily dissuaded. 'We think that had the arsenic been found, the lives of the other two women might have been saved. It was a very unfortunate error.'

The coroner agreed that it was unfortunate, but reminded them that a second body had been examined on the same day and it was thus going too far to speak of a definite mistake – the unspoken inference being that if a mistake had been made, it was not necessarily on the part of the analyst.

This was not going far enough for Professor Candy, who asked permission to make a statement. In a voice shaking with emotion, he said:

> As my conduct has been challenged, perhaps I may be allowed to say a few words in my defence. An English audience is, as a rule, willing to give fair play. I had certain organs submitted to me for chemical examination and I conducted a careful examination of those organs. I came to a certain conclusion which I reported to the coroner. I grant that a year afterwards, on justifiable grounds, the body was exhumed for further chemical examination and arsenic was found. I can only say that I did not find arsenic and it would have been absurd for me to have said I had when I had not. I am willing to say that there is a possibility of error in every human examination, but that is as far as I can go. I can say that if twelve months later, in the light of events, I examined those organs on the understanding that arsenic must be there and that I had got to find it, it is possible that I should have pegged away until I did find it. I think it is a grave thing for you gentlemen to charge me, after thirty years' reputation for care and skill in analysis, with criminal carelessness, for that is what it amounts to.

Professor Candy then thanked the coroner for giving him the opportunity to make a statement. The coroner turned to the jury and said, 'I really think you are going too far. In fact I think this is outside your province and I don't know whether I should be legally justified in accepting it.'

The foreman continued to argue with the coroner, while the rest of the jury indicated that they wanted their rider recorded, but after debating for some minutes, Dr Jackson refused to accept it: an announcement with which Tom Sidney evidently concurred, as he thumped the table and shouted 'Hear, hear!'

The formal inquests were finally over: more than 200 hours of testimony, 1,000 sheets of foolscap notes, acres of newsprint – but the mystery remained unsolved. As the room began to clear, Grace Duff, leaning on the arm of her son John, was observed walking up to Dr Jackson, and after a short conversation she shook his hand. Outside the building, as she and John were escorted to their car by policemen, they had to run the gauntlet of some female spectators who had waited outside the gates in order to 'vent forcible expressions of opinion', as the *Croydon Advertiser* cautiously put it.

Although she initially refused to speak with the waiting reporters, Grace later relented and issued a brief statement: 'I cannot say I am glad it is over, because I do not yet know whether it is over.'[6]

In the immediate aftermath of the verdicts on her mother and sister, the *People* had managed to obtain a slightly longer interview, in which Grace had commented that the verdicts were inevitable in the light of the evidence presented. 'The truth cannot remain hidden. It may take time, but it will come out in the end ... the investigation cannot be allowed to rest until the truth is known.'[7] This interview had clearly taken place at Grace's house in Birdhurst Rise, but at the conclusion of Edmund's inquest, both Grace and Tom's households had taken the opportunity to separately decamp from their Croydon homes – in part, at least, to avoid the attentions of the press.

Tom Sidney also made some brief comments on his way out of the final hearing, saying that the verdicts had come as no surprise and that the inquests had been thorough and fair, although they had been to both himself and Grace, '...absolute agony. Only the knowledge that the inquests were being held in the interests of us all kept us from breaking down under the strain and worry they entailed and the limelight of publicity.'[8]

Professor Candy was also surrounded by reporters as he left the building and said he had been 'staggered' when he heard the jury's rider and thought the coroner was too. The slight had clearly wounded him deeply and his perceived failure would continue to attract adverse public comment for some time to come, with letters on the subject appearing in newspapers such as *The Times*, suggesting that in future, analysis should only be done by 'top' Home Office men and implying that Candy had botched the job.[9]

Grace was right to assume that the verdicts did not represent the end. The same issue of the *Croydon Advertiser* which reported the concluding session of her husband's inquest, included the news that the exhumation of Miss Maria Kelvey's body was again being considered. According to the *Advertiser's* source, both this and the possibility of exhuming Grace and Edmund's two little daughters had been discussed during recent case conferences at Scotland Yard – and in the meantime, all papers relating to the case had been handed to Sir Archibald Bodkin, the Director of Public Prosecutions.[10] Whatever the verdict of the inquest jury, the police were leaving the press in no doubt that they considered Violet Sidney's death to have been a third murder and the *Croydon Times* was able to inform its readers that the police 'hold strongly' to the view that 'all three murders' were committed by one person.[11]

The suggestion that further bodies might be exhumed continued to surface for several weeks, with at least one newspaper noting that the headstone and coping had yet to be restored to the grave where Edmund Duff and his two daughters lay.[12] Meantime the Duff and Sidney plots in the Queen's Road Cemetery continued to attract the attention of sightseers; one morning in mid-August, a rumour spread that the promised exhumations were about to take place and a large crowd gathered in the cemetery, only dispersing after a fruitless wait of more than an hour, when it became plain that nothing was going to happen.[13] The papers also published more details about Maria Kelvey, stating that she had lodged with the Duffs and died at their home in South Park Hill Road, the implications of which were somewhat obvious.

The *Sunday Express* attempted to whip up more interest in their edition on 1 September, which contained an article by ex-Inspector Walter Dew of Scotland Yard, headlined, 'New Police Moves in Croydon Mystery', though Dew's piece was little more than a résumé of the scale and cost of the investigation and proceedings to date and contained no new information, save that the Director of Public Prosecutions had returned from his holidays and was now looking at the file. Other papers repeated the mantra that developments were expected shortly, but no arrest or further official announcements were forthcoming.

Tom Sidney had spoken of resuming his career as an entertainer once the inquests were over, but by the end of the summer his plans had changed and on 3 September he attempted to auction his house in South Park Hill Road, together with most of the contents, prior to departure for America.[14] The auction was held at the property and attracted such enormous interest that it had to be moved from the drawing room into the garden, but unfortunately many of those who attended were recognisable as the same women who had been regular spectators at the inquests. The house failed to reach its reserve of £1,700 and was withdrawn, although many other items, including a baby's perambulator and a Crown Derby tea service, found willing buyers.

Grace stayed on a while longer, but soon she too looked for fresh pastures in which to raise her family – somewhere they could walk down the street without heads turning, fingers pointing, or remarks being made. For Grace Duff, so long as the Croydon Arsenic case remained an unsolved mystery, it would never be 'over'. Within days of the final inquest verdict, a piece by Edgar Wallace, originally published in the *New York Times*, appeared in British papers.[15] Wallace was careful to stay on the right side of libel, but the implication of the piece was that Grace Duff was the murderess – the key death, he wrote, was that of Edmund Duff and it was here that the motive might be found.

There was little chance of the Croydon Mystery being forgotten. Within less than two years, it had been included in a murder compendium[16] and many such accounts would follow. The Metropolitan Police files on the case were initially closed, but under the 30-year rule then in operation they were reopened in 1959, affording the journalist Richard Whittington-Egan the opportunity of using them to undertake his own investigation of the case. He concluded that Grace Duff had committed all three murders and during the next three or four years, he managed to trace a number of the people who had originally been involved, including Grace herself. He called at her home on two occasions and reported her resulting hostility as if indicative of guilt[17] – although her look of 'undisguised hatred' may well have been the result of Whittington-Egan's turning up on her doorstep and accusing her point blank of murdering her relatives. Her daughter Mary, to whom Richard Whittington-Egan generously offered the opportunity of setting forth a limited rebuttal in his book, certainly took this line, saying that only those who have experienced the hounding of reporters can understand the revulsion that such tactics engender: by the time of these encounters on Grace Duff's doorstep, she was approaching her eightieth year.

Whittington-Egan completed his book on the case and it spent the next decade in his publisher's safekeeping until Grace Duff's death in 1973, when it could safely proceed to publication without legal action.[18] Once it was safe to name Grace, publishers were not slow to take advantage. 'Did Grace Duff cold-bloodedly kill three members of her own family?' asked the author of Murder Casebook no.53.[19] But if the police files made out such a strong case against Grace Duff – if there really was such a weight of evidence against her – why was no prosecution ever attempted?

CHAPTER EIGHT

SPECIALLY TRAINED

A t the conclusion of the three inquests, Coroner Jackson paid tribute to the
efforts of Inspector Fred Hedges. That was universally the official line – a
good job done by a dedicated, tireless officer. Yet in the small print of one or two
newspapers in early September 1929 there is a clue that all may not have been
what it seemed. On 7 September, under the headline 'Arsenic Mystery Sequel',
the *Croydon Times* reported a recent announcement to the effect that in future a
special corps of Scotland Yard detectives would be called in to deal with cases of
'unusual gravity or importance'. Officially this was because it was 'too much to
ask' that such cases should form part of the day-to-day work of busy divisional
offices, but unofficially it could be conjectured that some divisional inspectors
were not up to the job – and it is somewhat suggestive that this announcement
came not long after Sir Archibald Bodkin was confronted with the case file prepared by Inspector Hedges.

The Metropolitan Police file dealing with the investigation into the deaths of
Violet and Vera Sidney and Edmund Duff runs to hundreds of foolscap pages,
punctuated at regular intervals by Inspector Hedges' own reports on the case,
which at times make for astonishing reading. The first report submitted by
Hedges was written on 13 March 1929, eight days after Violet Sidney's death, and
it sets out not only the circumstances of Violet's death, but also those of Vera and
Edmund.[1] Hedges paints a picture of a deeply suspicious series of events, which
has created such unease in the minds of Dr Elwell and Dr Binning, that since
the death of Edmund Duff in 1928, both men 'have been extremely careful' in
their dealings with this family. Given that Dr Elwell had originally certified Vera's
death as due to natural causes, this does not entirely ring true and indeed there
is nothing in the statement Elwell made to Hedges on 11 March to suggest that
he had previously been entertaining any suspicions whatever.[2] Later in this first
report, however, Hedges mentions that he has had a confidential conversation
with Dr Binning, who told him that he and Dr Elwell were highly suspicious
of the similarity of symptoms in the three cases, so perhaps this 'unease' was not
mere assumption on Hedges' part.

By the time he wrote this report, Hedges had interviewed the surviving adult members of the family, and it is already clear where his suspicions lay. Tom and Margaret Sidney are respectively described as 'affable' and 'very refined', with the Inspector at pains to emphasise that they have no apparent motive. His impression of Grace Duff is very different – and his hostility to her apparent in every word. Hedges describes her as 'an exceptionally clever woman' who would 'benefit considerably from the death of her sister and considerably more by the death of her mother.' A week into the enquiry, with no definite evidence to support the idea that either Violet or Vera Sidney had been murdered, let alone anything which pointed to any one individual being responsible, Hedges had already identified Grace Duff as his prime suspect, although the worst he could say of her conduct was that during a lengthy interrogation she was at times in a very hysterical state, sitting sometimes on the couch and sometimes on the floor and at no time 'did she disclose any point on which I could enlarge.'

At the time of writing this report, Hedges had not received the final results of the analysis performed in respect of Violet Sidney (though Ryffel had confirmed to him the presence of arsenic) but he was already confidently concluding his report to the effect that 'in all probability Dr Jackson will press for the exhumations of Vera Sidney and Edmund Duff.'

Ten days later Hedges was again reporting that the more he saw of Tom and Margaret Sidney, the less likely he thought it that they were implicated in any crime.[3] He had now discussed Grace Duff's sanity with Elwell and Binning, who had told him they 'would have great difficulty' in getting her certified as mentally unbalanced, although they allegedly agreed with him that she was a 'peculiar type of woman' – a contention which is particularly strange, given that both doctors' names would later be romantically linked with Grace.[4]

By now Vera Sidney's body had been exhumed, and Hedges still hoped the investigation would extend to Edmund Duff, stating that from 'private conversations' with various unidentified people, he was convinced that arsenic would be found in Edmund's remains and that this would enable him to arrest Grace Duff. The report then ends on the slightly ludicrous note that if arsenic was not found in Edmund Duff's body, he would have to look very closely at the statements and antecedents of Kathleen Noakes, which rather suggests that Hedges' certainty about the guilt of Grace Duff was based on somewhat dubious foundations.

Hedges did not file another report on the case for almost a month, although he had been very busy in the interim; the inquest sittings were now in full swing and he had been revisiting his crime scene and interviewing some witnesses for a second and third time. Not surprisingly stories were starting to change, as recollection and event became further removed from one another. For example, another interview with Kathleen Noakes had generated the information that on the day of Violet's death, Violet went upstairs for a few minutes to fetch her purse, conveniently leaving Grace alone in the dining room with the medicine bottle.[5]

In his original report on 13 March, Hedges had dismissed Kathleen Noakes as 'not a very intelligent person',[6] and inferred that she was not a very nice one either, opining that when she gave notice on the night of Vera Sidney's death, it was probably because she feared that having nurses in the house would make extra work. He noted in addition that she had not offered to give up her half day in order to help out when Vera was seriously ill, and listed the various grumbles she aired to him about her time at Mrs Sidney's. By 21 April, however, Inspector Hedges had come to see a potential ally in Kathleen Noakes, who was stupid enough to be suggestible and regularly changed her story – often in order to present herself in a better light – which made her somewhat reliant on a sympathetic policeman who would not bring the contradictions in her various statements to the attention of the coroner. When, for example, Kathleen Noakes swore that she had been happy in her employment and had not given notice on the night of Vera's death, Inspector Hedges did not draw the coroner's attention to Kathleen Noakes' earlier admission that she had indeed given notice that night, and nor did he contradict her assertions that she had been happy at 29 Birdhurst Rise by bringing to light the various complaints which had emerged during his first interview with her, such as not being given enough to eat while in Mrs Sidney's service. On the contrary, Kathleen Noakes was fast becoming Hedges' star witness and in his 21 April report he notes approvingly that she was 'an excellent witness … [who] no doubt greatly impressed the jury.'

In the meantime, he had increased his list of hoped-for exhumations by three, having received an anonymous tip-off that a Miss Maria Kelvey died while a lodger at Grace Duff's house and that Mrs Duff, her children and even Dr Elwell had benefited from the old lady's will. In addition, two of Grace Duff's children had 'died suddenly' and this was obviously 'suspicious'.

By the time he prepared his next case report on 30 April, Hedges was cock-a-hoop over Kathleen Noakes' latest recollections.[7] On 27 April Mrs Noakes had finally been persuaded to recall that she had seen Tom Sidney in the hall of his mother's house on the day she died. 'It will be difficult for him to explain how he got into the house…' Hedges wrote, somewhat gleefully. It is evident from the tone of this latest report that the Inspector's previous good opinion of Tom had been marred – perhaps by the episode of the empty weedkiller tin discovered in Violet's shed, which Tom had insisted on drawing to the coroner's attention. Hedges certainly grumbled about this 'interference' in his report, protesting that he had not overlooked the tin during his earlier searches of the house, rather he had ignored it, because it had obviously not been touched for a very long time.

Although Tom Sidney was very much in the frame again, Hedges' interest in the Duff family was unabated. By the end of April he had taken statements from Grace's two elder children and interviewed the headmaster at John Duff's school to ascertain whether the boy had access to any arsenic there. He had also tracked down and interviewed various domestic servants who had worked for the Duffs, but had been unable to 'elicit anything which would be of value'. The perceived value of evidence is invariably dependent on what the assessor is trying to prove. Had Hedges been looking to support the contention that Grace and Edmund

Duff had been happily married and that Grace appeared genuinely devastated by the deaths of her husband, sister and mother, he would have found this testimony very useful indeed.[8]

From the outset Hedges' reports had exhibited bias and prejudice, but by the middle of May these traits had escalated to a frightening degree. He began his 11 May report by setting out a glowing character reference for Kathleen Noakes: 'a sympathetic, affectionate woman, always ready to do anyone a good turn', claiming that, 'the guilty parties have done their utmost' to discredit this unfortunate woman.[9] Given that Hedges cannot have known with any certainty who the 'guilty parties' were, and that he had sat time after time in court listening to Kathleen Noakes effectively discrediting herself with constant changes of story and fib after fib, this is at best a somewhat blinkered perspective for the person charged with running a major criminal investigation.

From Mrs Noakes the report moved to Grace Duff, described by Hedges as 'an erratic, irresponsible woman … a clever actress … typical of the type of woman who would be likely to carry out a system of poisoning and her subsequent conduct is such as would cast aside all suspicion, unless one is specially trained in the investigation of crime.'

The problem with possessing this marvellous ability to see the true nature of a suspect when all others were blind to it – an ability which Hedges clearly believed himself to possess – was that convictions could not be secured by clairvoyance alone. Hard evidence was needed and despite exhaustive enquires, Hedges had been unable to trace any arsenic to Grace Duff apart from the liquid weedkiller, which Ryffels' experiments had effectively demonstrated not to be the poison found in Violet's medicine bottle. Although the headmaster of John Duff's school had assured the police that there was no possibility of young John getting hold of any arsenic there, Hedges continued to persist with enquiries in that direction. He was also chasing up Tom Sidney's purchase of Eureka Weed Killer and considered it 'very suspicious' that Tom could not recall from whence he had bought it two years previously. He was still grumbling about the various items Tom Sidney continued to discover in Violet's house and submit for analysis, claiming that this was a deliberate attempt to 'throw dust in the eyes of the jury', 'draw attention away from the tin of weedkiller in his own shed' and perhaps most heinous of all, 'to show up my search of the house'.

Hedges had now decided that Tom and Grace were probably acting together – an assumption he considered to be supported by Kathleen Noakes' latest allegation, that she overheard Tom telling Grace on the night of Violet's death that, 'It is the best thing that could happen, as she would only fret after Vera.'

In spite of an enormous weight of testimony to the contrary, Hedges was still convinced that Grace and Edmund Duff's marriage had been unhappy and moreover that Grace might have been enjoying a flirtation with Dr Elwell. He had taken a statement from Elwell back in March, but that had been confined to the last illnesses of Violet and Vera Sidney. On 22 May he went to see Dr Elwell again and on this occasion his questions took a somewhat different line.

Dr Elwell told Hedges that he had originally become the Duffs' family doctor in December 1920, having been recommended by Violet, who was already his patient.[10] He had not regarded the Duffs as intimate friends, but if he called at teatime, he would stay for a cup of tea and a chat, and they had been friendly enough that Dr Elwell had stood godfather to the Duffs' youngest son Alastair. After Edmund's death, he had done his best to help and advise Grace, and felt considerable sympathy for her, but he had never visited unless she rang for him. She often rang about her children, but seldom ever for herself, indeed on one occasion he had been summoned by Violet, who had found Grace 'very poorly' and felt a doctor should be called. He emphatically denied that he had ever visited London with Grace and also that there had been any problems in the Duffs' marriage. 'They appeared to me a devoted couple and she never complained to me of her husband's ill treatment.' On one occasion he had remarked on some bruises on her shoulders, at which Grace had 'reluctantly told me they were caused by her husband, who was very excitable in moments of sexual passion.' Elwell had raised the subject of the bruises with Edmund, who said they were only the result of 'ruxing'[11] together.

Hedges continued to track down Grace Duff's ex-servants, in the evident hope of uncovering matrimonial discord, but he got no further with this line of enquiry. Jessie Bonfield, who spent six months with the family, starting in October 1926, said the Duffs were 'a devoted couple', she had never heard them quarrel and had no suspicions whatsoever that Mrs Duff's relationship with Dr Elwell was anything other than that between doctor and patient.[12] Barbara Smith, who did three months with the family, starting in November 1927, said exactly the same.[13] All told, Hedges eventually traced and interviewed all seven domestics who had worked for the Duffs between 1926 and the beginning of 1929, plus two nursemaids who had been engaged to help with the older children before that, but not one of them deviated from this picture of a happy couple, who got on well with one another and indeed their wider family – nor had any of them heard of the slightest rumour concerning Dr Elwell and Mrs Duff, nor themselves observed anything other than a normal relationship between patient and family doctor.[14]

In spite of this remarkable unanimity, Hedges' next report on 28 May (which ran to seventeen typewritten foolscap pages) contained a number of observations about the Duff marriage which were at complete odds with all the evidence he had collected to date, including the assertion that he had no doubt 'Mrs Duff was secretly in love with Dr Elwell'. He added that Tom Sidney endorsed his opinion that 'there is something between Dr Elwell and Mrs Duff' – although no contemporary statement or deposition backs this up.[15]

Still convinced that Tom and Grace were accomplices, the policeman speculated that perhaps Tom had been enjoined to take part in Edmund's murder when Grace informed him of her husband's violence. This was of course a dangerously misleading statement for Hedges to make – there was no evidence that the Duffs' marriage had been violent apart from a single mention of bruised shoulders, and a wealth of evidence that it was not. In similar vein, the occasion when Edmund had walked out of the room, probably due to his irritation with his brother-in-law, becomes in this report 'a very serious quarrel' during which Edmund was 'livid with rage'.

Hedges also considered it 'remarkable' that Grace 'never slept with her husband' – although Grace herself had explained that this arrangement had been the norm from the outset of their marriage, because Edmund not only snored, but he preferred to sleep alone so that he could read late at night.[16] Possibly Hedges was unaware that such sleeping arrangements were considered perfectly normal among upper and upper middle class couples in the 1920s and did not automatically denote a relationship in which love and sex formed no active part. He also drew attention to the substantial age difference between the couple, claiming that Grace could not possibly retain an interest in fifty-nine-year-old Edmund when Dr Elwell, a man in 'the prime of life', might be available.

Grace was again described as 'typical of a person' who would commit such a crime and 'a born actress'. 'Her sorrow for the loss of her relatives is only on the surface.' Hedges' special powers of insight were not just confined to divining the true character of his chief suspect. While admitting that at the time of writing he had not been told the results of the Duff exhumation, he wrote confidently that, 'There is no doubt that arsenic will be found in the organs of Edmund Duff' and 'it will be conclusively proved that Edmund Duff died from arsenical poisoning.'

By early June, if not before, Tom Sidney and Grace Duff had ample reason to distrust Inspector Hedges and his methods. The Inspector's normal way of obtaining a statement was to arrive with a colleague and pose a series of questions, with the witness's answers taken down in shorthand. The following day, the typed up 'statement' would be returned to the witness for signing, having been reproduced as a single narrative, linked together with police-ese phrases, such as, 'I now wish to speak of my sister Vera'.[17] At the hearing on 1 May, Tom Sidney stated on oath that he had not even been aware that he was making a statement during one of Hedges' visits, until he was required to sign it next day and at that same hearing complained of the policeman 'putting words' into his mouth. (In the case of Kathleen Noakes these arrangements were particularly dubious, because she was illiterate.[18]) Thus it is hardly surprising that when Hedges visited Grace Duff for a further statement on 3 June, she insisted on writing it herself – a perfectly reasonable request which only served to irritate the Inspector still further, as he made plain in his report dated 12 June.[19]

By now Hedges was extending his investigation to encompass the Duffs' one-time lodger, Miss Kelvey, and their two daughters (Margaret, who had died in 1919 as a result of a failed operation to remove a colonic obstruction and Suzanne, who succumbed to meningitis in 1924). Having successfully pressed for Edmund Duff's exhumation, the Inspector's reports reveal that he was now pestering Dr Jackson about these two children, but 'Dr Jackson is of the opinion that the circumstances are hardly sufficient' to justify an exhumation. Undeterred, Hedges had found a doctor (unnamed) who assured him that the symptoms of meningitis could be confused with arsenical poisoning, and went on to remind his superiors that although two doctors had diagnosed Suzanne's meningitis, three doctors had failed to spot that Vera had been poisoned and two had mistaken Edmund's death as due to heart disease. He also included the dubious claim that Dr Elwell 'would be much relieved if the body [of Suzanne Duff] is exhumed.' Alas, the tenor of the report is less that of a senior policeman conducting a serious investigation, than of a whiny child who is being denied his way.

Hedges' reports were naturally confidential, but in the same week that he first mentioned his hopes for three more exhumations, the local papers carried a story that the police were looking into Miss Kelvey's death and, soon afterwards, speculation about exhuming the two little girls similarly appeared in the public domain. This leads to the inescapable conclusion that Hedges, or someone close to him, was systematically leaking this information, which implies a policy of notching up every possible pressure on Grace Duff.

Grace was not the only one under pressure. As the inquests went on and on, no one endured longer and more searching cross-examinations than her brother Tom. In the initial stages of the investigation, both Tom and Grace were probably in a state of disbelief, but this was gradually replaced by a terrible certainty – there appeared to be incontrovertible evidence that three members of their family had been murdered, and by logical inference a member of the family must have administered the poison.

Tom and Margaret Sidney must have discussed the situation endlessly and in July a chance remark from their six-year-old son, Cedric, set them thinking. According to Cedric, his cousin John sometimes unlocked and entered their garden shed to get Cedric's bicycle out for him. Moreover, John did not always enter the Sidneys' garden via the house when he came round to play: sometimes he climbed over the gate.[20] Although the Sidneys were convinced that Grace could not have got any weedkiller from their shed, Cedric's story did open up the possibility that John had obtained it for her.

In the wake of Cedric's innocent recollections, Tom Sidney contacted Inspector Hedges, who first took a statement from Margaret Sidney and the next day, travelled to John Duff's boarding school in Bath, accompanied by Tom. Via Hedges' report, dated 21 July, we get an insight into the way Tom Sidney's mind was starting to work. On the journey down, he allegedly confided in the policeman: 'It seems an awful thing to say against your own family … I have weighed up the situation in my own way and after eliminating the servant, I must come to the conclusion that it is either my sister alone, my sister and John together, my sister and her daughter together, or the daughter and John together, or one of them alone.'

Yet Tom's agony of doubt surfaced later, when he told Hedges, 'I don't want you to think that I don't love my sister.' He commented that in the past, Grace had often remarked when one of the children had annoyed her, 'I could soon give them something and finish them off.' He had always taken this as a joke, but now he was not so sure. As a precaution he had moved himself and his family down to Bexhill-on-Sea.[21]

When they arrived at Monkton Coombe School, the headmaster gave Hedges permission to question John Duff alone – a somewhat surprising decision, given that the boy's mother was not even aware that this interview was taking place. Hedges questioned John at length, but the boy admitted nothing beyond climbing the garden gate and retrieving his cousin's cycle from the shed. Eventually Tom Sidney and the headmaster were invited back into the room while John made his statement, as Hedges 'deemed it advisable' to have witnesses for this part of the process. Altogether the detective spent three hours with the boy.

If this was distasteful enough, Hedges followed it up next day with another long interview with Mary Duff, during which the girl eventually burst into tears, saying, 'Oh mother, what have I said? I have got a bad memory and I'm afraid I shall say something that is not right.' Hedges questioned her not only about her father's death and the tin of liquid weedkiller once kept in the cellar, but also about various pets which had died and the detective games she had played with John, in which they had pinned notes on the doors, using secret code. 'Neither of us did anything really wrong,' the child's rather pathetic testimony reads. 'John would never touch weedkiller. He is good and kind.'[22]

Grace Duff again incurred the ire of Inspector Hedges by insisting that he take down her daughter's answers in longhand, in order that she could see exactly what was being written. Hedges claimed that during the process, 'It was obvious to me that Mrs Duff spoke sharply to the child, as she is anxious to convince us and the jury that the tin of weedkiller traced to her possession had not been opened until the house was searched by the coroner's officer, just after Mr Duff died.'[23]

In many ways this comment epitomised his jaundiced portrayal of Grace Duff's every word and action. The tin of weedkiller had not been 'traced to her possession' – she had volunteered its whereabouts to the coroner's officer when he visited (rather than searched) her home and it was this same coroner's officer who had deposed that the tin gave every appearance of not having been previously opened. Faced with a policeman who is determined to badger one's child until she says something potentially incriminating, any parent might betray a degree of tension in their voice. (One wonders whether this sharpness of speech was discernable to anyone else, or whether it was yet another instance where Grace's behaviour was only apparent to a man 'specially trained in the investigation of crime'.)

Since the expedition to Bath, Tom Sidney had become Hedges' new best friend – all those strongly held convictions about his involvement in the crime had magically evaporated, and the latest batch of medicine bottles which Tom had handed over to the coroner were no longer seen as an attempt to undermine Hedges, but were explained in the policeman's report as having been 'in places where they could not be seen until after the furniture was taken away.'

Clearly upset and annoyed by Tom's involvement in the interrogation of her son,[24] Grace, who had until then apparently held back from expressing any suspicions of her own, gave voice to one now, intimating to Tom that Margaret was in a position to have committed all three murders and reminding him that he had once told her Margaret had an aunt who 'was not quite right'.[25]

Needless to say this did nothing to improve relations between the siblings. Suitably provoked, Tom made another statement to Hedges which was hostile to his sister, then took the Inspector round to meet the local vicar, Revd Deane. Essentially Hedges derived nothing from this encounter, other than a character reference for Tom, coupled with a series of gossipy observations to the effect that Grace Duff's behaviour was in various ways 'abnormal' and alleging that she had not appeared particularly sad at her husband's funeral.[26] In the light of considerable evidence to the contrary, this isolated suggestion that Grace had appeared less than devastated by Edmund's death can perhaps be put into context by the fact that later both Tom himself and Grace's daughter would separately recall that Revd Deane and Grace had long entertained a strong mutual dislike.[27]

Revd Deane informed Hedges that he had no desire to become involved with the case and had only turned up to one of the hearings so that, if necessary, he could speak up about what a straightforward sort of chap Tom Sidney was – perish the thought that he was merely drawn by curiosity. He went on to say that he had discussed the case with his wife and 'long suspected' that Edmund Duff had not died a natural death. Better yet, he claimed to have told his wife, when Vera died, that she had been 'put out of the way' – in fact his uncanny intuition went right back to the funeral of Suzanne Duff in 1924, when he had thought Grace Duff's behaviour 'peculiar'. In the light of these suspicions, one may think it somewhat surprising that the vicar of St Peter's had not considered it his duty as a citizen to report these matters to the relevant authorities well before July 1929.

Yet the Revd Deane's attitude appears to epitomise the kind of collective hysteria which was building up around the case. Faced with the likelihood that a murderer dwelt in their midst, citizens of Croydon took whatever action they thought best. When Albert Taylor, whose grocery business in George Street Grace Duff had patronised for a number of years, received an order from her which included Harpic and spirit of salts,[28] he consulted with Frederick Rose, the chemist whose premises happened to be next door. On Rose's recommendation he refused to supply the spirit of salts, 'as the two are used for the same purpose'. Mr Rose told Dr Binning about the order and Dr Binning mentioned it to Tom Sidney, who dutifully informed Inspector Hedges, who recorded this game of Chinese Whispers in his report dated 28 July. Perhaps never in the history of criminal investigation had the attempted purchase of routine household cleaning materials occasioned so much interest.

By now a kind of alliance had grown up between Fred Hedges and Tom Sidney, which resulted in Tom passing on various tittle-tattle which was hostile to Grace. At no stage does it appear to have occurred to Hedges that one of his suspects could have been stitching up the other, in order to keep his own neck out of a noose.

Among the anonymous letters received by the Sidneys in July was one which claimed that Margaret was Edmund's 'cast off tart' and that this had been Margaret's motive for murdering Edmund. The timing was somewhat unfortunate, in that the letter's arrival coincided with Grace's suggestion that Margaret might have been responsible for the murders. This led Tom to suspect that his sister was the author of the letter – an idea which Hedges seized on with alacrity. When Tom taxed Grace about the letter, she claimed to have received a similar one, which she said she had thrown away, although she accurately described the distinctive envelope in which her letter had arrived, which was a match for the one received by her brother. This merely reinforced Tom's theory that Grace was behind the communication, although the fact that all three members of the family knew there had never been anything at all between Margaret and Edmund logically argued against this conclusion.

From the outset of the enquiry, Hedges had been intimating that the way forward was to arrest Grace Duff, in spite of an acknowledged lack of evidence against her, and in his 28 July report he urged the course ever more strongly, stating that, 'If no proceedings are taken in these three cases, I feel convinced that we shall have a series of similar murders to deal with. It is obvious that in future, a potential murderer will not be slow to take advantage of what must appear to him as a problem for the police.'[29]

Elsewhere in the same report Hedges repeats his concerns about the possibility of chalking up three unsolved murders in his district; unfortunately, the message a conviction would send out to other would-be criminals appears to have been far more important to him than the possibility of an innocent person being hanged.

At the conclusion of the three inquests, Hedges set about writing another report, in which he made no secret of his disappointment at the outcome – had just one of the juries named the person they believed to be the murderer, automatic arrest would have followed, but as things stood, Hedges still had to persuade his superiors to authorise any arrest. He was extremely critical of the coroner, who 'throughout this enquiry … has been extremely kind to this woman…' (the woman in question was of course Grace Duff). Hedges felt the coroner had 'shown extreme weakness' in his summing up of the evidence, and he went on to explain at some length just what he considered the coroner *should* have said – needless to say all of it detrimental to Mrs Duff.[30]

Hedges was particularly infuriated by the advice Dr Jackson had given to the jury, discouraging them from naming any one individual. In a style reminiscent of a sulky schoolboy, Hedges put these numerous errors down to the fact that the coroner had become 'bored with these protracted enquiries'… 'but I doubt whether he has suffered more than Inspector Morrish and myself, as we have strained every nerve for exactly five months to bring this case to a successful termination.' He went on to dismiss the coroner's suggestion that a third party might have entered the house via an unlocked door and tampered with the food as absurd and improbable, ending as ever with another diatribe against Grace Duff.

In a letter to the Commissioner of the Metropolitan Police the following day, Sir Archibald Bodkin firmly turned down the idea of arresting Grace, saying that, 'this step is a somewhat rash one and one which would end to a certainty in her acquittal.'[31] Bodkin did, however, invite Hedges to submit a report summarising the evidence against both Tom Sidney and Grace Duff, to which the Inspector responded with alacrity, despatching another lengthy document for the attention of the Director of Public Prosecutions on 12 August.[32]

Here, at last, was an opportunity for Hedges to set out a coherent case against Grace Duff. He began by listing nine motives for murdering her husband Edmund, beginning with the fact that the 'deceased was twenty years her senior and she teased him about it.' This might have been a pretty weak motive, but at least it was based on a kernel of fact. Motive number nine was provided by 'an alleged violent quarrel' between Edmund and Grace before he left for Fordingbridge. In spite of months of investigations and dozens of interviews, the police had failed to find a single witness who was prepared to say they had ever seen the Duffs exchange so much as a cross word, still less engage in a violent quarrel – yet Hedges was still prepared to put this allegation in writing, in the hope of effecting an arrest. In a similar vein, motive number three claimed that 'Mrs Duff is known to have a strong liking for Dr Elwell and entertained him.' This too was mere conjecture on Hedges' part and lacked any testimony to back it up. Included in the general character assassination was an accusation that Grace Duff's conduct on the night her husband returned from Hampshire was 'callous', because on her own admission she had not bothered to go to him during the night, when she knew he was unwell. This too was untrue – Grace's statements consistently claim that when she heard Edmund moving about she went in to him, only to be told to go back to bed.

The other six motives related to money; according to Hedges, Grace stood to benefit considerably by her husband's death. Again the evidence of Grace's finances suggested otherwise – it was true that she had received £1,500 from Edmund's life insurance, but she had also lost his regular income and most of his pension.

When it came to Grace's opportunity to murder Edmund, Hedges was on much more solid ground. She had access to the beer and access to the Noble's Liquid Weed Killer and this 'singled her out' as the one person who had motive and opportunity in all three cases. Tom Sidney was dismissed in a few sentences as having no real motive or opportunity to murder his brother-in-law.

In Vera's case, Grace's motive was again alleged to be financial and, according to Hedges, since she visited her mother's house almost every day, she had ample opportunity to slip some weedkiller into the soup. The origin of the weedkiller was more troubling – by the time of Vera's death, Grace had long given the tin of liquid weedkiller to Lane the gardener, but Hedges conjectured that either Grace had obtained some weedkiller from her brother's shed, or else had a secret supply of arsenic, from the time when she had lived in Nigeria, where Edmund had used it to doctor their horses. (He did not bother to mention that Grace had not lived in Nigeria for the best part of fifteen years.)

In Vera's case, Hedges again exonerates Tom Sidney, saying he had no motive and had not visited the house for several days before his sister died. Nor did he consider that Tom had a strong motive in the case of his mother, Violet. The strange incident of Tom's alleged appearance in the hall on the day of Violet's death is entirely absent from this report, its supposed significance forgotten. Instead Hedges majors on the other Kathleen Noakes story – of Grace being left alone in the dining room when her mother went upstairs to fetch some money for Grace's errand. Again, it is Grace who is perceived as having both motive and opportunity: 'she undoubtedly knew where her mother kept the medicine bottle,' the Inspector opines, going on to say that she probably still had some arsenic left from the 'secret packet' which had provided the arsenic to see off Vera – a secret package which to all intents and purposes had never existed beyond the fertile imagination of this man 'specially trained in the investigation of crime'.

When it came to Violet, 'Suicide can be safely eliminated', Hedges wrote, reminding his superiors of Violet's strongly-held religious beliefs. No – it was Grace and Grace alone who had planned and executed all three crimes; moreover, Hedges explained, Tom Sidney himself was now convinced that this was the case, believing that she must be a 'homicidal maniac'. One of the underlying themes in a number of Hedges' reports is his apparent conviction that the more people agreed with his suspicions, the truer they became. His inability to distinguish fact from opinion is one of the numerous disturbing features which emerge from the way he handled the investigation. In a report dated 20 September, Hedges would write, 'after the inquests many members of the public mentioned to me that they thought Mrs Duff was exceptionally lucky'[33] which, while no doubt a true reflection of some sections of public opinion, is hardly evidence on which to argue for an arrest.

Hedges was certainly not alone in his conclusions. Support came from Messrs Wontner & Sons, the firm of solicitors who had been appointed to act for the Commissioner of Metropolitan Police throughout the Edmund Duff inquest. Having attended many of the hearings in person and then read the depositions from those at which they had not been present, they submitted an eight-page letter, stating that after the three verdicts, 'for all practical purposes three verdicts of murder', they had 'formed a very strong impression that the only person who can be held responsible for these three separate deaths is Mrs Grace Duff'.[34] Wontners had essentially arrived at this by process of elimination, arguing that of the three suspects, Kathleen Noakes could not have killed Edmund Duff, Tom Sidney could not have killed Vera and logically, therefore, the culprit had to be Grace Duff, the only person in a position to have killed all three – although they doubted whether there was sufficient evidence to put her on trial. With regard to motive, in a neat twist of double think, Wontners concluded that if Grace Duff had committed the three murders, she must be a homicidal maniac, and therefore being a homicidal maniac, she needed no motive to commit three murders.

The Director of Public Prosecutions agreed with Wontners that there was insufficient evidence to put Mrs Duff on trial, but Hedges kept on trying. In

September he submitted a further report, including full details of Grace Duff's bank accounts and complaining that insufficient evidence of her financial position had been placed before the inquest juries.[35] Sir Archibald Bodkin wrote back, saying he did not consider 'the contents of the report add anything materially to the position as already ascertained.'[36]

On 9 October 1929 Hedges compiled what would be his last formal report on the case.[37] It contained nothing new about the murders, but did bring the activities of his two principal suspects up to date. Tom Sidney was shortly leaving for America, but in conversations with Hedges had expressed concern about the way his sister Grace was running through her inheritance. Grace had bought a motor car and a bungalow in Seaford, although Tom did not know the address – a strong indication of the rift which had developed between two households who at one time had scarcely sneezed without the other being aware of it.

Hedges concluded by expressing the hope that some evidence might still be forthcoming and drawing his superiors' attention to the fact that the coroner, Director of Public Prosecutions and even Wontner & Sons had all 'commended police action' in connection with the case. The heavy hint achieved its objective. Police Superintendent Wilson added a note to the bottom of the report, recommending that the three officers principally involved, Hedges, Morrish and Sergeant Carl Hagen, be 'granted a high commendation from the Commissioner.'

CHAPTER NINE

AN AFTERTASTE OF OXTAIL

The reports written by Inspector Hedges in 1929 were coloured by a particular perspective: that Grace Duff was the guilty party and that every piece of evidence could be turned to that conclusion. Unfortunately, Richard Whittington-Egan's book published in 1975 ultimately takes the same line. It is perhaps understandable that Whittington-Egan would be reluctant to highlight or criticise Hedges' prejudices, methods and lack of objectivity, for although Hedges himself died in 1954, the author had received generous co-operation from his widow, son and daughter[1] including access to Hedges' own notes on the case; and, in pursuit of the theory he shared with the Inspector, he had managed to track down a number of people who were willing to provide unfavourable recollections of Grace Duff, including an erstwhile neighbour who alleged that Grace had enjoyed the notoriety of the case and posed for press photographers in her front garden.[2] This is something which the present author finds rather difficult to swallow, given that these photographs are strangely absent from the contemporary news reports, which if anything tend to give the impression that Grace was a distinctly reluctant interviewee. Similarly, although ex-neighbours were prepared to state some thirty years after the event that, following Edmund's death in 1928, Dr Elwell's car was seen night after night parked outside Grace Duff's house,[3] all Inspector Hedges' determined efforts to dig dirt in 1929 failed to uncover this information.

It is also conceivable that just as recollections blur with time, they also shift as a person's guilt moves from mere speculation to generally accepted fact. Eventually even Grace's own brother became convinced that she was a murderess and his perception of her altered to encompass that. Agatha Christie summed up the terrible dilemma facing members of a family, one of whom must logically be guilty of the murder of another, when one of her characters states, 'If one of the family was guilty ... they would look at one another and wonder ... perhaps the suspicion affecting one's relationships with people. Destroying love, destroying trust...'[4]

In their letter summarising the case, Wontner & Sons made the point that the inquests had been marred by 'improbable theories' and 'many red herrings'[5] – a contention which anyone who has read the long drawn-out saga of proceedings would find it difficult to argue with. For Wontners, as for almost everyone else, the key lay in how arsenic could have been introduced into the vehicles by which it was administered.

In the case of Violet Sidney the *modus operandi* appeared clear-cut. Violet had taken the last dose of her tonic and almost immediately remarked on its gritty texture and unpleasant taste – sensations which had not been present with any of the earlier doses. Within about thirty minutes of this she began to exhibit symptoms of some form of poisoning and subsequent analysis demonstrated that arsenic was present in both the medicine bottle and wine glass she had used to take it.

The question of who had introduced the arsenic into the medicine might have been more straightforward if Violet had been taking her tonic regularly, but she had not. Dr Elwell and Grace Duff both testified to Violet's admission that she had not been taking the medicine and no one knew how long the bottle had stood since the previous dose. Nor was anyone prepared to say that they had seen the bottle from the time it was delivered on 25 February, until Violet had it in the dining room on 5 March. John Duff at one stage said he thought he had seen a medicine bottle on his grandmother's dressing table, but there was no particular reason to assume this was the Metatone bottle.

In this context, Kathleen Noakes' sudden realisation, more than a month after the event, that Grace had been left alone in the dining room for a few minutes on the morning of Violet's death loses all its significance, because the arsenic could have been added to the bottle several days before: by Tom, Margaret, the Duff children, or even Mrs Noakes herself. The allegation that Kathleen Noakes encountered Tom Sidney in the hall of 29 Birdhurst Rise that morning is equally meaningless, although the story of this sighting does help to expose the level of chicanery Inspector Hedges was willing to employ in his quest to pin the crime on one or other of his suspects.

It was 27 April when Kathleen Noakes made her statement about encountering Tom Sidney in the hall – and William Fearnley-Whittingstall would subsequently question her very closely about the circumstances in which she had come to make it. By 27 April Mrs Noakes had already made three lengthy formal statements to Hedges describing in considerable detail the events of 5 March, to say nothing of having given evidence before the coroner, without ever giving so much as a hint of this memorable appearance in the hallway. Fearnley-Whittingstall rightly smelled a rat, although we have no way of knowing if he had spotted the most significant element in the chronology of this episode.

In fact Kathleen Noakes had not been the first person to place Tom Sidney in Birdhurst Rise that morning. When Grace Duff gave her evidence at the inquest held on 22 April,[6] she was asked to provide a full description of her activities on the day of Violet's death, during which she said that she had returned to her mother's house at about 1.15 on 5 March, mentioning that as she walked up the road she met her brother Tom, coming in the opposite direction with one of his children. When she asked if he had called in on their mother, Tom said he had not as the child would annoy Violet if she was still eating her lunch.

It is surely stretching coincidence that a mere five days later, and only after several conversations with Inspector Hedges, Kathleen Noakes suddenly remembered that she had seen Tom Sidney in the hall on 5 March, but placed the encounter about ninety minutes earlier than Grace Duff had done, when the time was ripe to tamper with Violet's medicine. Had Kathleen Noakes' story been true, one way of rebutting it would have been for Tom to suggest that she was mistaken about the date, but when questioned by the coroner, Tom Sidney denied that this episode had taken place on that day or indeed any other. The real giveaway, however, lies in the detail of Kathleen Noakes' testimony. Pressed to confirm whether the child accompanying Tom that day was a boy or a girl, Mrs Noakes could not 'remember' – Grace's original testimony merely said 'one of his children' and if Kathleen Noakes guessed wrongly, no doubt Margaret Sidney and her daily help could have testified that the child in question had been at home all along.

With the field on who had slipped arsenic into Violet's medicine wide open, could the list of suspects be narrowed down in the case of Edmund's beer? One of the first obstacles in bringing home the administration of arsenic lay in an element of doubt as to whether the poison had been administered in his beer at all. There was incontrovertible evidence that Edmund Duff was already feeling unwell before he arrived home from his fishing holiday, but the Home Office experts all considered this illness was coincidental to what had killed him, a situation which appeared to fit with the hypothesis that the killer always took advantage of some kind of unrelated minor illness to mask the administration of poison, thereby increasing the possibility that the symptoms would be put down to something else.

Edmund's beer had been put forward as the most likely substance in which to dissolve the arsenic, principally because all the other foodstuffs consumed by Edmund had also been consumed by others without ill effect. However, there were several snags inherent with the theory about the beer, not least that it was kept in the larder, in a crate where there would generally be several bottles at any one time, which made it difficult for the would-be assassin to know exactly which bottle Amy Clarke would select for inclusion on the supper tray. Moreover, although Amy Clarke said she took out the stopper immediately before carrying in the tray, whereas Grace said that Edmund opened the beer himself, whichever of them actually performed this task, there was a significant chance that they would notice the paper seal and stopper had been tampered with.

Hedges always worked on the assumption that the arsenic was introduced to Edmund's beer on the day of his death; but like the medicine, the beer – which no one but Edmund was liable to drink – had not been sampled for several days. Once the period for introducing the poison was extended to the three days while Edmund was away in Hampshire, it encompassed all manner of people: Vera, Violet, Tom and Margaret were constantly in and out of one another's houses

– the former two had called half a dozen times between them on the day of Edmund's death alone.

The uncertainty regarding the beer increased still further in the light of Mr Fearnley-Whittingstall's questions about the effect of arsenic on beer.[7] Would not solid arsenic separate and leave an obvious residue? Would the introduction of arsenic make the beer go flat? Sir Bernard Spilsbury responded cautiously that he favoured the idea that the arsenic had been introduced in liquid form, without really addressing the points about the possible effects of arsenic on bottled beer. Indeed no one gave evidence about any experiments having been undertaken to see just what happened in the event that arsenic in any form was mixed into a bottle of Bass.

Apart from the beer, there was the flask of whisky Edmund had taken away on holiday, its provenance and time of consumption unknown. Finally there was the possibility that Grace had actually slipped the poison into a cup of tea between supper and bedtime: who but she was left to confirm that Edmund had nothing to drink that evening, after his beer?

Ultimately there is Vera's soup. Again the soup appeared to be the perfect vehicle if the poison was intended for Vera, because Vera was the only member of the household who was in the habit of eating it. During his summing up, Dr Jackson pointed out that since Vera ate soup every day, there would be no need to add poison to it on a day when a third party was expected to lunch, thereby attracting the very suspicion which coinciding the murder with a minor illness was designed to avoid. This was a potential stumbling block for Hedges and in several of his reports he tried very hard to convince his superiors (and possibly himself) that Grace had not known her aunt was expected to lunch until after she added the arsenic to the soup, by which time it was too late to do anything about it. However, Grace consistently claimed that she had known several days in advance that Mrs Greenwell was expected, which on balance, given that Vera, if not Violet, was in the habit of conveying every major or minor item of news around the entire family, seems likely to have been the case.

The evidence regarding the soup is another confusing tangle of testimony, reliant for the most part on the distinctly suspect recollections of Mrs Noakes, although it was universally agreed that Vera took soup every day, while Violet scarcely ever did and that Mrs Noakes was forbidden soup by Violet, who thought her servants did not need a three course meal. According to Mrs Noakes, the soup was always made using Symington's Oxtail Soup Powder, with which she would boil up a variety of vegetables, sometimes in combination with leftover meat or bones, after which she strained the soup and placed it in the cellar, reheating it as required.

The soup was made in 'a big heavy metal saucepan' and Mrs Noakes claimed that she made up a fresh batch every second day. Yet the use of a 'big heavy pan' implies that quite a large quantity of soup was made at a time, and even if Vera had soup at lunch and again in the evening, she would surely not have got through more than 1½ to 2 pints of the stuff every couple of days at most. This does lead to the possibility that soup was not always freshly prepared every second day, but may have been covertly kept for somewhat longer on occasion, in order to save Mrs Noakes the labour of preparing it so frequently.

No one was required to give a statement on the subject of the soup until more than a fortnight after Vera's death, so it would be entirely understandable if Mrs Noakes experienced some difficulty in recalling the preparation of any one particular batch of soup among so many. In her first statement on the subject, made on 11 March,[8] she said that herself, Vera and the cat had all been sick on 'Monday or Tuesday' after eating the last of a batch of soup. By 16 April she 'was certain' that this sickness had occurred on the Tuesday[9] – the day before Mrs Greenwell's visit. This was supported by the fact that on 12 April Mrs Greenwell had recalled her visit in a statement to Newcastle police,[10] saying that when lunch was served, Vera had commented that she didn't want any soup, as 'This is the soup that made me sick yesterday'. (Mrs Noakes' uncanny ability to alter her story in response to statements made by other witnesses, the contents of which she ought properly to have been entirely ignorant, was truly remarkable.)

By the time she was called to give evidence at the inquest on 1 June Mrs Greenwell was no longer sure exactly what had been said, although she still thought Vera said 'yesterday.'[11] By this time, however, a further element of doubt had been introduced into the proceedings, when Grace said in a statement taken on 18 April that she was told that Vera and the cook had been sick the previous evening, when she visited on the Tuesday.[12] By then she was trying to recall the details of a conversation which had taken place two months previously and her memory could easily have been at fault, not least because she was also in the house on Wednesday afternoon, at which point Vera's and Mrs Greenwell's nausea was also being discussed – making this an entirely logical time for her to have heard about the illness of the cat and the cook.

By 9 May however, Kathleen Noakes was shifting her ground. She was now 'almost positive' that she had been sick on the Monday.[13] This fitted rather conveniently with her insistence that the soup which made everyone ill was not one, but two separate batches.

Time then to look at the fate of the soup made on Sunday. According to Mrs Noakes, although it had been Vera's usual habit to have soup for supper on Sunday evening, she had not done so the Sunday before she died. Mrs Noakes said she knew this because although she left the soup out in the dining room to be heated on the jet when wanted, she could tell it had not been heated up by its 'jelly state' when she returned home from her afternoon off and tidied things away.[14] Incidental corroboration that the soup was untouched comes from Grace Duff, who spent part of that Sunday evening with her mother and Vera and recalled that no one bothered with any supper while she was there.[15] On Monday, as Mrs Noakes originally remembered it, Vera was out to lunch and thus, although the soup was made on Sunday, no one consumed any until Monday evening, when Vera had her usual portion, Mrs Noakes had 'half a cup full' and the remains were put down for the cat, which according to Mrs Noakes finished off the batch.

There are three reasons for concluding that this was not correct. Firstly Vera Sidney's diary proved that she was not out to lunch on Monday, which means that in all likelihood she consumed some of the soup at lunchtime without any ill effect. Secondly the soup made on Sunday would in the normal course of events have lasted two days, so if only two portions had been consumed – that served to Vera at lunch and suppertime on Monday – there must have been a significant quantity of soup left over, considerably more than Mrs Noakes's half a cup and the cat's leftovers. Mrs Noakes was certainly not authorised to waste large quantities of food by feeding it to the cat, so in attempting to prove that no one touched the soup until Monday evening, Kathleen Noakes tends to disprove her own assertion that the soup consumed on Monday evening was the end of the batch.

Mrs Noakes always stood by her contention than an entirely fresh lot of soup was made on Tuesday, which was untouched until Wednesday lunchtime: a theory which partly relied on the entry in Vera's diary stating that she was so unwell on Tuesday that she had nothing at all to eat. Vera's diary was produced in evidence to corroborate this,[16] and states that Vera stayed in bed until teatime and did not 'do any eating during the day only tea and Oxo'.

Quite aside from the fact that Mrs Noakes was a demonstrably poor witness who frequently contradicted herself, there is evidence that she also told self-serving lies. Many years later Kathleen Noakes admitted to Richard Whittington-Egan that she had even obtained her position with Mrs Sidney by lying: pretending to be a widow in need of a situation, when in fact she only wanted a temporary job to put money aside for something specific. In reality the 'widow' was living with a married man and her husband was in the process of divorcing her – but no woman admitting to such a situation would have gained employment in a respectable household in 1928.[17]

Terrified of being blamed for the death of either of the Sidneys, whatever happened she was not going to admit anything which incriminated her, or made her appear in any way responsible. She knew she was supposed to make a fresh batch of soup every second day – but if a substantial quantity of the soup she made on Sunday was still left by Tuesday, might she have been tempted to cut corners and heat it up for lunch on Wednesday? The potential for food poisoning via constantly reheated food was little understood in the 1920s, when reheated leftovers were part of most people's regular diet. It is entirely possible that the veal cooked on Friday or Saturday was then turned into soup on Sunday, rather than Tuesday. The soup would then have been left in the cellar to cool for several hours, before being carried into the dining room, where a fire would have been lit throughout the evening, and the soup left to stand there at room temperature until about 10.30, when it was taken back down to the cellar. Here it sat until Monday lunchtime when it was heated up in its entirety[18] to provide Vera's lunchtime portion, and then it was reheated again on Monday evening, when part of it was consumed by herself and Vera – allegedly making them both sick – although neither initially attributed their illness to the soup. If this was not in fact the last of the soup, and Kathleen Noakes elected to return it to the cellar, then on Tuesday it may have been heated up again, before Mrs Noakes discovered that no one wanted any soup. Did Mrs Noakes at this point discard whatever was left and make a fresh batch in readiness for the next day – or did she save herself the trouble by adding a little water to the thick, jelly-like soup which remained, and on Wednesday reheat the mixture yet again, by which time any remnants of veal would now have been cooked, cooled and reheated at least four times – a perfect recipe for food poisoning.

There are several circumstantial titbits to support this idea. If Mrs Noakes heated up the soup on Tuesday, then found it was not wanted, she might have been tempted to take half a cup, thinking that it would not be missed. Her story of originally accounting for her sickness because she had eaten some rich cake on Sunday made no sense at all; in fact, in the copy of Kathleen Noakes' deposition in the coroner's file, Dr Jackson has annotated the story of suspecting that the cake induced her sickness with an obvious query[19] – 'surely this would have made her sick on Sunday, rather than Monday or Tuesday?'

An admission that she had drunk some soup on Tuesday which she suspected had made her ill, but which she had nevertheless served up the following day for lunch, would hardly have shown Mrs Noakes in a good light. Moreover, it would have been entirely consistent for her to have woven some fabrication to cover up for the fact that instead of making fresh soup, she was still using up the batch she had made on Sunday.

Then there is Vera herself, who apparently recognised the soup as that which had made her ill previously. The soup served at lunch on 13 March was described by Mrs Greenwell as 'brown soup' and this would presumably have been its appearance every day, irrespective of the slightly varying ingredients. Vera ate soup regularly and it had never made her ill before, so she had no reason to be suspicious of soup in general. Did she somehow realise that Mrs Noakes had presented them with the same batch of soup which had been prepared several days before – something she might have hesitated to mention outright in front of a lunch guest?

This is hardly conclusive, but coupled with another event, it becomes highly suggestive. Vera fell ill immediately after the lunch party, when the vomiting which had troubled her after the first lot of soup recommenced with a vengeance. The only other person to sample the soup had also succumbed to an attack of vomiting. On Thursday night, when Kate Noakes returned from her afternoon off, she abruptly informed Violet Sidney that she intended to leave. With Vera desperately ill, and the house full of doctors and nurses, anyone might think this a curious time to give notice and later Kathleen Noakes would try to deny that she had done so, claiming that she had only suggested she might need to get away on account of her health – although apart from an upset stomach on the night she drank the soup, there was never any suggestion at all that Mrs Noakes had been in poor health. Is it possible that she gave her notice in a fit of panic, thinking that she might be blamed for serving up the leftover soup which had made Miss Vera so ill?

When Kathleen Noakes denied having given notice that night, it provoked an angry outburst from Tom Sidney, who asked if Mrs Noakes was calling his mother a liar.[20] It was not Violet, however, but Kathleen Noakes who was lying – nor is corroboration that the cook gave notice that night solely reliant on the family's recollections of what Violet had told them. In her very first statement to Inspector Hedges on 7 March, Kathleen Noakes mentions that she had given notice on the night of Vera's death and on 5 March, Violet was writing that her maid would be leaving in ten days time – which precisely equates to the month's notice Kathleen Noakes had given her on 14/15 February.[21]

Even more suggestive testimony comes from Mary Keetley, one of the professional nurses called in to help nurse Vera, who gave a full statement to the police accounting for the time she spent at 29 Birdhurst Rise, from her arrival at around 11.30 on Thursday morning until her departure the following morning.[22] She independently mentions that she tried to persuade Kathleen Noakes not to leave on Thursday night – the wording of the statement implying that Mrs Noakes might have been proposing to leave there and then.

Another curious episode occurred on the morning after Vera's death, when Mrs Noakes failed to appear at the usual time to go about her duties. This was recalled by Daisy Geer, the nurse brought in late on Thursday night to relieve Mary Keetley. Daisy Geer too had been approached for a statement and remembered that Mrs Noakes had been so slow to get up on Friday morning that Grace Duff had eventually taken the nurse down the road to her own house, in order to provide her with some breakfast. According to Miss Geer, Mrs Noakes only appeared after repeated attempts were made to rouse her – Miss Geer at one stage exclaiming, 'Whatever is the matter with her? Why won't she get up?'[23]

Had Kate Noakes really overslept on this of all mornings – or was she hiding behind her door, afraid to come out and face the music? Kathleen Noakes had evidently been somewhat agitated on Thursday night and was presumably aware of the gravity of Vera's condition. It seems highly unlikely that she simply went to bed, fell into a sound sleep and was completely unaware of what was taking place in the house. People were crying, doctors and nurses were entering and leaving the sick room; at one stage Grace stood outside her mother's door, remonstrating with Violet, who was so grief-stricken she had locked herself inside. The nurse joined Grace in persuading the old lady to come out and take a sleeping draught – both necessarily having to raise their voices to be heard through Violet's locked door[24] – yet we are supposed to believe that Kathleen Noakes was deaf to all of this and that until she emerged from her bed and came downstairs next morning, she was unaware that Vera was dead.

It has always been assumed that Gwendoline Greenwell and Vera Sidney both suffered from the effects of arsenical poisoning, which Mrs Greenwell survived because she had drunk very little of the soup. However, no doctor was ever asked to provide a statement describing Mrs Greenwell's symptoms, or to state a definite diagnosis. No samples were taken from her for analysis. Had Vera Sidney lived, a different conclusion might have been reached – that they had both suffered an attack of food poisoning.

It is pure assumption that Mrs Greenwell survived because she took less soup than Vera. In her original statement on 12 April, Mrs Greenwood's exact words were, 'I only took three or four spoonfuls [of the soup] and I noticed that Vera did very much the same.' By the time she gave evidence in court on 1 June, Mrs Greenwell could only say, 'I did not notice how much soup Vera took, but she left a lot in her plate.' Mrs Noakes' statements are equally vague. So while it is possible that Vera drank much more soup than her aunt it is far from proven and, considered in this light, the supposition that Vera Sidney received a fatal dose of arsenic via her soup becomes far less certain.

In addition to the three accepted victims of the Croydon poisoner, suspicions about the possibility of three more had found their way into the press. The first of these was Miss Kelvey,[25] who had lodged with the Duffs towards the end of her life. Dr Elwell had been her medical attendant and like Grace Duff and her children, he had received a small legacy in the old lady's will. Such gestures were hardly unusual from childless women, who felt a degree of gratitude for the kindness they had received in their declining years, and Miss Kelvey's will included a number of similar bequests to other friends and their children, her executors and professionals from whom she had enjoyed good service towards the end of her life, including £10 to her bank manager.[26] Miss Kelvey died in January 1927 as a result of suffering a third stroke. She had been failing for some time and was being cared for by Grace Duff during the day, while a professional nurse stayed with her overnight. In spite of interviews with a variety of witnesses, Inspector Hedges was unable to winkle out anything which was inconsistent with the idea that seventy-six-year-old Miss Kelvey's death had been a perfectly natural one.[27]

The Duffs' eldest daughter, Margaret, had died back in 1919 and Hedges decided to investigate this too. The family medical practitioner from 1917 to 1919 had been Dr Francis Gaynor, but he turned out to be far from helpful to Hedges' cause, informing the policeman that Margaret had been a sickly child, who suffered badly from rheumatoid arthritis and in 1919 had to be treated for an unrelated internal obstruction. It was a time when operations on small children were extremely risky and although Margaret survived the surgery, which was performed by Sir William Arbuthnot Lane, she died within a few weeks.[28]

When Hedges turned his attention to the Duffs' fourth child, Suzanne, who had died age two in 1924, he was initially more optimistic. Suzanne had died 'suddenly' and this time there had been no operation performed by an eminent specialist. But although Suzanne's nurse told him a somewhat confusing story of the child becoming ill after a fall, both Dr Elwell and Dr Purdom (who had been called in while Dr Elwell was temporarily out of the district) considered the symptoms entirely due to meningitis.[29] As we have already seen, this did not prevent Hedges from trying to find a medic who would agree that the child's fits, even coupled with a complete absence of vomiting and diarrhoea, might still have been due to arsenical poisoning.

By the time Richard Whittington-Egan wrote his book, a number of people had come forward to allege various instances of peculiar or suspicious behaviour on the part of Grace Duff, either immediately preceding or following the deaths of Suzanne Duff or Miss Kelvey[30] but like the tales of Dr Elwell's ever present motor car, not one of them is substantiated by contemporaneous testimony. The worst that any of the various maids could say of Grace was that she appeared a somewhat over-anxious mother, who was inclined to call the doctor to her children for minor ailments – which was perhaps not surprising when she had lost two of them to illness. Marian Hartley, who went to work for the Duffs when her husband lost his job in 1927 and stayed with them for a year, recalled an occasion when she had taken her own daughter with her to work and Grace had begun to cry, explaining that the little girl bore a very strong resemblance to Suzanne, and asking Mrs Hartley not to bring the child again.[31]

Even the judgement that Grace was over swift to call in the doctor needs to be put into the context of both the times and the witnesses making the observation. Before the inception of the National Health Service in 1948, patients paid for every house call from their doctor, and as a result working class families – from whom domestic servants were drawn – tended not to consult a doctor for any but the most serious complaints. These were also the days when a doctor was expected to exhibit a 'good bedside manner', otherwise his patients were perfectly at liberty to take their business elsewhere, and the friendly, almost over-attentive service with which both Dr Elwell and Dr Binning provided the Duff and Sidney families must also be seen in this light. Moreover, Grace's tendency to call her doctor out predated any possible infatuation with Dr Elwell. Her previous practitioner, Dr Francis Gaynor's records revealed that he made seventy-seven visits to the Duff children over a period of two years.[32]

If Inspector Hedges' pursuit of evidence in respect of these three entirely natural deaths appears somewhat hysterical, it is none the less very much in line with his approach to the rest of the investigation. It goes without saying that no detective wants three unsolved murders on his patch but even so, Hedges' anxiety that copycat criminals would 'not be slow to take advantage' if the police failed to bring about a conviction reads very strangely indeed. Did Hedges really believe that domestic murder by arsenical poisoning was a widespread problem, which might worsen if any perpetrators were seen to be getting away with it? The truth is that he may have done. During the first decades of the twentieth century there were a series of high profile murders involving arsenic and they all have an important bearing on the Croydon case and its investigation, in one way or another.

CHAPTER TEN

THE POISONING TWENTIES – ARSENIC'S LAST HURRAH

B y the 1920s arsenic had been synonymous with murder for centuries, even nicknamed 'inheritance powder' in some parts of continental Europe, in a half joking nod to its potential for the removal of wealthy relatives; but in spite of popular folklore, murder by poisoning is statistically negligible and always has been. For as long as records have been kept, they reveal that our favourite methods of despatching our fellow human beings involve physical weaponry in the form of guns or knives, violent battery, or asphyxiation; however, poisoning cases had a habit of making the headlines, which suggested to the general population that they occurred with a much greater frequency than was actually the case.

Throughout the latter part of the Victorian era an arsenic case – either murder or attempted murder – had come before the British courts on average roughly once a year. Many cases, like that of Mary Lelly in Lincolnshire[1] or Philip Cross in County Cork[2] were short-lived sensations, quickly forgotten beyond their own localities, but a handful of alleged poisoners, for example Madeleine Smith,[3] Mary Ann Cotton[4] and Florence Maybrick,[5] became household names, mainly thanks to the prolonged and hysterical coverage afforded to their cases. Their names became synonymous with arsenic, even if very few people could recall which of them had ultimately been found guilty.

At the beginning of the twentieth century, the number of arsenical poisoning cases coming before the courts began to decline. The trial of Elizabeth Nicholson in 1904 created little more than a flicker of interest.[6] Nicholson was a housekeeper accused of poisoning her elderly employer in order to obtain a small inheritance. However, the accused belonged to the servant class and the crime took place in Westmorland, with the trial held at the Appleby Assizes, far away from the London dailies, so the story created barely a ripple of interest beyond the north country. Nicholson was acquitted, as was twenty-nine-year-old Edith Bingham, another northern lass tried for murder by arsenic a few years later.

Edith Bingham's trial generated marginally more attention, not least because it was alleged that she had murdered several members of her family.[7] Suspicions arose when her brother, James Bingham, died on 15 August 1911 after a brief illness, the symptoms of which were consistent with arsenical poisoning. When the county analyst found traces of arsenic in James Bingham's organs, the exhumations of Edith's father and two of her sisters were set in hand and two out of three of these bodies also tested positive for the poison.

No arsenic was traced to Edith Bingham, although empty tins of the arsenic-based Acme Weed Killer were found on a rubbish tip in the grounds of Lancaster Castle, where her brother James had succeeded his father as caretaker. Edith had no obvious motive, unless her father ticking her off for various failures in house-keeping could be construed as such. Moreover, the death of her brother James effectively rendered her homeless, because their dwelling inside the castle precincts went with the job: but she did have opportunity, being the member of the household responsible for preparing all the meals.

During the evidence it emerged that Edith Bingham was not a very bright girl and her standards of housekeeping had been noticeably deficient. She did not always clean the kitchen pans and utensils properly, but this was rather a long way from actively poisoning three members of her family. The prosecution had taken the step of bringing in a prominent London expert, Sir William Willcox, but although Willcox opined that death was due to arsenical poisoning, he had to admit that he was basing this opinion solely on having read the reports prepared by the doctors and chemists who had actually performed the post-mortems and analyses.

The jury took a mere twenty-five minutes to decide that Edith Bingham was not guilty of the murder of her brother James, at which the prosecution announced that they would not be bringing evidence on the two outstanding charges of murder and the judge formally declared Edith innocent of those charges as well. There were some audible hisses in court and the question of how arsenic got into the remains of three members of her family continues to be debated.

Within less than a month of the Bingham trial, Sir William Willcox became involved in an arsenic case which made much bigger headlines. When Miss Eliza Barrow passed away on 14 September 1911 her landlord, Frederick Seddon, had her buried in a common grave and pocketed the proceeds of her estate.[8] However, when a nephew of Miss Barrow's confided his suspicions to the police, her body was exhumed and a post-mortem carried out in the presence of Willcox, by his up-and-coming young protégé, Bernard Spilsbury. The duo decided that the body was in a surprisingly good state of preservation and on analysing the organs, Willcox detected arsenic.

Seddon was arrested, tried and found guilty. The motive had apparently been sheer avarice and Seddon's name became a byword for killers of a particularly cold-blooded stamp. Although the old queen had been dead for more than a decade, the case has a distinct whiff of Victoriana about it. The prosecution suggested that Seddon had obtained the poison by soaking arsenic-impregnated fly papers in water, then adding the resulting liquor into his ailing lodger's food: a method redolent of several cases in the previous century. It would be the last British murder trial involving arsenic for almost ten years and, as the country advanced into determined modernity, it seemed for a while that such cases were a thing of the past.

Then, on 9 March 1920, the Chief Constable of Carmarthenshire wrote a letter to the Home Office seeking permission to exhume the body of a woman called Mabel Greenwood, who had died on 16 June the previous year.[9] The Chief Constable belonged to the Frederick Hedges school of policing and thus the evidence that Harold Greenwood, a Kidwelly solicitor, might have poisoned his wife, included the fact that his professed willingness to help the police with their enquiries, coupled with his readily agreeing to have the body exhumed, were 'suspicious'. Since it is reasonable to suppose that any unwillingness to co-operate, or opposition to an exhumation would have been construed as equally suspicious, it is fairly clear that the operation of a heads we win, tails you lose philosophy was under way. Similarly, when the evidence of one of the nurses who had attended Mrs Greenwood during her last illness proved less than helpful to the police case, this was put down to her alleged friendship with Greenwood. Greenwood's principal sin, however, was that he had remarried 'too soon' after his wife's death.

The body was exhumed and Dr John Webster, a pathological chemist at St Mary's in London, detected arsenic. The Greenwood case was soon dominating the headlines, with first the inquest, then the proceedings in the magistrates' court and finally the trial, appearing in the national papers over a period of nearly six months. The prosecution again wheeled in Sir William Willcox to offer an expert opinion. The situation had begun to look very black for Harold Greenwood, in whose garden shed Eureka Weed Killer had been discovered.

This particular Eureka Weed Killer was a shade of rose pink, which, when added to most foods, marginally altered the colour, but its rosy hue was undetectable in port wine. Mabel Greenwood had taken a glass of port wine with her lunch on the day she became ill and the prosecution contended that Harold Greenwood had slipped a fatal dose into the bottle before their meal. Everything else consumed by Mabel Greenwood before her final illness had been eaten or drunk by other members of the household with no untoward effect, but Mr Greenwood had taken whisky rather than wine with his lunch.

The police had revisited the Greenwood household on numerous occasions to question the servants, but there was one vital witness they had overlooked. The Greenwoods' eldest daughter, Irene, went into the witness box at her father's trial and testified that she too had drunk a glass of wine at lunch on the last day of her mother's life. It was the evidence which literally saved her father's neck. Harold Greenwood was acquitted on 9 November 1920.

Almost a year to the day that Harold Greenwood was acquitted, Mrs Annie Black expired at her home in Tregonissey near St Austell. She had been ill for some time, and her various symptoms had included vomiting and a burning sensation in her throat – but it was less Mrs Black's symptoms that initially excited suspicion, than the fact that two days before she died, her husband, Edward Ernest Black, had absconded.[10] The family doctor refused to issue a death certificate and, following a post-mortem, Annie Black's body was found to contain arsenic.

The police ran Edward Black to ground in a hotel room in Liverpool on 21 November where, when they forced the door of his room, they found he had attempted to commit suicide by cutting his own throat. Black recovered from his self-inflicted wounds and stood trial for his wife's murder the following spring.

The case differed substantially from the Greenwoods', not least in that Black's stepdaughter gave damaging testimony against him, including allegations that he had been interfering with her sexually for a number of years. This, coupled with the fact that Black had originally left home in a hurry to avoid arrest in connection with a series of fraud charges (he had been defrauding his employers, the Refuge Insurance Company), hardly painted a complimentary picture of this ex-member of Tregonissey Church choir. Although Black protested his innocence, the jury found him guilty and he was executed.

The public did not have to wait a year before the next big arsenic story hit the headlines. The case against Herbert Armstrong bore uncanny similarities to that of Harold Greenwood. Both men were solicitors, practising in small country communities, both had been apparently devoted to wives who had suffered poor health for some time, both wives had initially been consigned to the local churchyard without occasioning suspicion, but both men would later be accused of using forms of arsenic weedkiller to despatch their spouses.

Katharine Armstrong's body had been buried in Cusop churchyard, near Hay-on-Wye, for almost a year before it was exhumed on 2 January 1922.[11] As in the Greenwood and Black investigations, the Home Office experts Webster and Willcox became involved from the outset, and on this occasion Spilsbury was appointed to perform the belated post-mortem. Arsenic was discovered in Katharine Armstrong's remains and this time there was no daughter to cast doubt on how it had arrived there – the three Armstrong children were kept sufficiently far away from the trial that Armstrong's youngest daughter, Margaret, never knew the circumstances of her father's death until she chanced to read about it in her teens.[12]

Suspicion that Armstrong had murdered his wife initially arose not from anything in the couple's own relationship, but from unproven allegations that he had sent a rival solicitor, Oswald Martin, a box of poisoned chocolates, then made a further attempt on Martin's life when the latter accepted an invitation to tea. It has been suggested that Herbert Armstrong and his counsel thought the prosecution case so inherently flawed that acquittal was almost guaranteed, but the jury thought otherwise and Herbert Armstrong was executed on 31 May 1922, protesting his innocence to the very end.

The poisoned chocolates in the Armstrong case quickly inspired a copy-cat attack on Sir William Horwood, Commissioner of the Metropolitan Police. Horwood received a box of chocolates on 9 November 1922 and became very ill after eating just one of them. The chocolates had been laced with arsenic and Horwood was hospitalised for a fortnight, during which time he received more anonymous gifts of poisoned chocolate, as did a couple of other senior police officers, who fortunately did not eat them. The donor turned out to be a market gardener called Walter Frank Tatham, who had a history of mental illness and had been certified insane and detained on at least one previous occasion. Brought before the courts in respect of the poisoned chocolates, Tatham was decreed unfit to plead and detained at His Majesty's pleasure.[13]

Meanwhile, the annual arsenic murder sensation for 1923 was again provided by citizens of Wales and its borders. When forty-seven-year-old Jenny Morgan of Newport, Monmouthshire, died on 22 January after a long and trying illness, her doctor was uncertain of the cause of death, so a post-mortem examination and analysis of organs followed.[14] When the county analyst discovered traces of arsenic in her remains, an immediate police investigation commenced and the coroner's inquest into Jenny Morgan's death soon developed into an integral part of this investigation.

Like the Croydon inquests, the proceedings which enquired into Jenny Morgan's death became bogged down in a skein of side issues, not least whether any arsenic could be traced to any particular member of her family. Fortunately for the widower, he appears to have been the only citizen in the country not routinely keeping a tin of arsenic-based weedkiller in his shed, but one of the Morgans' sons, William, was a storekeeper at a local wholesaler which dealt in weedkiller – and William, in common with the rest of the family, had helped to care for his mother as she lay bedridden in her final days.

The inquest proceedings had not been without their oddities, dramas and distractions. One witness testified to having a conversation with Jenny's husband Herbert, in which the latter had allegedly referred to his wife's being dead, before death had actually taken place. Another witness, Ethel Andrews, apparently became so distressed by the idea that she had to give evidence that it impelled her to commit suicide. She vanished from her home on 26 February and was not seen again until her body was fished out of the canal on 17 March, with the witness subpoena still in her pocket.

In summing up, the coroner stated that there could be no possible doubt that Jenny Morgan's death was due to arsenical poisoning. Accident and suicide were entirely out of the question and therefore the jury must consider by whom it had been administered. According to the coroner there were only three possibilities: her husband Herbert, and her sons Cyril and William. Both Herbert and William had given evidence which contained contradictory statements and according to the coroner in William's case, his behaviour appeared at times irrational and even unbalanced. Cyril had managed a more favourable impression and contradicted himself to a somewhat lesser degree, on which basis the coroner invited the jury to eliminate him.

To say that this was a thoroughly unbalanced and irregular method of arriving at an inquest verdict would be to put it mildly, but faced with an edict to choose between Herbert and William Morgan, after deliberating for almost two hours, the jury returned a verdict of wilful murder against William and the young man was arrested and taken away to Cardiff prison.

The next step in the proceedings was the magistrates' court and by now William Morgan had a solicitor, Mr Dauncey, to represent him. Dauncey told the

Bench that while he accepted that Mrs Morgan had died by arsenical poisoning, there was no *prima facie* evidence that it had been administered by his client and, 'a charge of murder has never been preferred before upon such flimsy evidence'.[15] After withdrawing to confer, the magistrates agreed that there was insufficient evidence to proceed, but were unable to discharge Morgan there and then as he was still technically held under the coroner's warrant. The young man spent another ten days in Cardiff prison before the legal wheels had ground out the *nolle prosequi*[16] which would gain him his release. No one else was ever charged with the murder of Jenny Morgan.

A charge of poisoning against another son called William was destined to go much further the following year in Edinburgh, when Willie King stood trial for the murder of his mother and attempted murder of his father in the summer of 1924.[17] King was a twenty-two-year-old trainee accountant with an interest in chemistry, who never denied buying a packet of arsenic, four days before his mother's death, for use in his home experiments. On discovering the opened packet of arsenic in her son's bedroom, Mrs King had removed it to the kitchen, from whence Willie covertly stole it back and returned it to his bedroom.

After a bread and cheese supper that evening, both the King parents were taken ill and Mrs King died. Professor Littlejohn, the analyst, found more than 3 grains of arsenic in Mrs King's body and estimated that during the course of her short illness, her body had expelled twice as much again. The professor had established by experiment that he could easily pick up as much as 2 grains of arsenic between his thumb and forefinger, which meant it would have been easy for anyone to covertly introduce the stuff onto the bread and cheese. Willie King's trouser pocket had been found to contain the equivalent of 1 grain of arsenic, which he claimed must have got there from his fingers, after he had handled the package.

As in so many cases, the motive was weak and hard evidence that the young man had contaminated the food non-existent. The judge summed up very much in Willie King's favour, drawing attention to the fact that he was 'well brought up' and came from 'a respectable family'. His father wept with relief when the jury brought in a verdict of not guilty.

For a couple of years it began to look as if the spate of arsenic murders was over. In 1927 Mrs Margaret Devigne was put on trial after she apparently assisted her invalid mother into the afterlife with a dose of arsenic. However, there was a significant level of doubt as to whether the old lady had died as a result of the arsenic, or from the effects of a malignant tumour on her liver. The case attracted little public interest, not least because Mrs Devigne was swiftly declared unfit to plead and detained under the then equivalent of the Mental Health Act.[18]

When Harry Pace died on 10 January 1928, his relatives immediately took their suspicions to the police, claiming that he had been murdered by his wife Beatrice.[19] The Pace family were part of a semi-invisible underclass of rural poor; married at seventeen years of age, the couple had produced ten children, only five of whom had survived to live with their parents in an isolated three-room cottage in the Forest of Dean, where Pace scratched out a living working as a quarry labourer and keeping a few sheep. They routinely kept arsenic-based sheep dip in the cottage and when Harry Pace's organs was analysed, arsenic was found.

The long drawn out inquest proceedings first opened on 16 January, and it soon emerged that Pace had been a volatile character, given to violent outbursts, morose fits of depression and what appeared to be occasional outright madness. He had more than once threatened suicide and not infrequently beaten his wife and children. The most hostile evidence against his widow came from Pace's mother and the expert testimony of Sir William Willcox, who insisted that his findings supported a death by murder, rather than accident or suicide. In the meantime, Beatrice Pace and her children were suffering considerable privations, as quite apart from the attentions of the Scotland Yard detectives who had been drafted in to handle the case, and the anxiety these proceedings must have generated, the State had elected to withhold her widow's pension until the outcome of the inquest was known.

On 22 May the coroner finally sent the jury out to consider their verdict. They returned after nearly an hour to state that Harry Pace met his death by arsenical poisoning, administered by some person or persons unknown. At this the coroner took the unprecedented step of refusing to accept their verdict as it stood, claiming that, 'No person can be committed by coroner's inquisition and so bring about a further inquiry into the case unless some person is named.' (This was a crafty mixture of fact and fiction. No person could be committed – i.e. arrested – on his order unless the jury named that person, but further investigation of a crime was in no way impeded if no one was named.)

The coroner then cleared the court to enable the jury to 'reconsider' their verdict. When the public were re-admitted, it was to hear the foreman announce with tears in his eyes, that the revised verdict was death by arsenical poisoning, administered by Beatrice Annie Pace. Uproar ensued. Women in the public gallery burst into tears. Other members of the public hissed and Mrs Pace herself became hysterical, sobbing, 'I didn't do it. I didn't do it. I wouldn't. I couldn't.' She eventually collapsed and had to receive medical aid.

Many of those who found themselves on trial for murder in the 1920s – whether innocent or guilty – evoked considerable hostility from the general public, but this was never the case with Mrs Pace. Perhaps it was because the press carried stories of her lengthy interrogations by the detectives from Scotland Yard, when she and her children were detained for hours on end at the police station. Or possibly it was the distasteful spectacle of her children being brought into court to give evidence against her at the hearing before the magistrates where, as nine-year-old Leslie took the witness stand, Beatrice Pace was overheard whispering to the wardress who sat beside her in the dock, 'That's my little boy.' Maybe it was the interview given by her seventeen-year-old daughter Dorothy, explaining how the police questioned her for more than four hours, until in desperation she lied to them so that they would let her go home to her mother. Perhaps it was the fact that Harry Pace, a brutal bully, did not make for a particularly sympathetic victim – maybe even that the evidence against Beatrice

Pace was wafer thin, verging on non-existent? Whatever the reason, each time Mrs Pace left court for her Cardiff prison cell, the crowds lining the pavement shouted out 'Shame' and 'God bless you'.

In spite of popular support from the general public and tabloids alike, and an impassioned plea from a counsel funded by popular subscription, who pointed out that there was absolutely no *prima facie* evidence against his client, the magistrates decided there was a case to answer and Beatrice Pace was committed for trial. She appeared before Mr Justice Horridge at the Summer Assizes and when at the conclusion of the evidence for the prosecution, her defence again submitted that there was no case to answer, the judge finally agreed, directing the jury to bring in a verdict of not guilty. The seven-month ordeal of Beatrice Pace was over.

Later the same year it looked as if the Welsh courts might be about to witness another arsenic murder trial, but after a series of inquest hearings into the death of Mrs Jessie Llewellyn, during which a variety of experts argued for and against a lethal dose of arsenic having brought about Mrs Llewellyn's demise, a verdict of death by natural causes was eventually returned and the case slid into obscurity.[20]

Viewed in the context of these earlier cases, the manner in which Coroner Jackson handled those long drawn out proceedings in Croydon in 1929 becomes increasingly creditable: it is not entirely unrealistic to suggest that the way he conducted the final days of them may have been responsible for saving Grace Duff's life.

The 1920s had seen an abundance of arsenic-related headlines, but only two cases made big news in the following decade. The first of these was the trial of Annie Hearn which took place in Bodmin in June 1931.[21] Like the suspect in an earlier Cornish arsenic case, Annie Hearn had somewhat damaged her credibility by making a run for it, once she realised that enquiries were underway, but unlike Edward Black, the forty-six-year-old widow was fleeing from nothing more than the possibility of being arrested for two murders she claimed not to have committed.

It was another case in which the two 'suspect' deaths had initially been ascribed to natural causes, with doubts only raised once the bodies had been buried in the local churchyard. After exhumations and analysis – with Dr Roche Lynch performing this service for the Home Office – it was concluded that death had been due to arsenical poisoning. The first alleged victim was Annie Hearn's spinster sister, Lydia Everard, with whom she had shared a bungalow in Lewannick, near Launceston. The sisters had begun to share a home after the death of Annie's husband and apparently got on well. Apart from obtaining sole custody of the bungalow, Annie appeared to have had little reason to murder her sister and when Lydia died on 21 July 1930 after a long period of poor health, no one initially seems to have entertained any suspicions.

Annie Hearn had become friendly with her neighbours, Mr and Mrs Thomas, and the trio sometimes undertook little outings together, including one on 18 October 1930, when Mrs Hearn provided a picnic lunch of salmon sandwiches. Unfortunately, soon after consuming these sandwiches, both Mr and Mrs

Thomas began to feel slightly unwell and when they got home, although Mr Thomas felt better after a nip of whisky, his wife became very unwell indeed. In fact, Alice Thomas was so poorly that Annie Hearn came over to help look after her and continued to do so for the next ten days, until Mrs Thomas's mother arrived and took over. These ministrations were to no avail and on 4 November Alice died – death initially being ascribed to natural causes.

The prosecution's theory ran that first Lydia Everard, and then Alice Thomas, had been put out of the way so that Annie Hearn could have Mr Thomas to herself. Annie Hearn had tended her garden with arsenical weedkiller, which got the prosecution case over the first hurdle of where the accused had obtained the poison. This did not help them much when it came to administration, however, because in line with the routine practice of always dying arsenic-based products a distinctive colour – a practice which derived from the numerous deaths which had occurred in the nineteenth century thanks to white arsenic being mistaken for salt, sugar and flour – Mrs Hearn's arsenic weedkiller was bright blue. The defence had arranged experiments which showed that when even tiny quantities were introduced to white bread, tinned pink salmon, or butter, these various foodstuffs very obviously turned blue.

The prosecution's problems were not confined to the question of how the arsenic could have got into the sandwiches. There was also significant doubt about the integrity of the samples taken from the exhumed bodies. The organs had been removed in the open air and put into jars which had been standing open on a nearby trestle table in the churchyard. The jars had been handled by various policemen and officials who were present at the scene. There were no facilities for hand washing and the possibilities for contamination were thus considerable.

Arsenic occurs naturally in soil and the level is particularly high in certain parts of the country, including Cornwall.[22] The soil in the churchyard had been tested and found to have a higher than usual concentration of natural arsenic and the defence contended that if even a few specks of earth had managed to get into a jar from someone's unwashed fingers, the discovery of arsenic in the two women's remains was effectively compromised. After a trial lasting eight days, the jury took less than an hour to find Annie Hearn not guilty.

Several of these cases all but form matching pairs. Armstrong and Greenwood, the two solicitors said to have put away their wives, William Morgan and William King, two sons accused of matricide on the slenderest of evidence, Elizabeth Nicholson and Edith Bingham, slapdash north country housekeepers, and the last of the murders with a bearing on the Croydon case was another such 'twin': the case of Charlotte Bryant in 1936.

Charlotte Bryant, like Beatrice Pace, was a member of the rural poor, who married in her teens and went on to produce a large family.[23] Her husband, Frederick Bryant, was a cowman and although their Dorset cottage was not large, the Bryants took in lodgers to help make ends meet. In 1933 Charlotte began an affair with the latest of these, Leonard Parsons, a ne'er do well who had children by various other women and made his living as an itinerant pedlar and horse dealer. He moved at frequent intervals, partly to avoid paying the various child maintenance orders which had been made against him. According to both Charlotte and Leonard, her husband Fred was aware of the fact that the youngest Bryant child had been fathered by Parsons and did not have a problem with it. The pair also claimed that Parsons had consistently been clear that he neither wished to go away with nor marry Charlotte Bryant, even had she been free to do so. Yet in spite of the fact that Parsons was self evidently not a marrying man, Charlotte's only motive for murdering her husband was said to have been her expectation that Leonard Parsons would marry her, once she was free.

After Parsons moved out, the Bryants took in other lodgers, the last of whom, a middle aged widow called Lucy Ostler, was still with them when Fred Bryant died.

Fred Bryant had been afflicted by some kind of gastric illness on and off since May 1935 and by December, when Charlotte belatedly tried to take out a policy on his life, he appeared so sick that the insurance agent declined the business. When Bryant fell victim to a particularly fierce gastric attack on 20 December, a doctor was summoned and suggested admitting the patient to hospital, but Bryant initially refused, only agreeing to be admitted on 22 December, a few hours before he died.

Gossip and speculation were not slow to follow. Dr Roche Lynch was called in to analyse the organs and calculated that there was in excess of 4 grains of arsenic in Bryant's body.

When Charlotte Bryant was arrested on 10 February, her five children (aged twelve, ten, six, four and fifteen months) were taken to Sturminster Newton Institution,[24] there being nowhere else for them to go. Two days later the local NSPCC inspector applied to move the children from Sturminster Newton to another district, where he had found a foster home for them. Via her solicitor, Charlotte refused, saying that, 'they will stay at Sturminster Newton until all this is sorted out.' She next saw her children briefly in the anteroom of the magistrates' court, some six weeks later. It would be one of the few meetings she would ever have with them again.

The trial opened at the end of May. The prosecution majored on various contradictory statements allegedly made by both Charlotte Bryant and her lodger Lucy Ostler, but for different reasons both women's statements should have been received with considerable caution. In the days immediately before Charlotte Bryant's arrest, rumours had flown around the district that Mrs Ostler's husband was to be exhumed and the unfortunate widow admitted under cross-examination that because of this she had been in 'a bit of a way' when interviewed by the police. Under the circumstances, any damaging statements which tended to incriminate her landlady, while obviously deflecting suspicion from herself, were distinctly suspect.

Charlotte Bryant could neither read nor write. Informed that there would have to be an inquest on her husband, she responded with the question: 'What's an inquest?' During her trial, when asked about something she had told the police which was patently untrue, she agreed that the information given was not correct, but said she had been confused when the question was put. 'I had the children all around me. One was crying and I cannot really understand what I did say.'

Like Beatrice Pace before her, Charlotte Bryant saw her children, Lucy aged ten and Ernest aged twelve, put into the witness box to testify for the prosecution. She listened in bewilderment to the evidence of Home Office expert Dr Roche Lynch, who appeared to be able to prove that she had attempted to burn an incriminating old weedkiller tin in the stove, even though she denied doing so.

Her defence contended that there was not a shred of evidence that Charlotte Bryant had ever handled arsenic, still less used it to poison her husband – who had regularly used arsenic for dipping sheep. They further suggested that Bryant could have poisoned himself accidentally, given that he was not in the habit of washing his hands before eating and that standards of hygiene in the Bryant household were generally poor – but the jury was not convinced. Charlotte Bryant was executed on 15 July 1936 after an unsuccessful appeal.

When Edmund returned from Hampshire, Grace met him at the corner of South Park Hill Road, seen here through the arch of the railway bridge. (*Croydon Local Studies Library & Archives Service*)

Edmund Creighton Duff.

Grace Duff with her
son John, *c.* 1918.

Violet Sidney in middle
and old age.

Vera Sidney photographed age twenty-one
and approximately ten years later.

Vera in nursing uniform during the First World War.

Tom Sidney saw active service during the First World War and was wounded at Vimy Ridge.

Tom at the piano. Before
the war he toured in Britain,
South Africa and Australia
and after the war in Britain
and America.

Margaret Sidney in
September 1929.

Tom and Margaret Sidney in 1923. *Below*: their children Cedric and Mary-Virginia, both pictured in 1929.

Grace with Suzanne in 1924.

A less flattering shot of Grace, on the reverse of which she wrote *Isn't this awful?*

Grace and Edmund's three surviving children: John (above), Mary and Alastair.

In the garden of 6 South Park Hill Road in 1927. Tom, Grace and Vera are standing; the man on the rug is believed to be Edmund.

George Street, Croydon, in 1927, where the premises of Frederick Rose, purveyor of arsenical preparations, faced those of the undertakers J.B. Shakespeare & Co., whose sign can be seen to the left of the tram. (*Croydon Local Studies Library & Archives Service*)

After its exhumation, the body of Edmund Duff is conveyed to the Mayday Hospital mortuary. (*J.B. Shakespeare & Co. Ltd*)

The Duff-Sidney grave in the Queen's Road Cemetery – the last resting place of Margaret, Suzanne and Edmund Duff, Vera and Violet Sidney. A child angel scatters flower petals from her skirt. (*© Diane Janes*)

The Duff-Sidney grave lies immediately to the right of the Chapel of Rest, obscured by a tree. The complex of buildings with a tall chimney and tower which lie immediately above the cemetery is the Queen's Road Homes, where Coroner Jackson conducted the inquests, and in the top left-hand corner the outline of the Mayday Hospital, where the various post-mortems were conducted, can just be made out.
(© *English Heritage. NMR. Aerofilms Collection*)

A section of the notes prepared by Coroner Jackson in advance of his summing up the evidence at the Edmund Duff inquest: Cause of death – no doubt.
(*Croydon Local Studies Library & Archives Service*)

Cause of death (no doubt)

Man's illness not serious until he arrived home, and after supper.

No direct evidence how arsenic was administered (in what, or by whom) — but he suddenly dies of arsenical poisoning.

Now you have got 4 alternatives : —

(1) he took it himself to kill himself (suicide - or killed while ground mind)

(2) he took it himself, in some way of which there is no evidence, accidentally;

(3) accidentally it was given to him. (that means it got into his food somehow.)

(4) he was poisoned by somebody else.

Number 29 Birdhurst Rise, the home of Violet and Vera Sidney. (*Peter Woolley*)

Advertisement for Eureka Weed Killer. (*DKC Collection*)

Grace Duff and Tom Sidney in later years – brother and sister separated by a gulf of suspicion.

Grace and Mary in Seaford, Sussex, late 1960s.

Margaret and Tom in the USA, 1970s.

CHAPTER ELEVEN

DEADLY CONTROVERSIES

The Hearn and Bryant cases took place in the 1930s, but in the annals of arsenic murder they belong naturally with the famous trials of the previous decade. After Bryant there would be no more than a handful of known murders involving arsenic throughout the rest of the century, and in two of these cases the guilty party would take his life before the law could catch up with him.[1]

In spite of numerous superficial differences, a series of common themes and shared traits run through most of the arsenic cases which made it to court in the 1920s and '30s. A surprising proportion of those accused were 'incomers' – people who had not always belonged to the neighbourhood in which the crime was said to have been committed. Neither Edward Black nor Annie Hearn were natives of Cornwall, both originating from the north of England; professional opportunities had brought Herbert Armstrong and Harold Greenwood into their respective communities – even Beatrice Pace and Charlotte Bryant were girls from other districts, who had married local men.

In the majority of these cases there was no obvious motive; several of the accused were rendered substantially financially worse off by the death of which they were accused. Harold Greenwood lost a significant annual income on the death of his wife, while Pace and Bryant lost their breadwinners (surely the fact that Harry Pace at least provided a roof over their heads had been one of the factors which encouraged his wife to put up with him?).

Quite a few of the victims went to their graves without initially exciting the slightest suspicion. The alleged victims of Herbert Armstrong, Harold Greenwood and Annie Hearn had all been buried for a considerable period before it occurred to anyone in officialdom that their deaths might have been due to anything but natural causes.

In almost every case the person who ended up (or nearly ended up) in the dock arrived under the spotlight of suspicion by process of elimination, rather than hard evidence. Once it had been determined that the deceased had been poisoned with arsenic and had not committed suicide, the obvious inference was that some third party must have adulterated their food and drink and that person must have been someone close to them. Operating on a similar basis to a traditional 1920s whodunit, the police ruled out the servants, if there were any, and concentrated on the family. In a family which comprised one surviving adult there was only one possible suspect, and even in households like the Kings or the Morgans, the finger of suspicion did not have a very wide arc to travel.

Another common factor in several cases was the presence of a whistle blower – a persistent accuser, thanks to whom the police investigation began. When Harry Pace died it was his mother who pressed for an investigation. Similarly, although the medical professionals involved in the death of Alice Thomas entertained no suspicions, Mrs Thomas's brother, Percy Parsons, accused Mrs Hearn at his sister's funeral and continued to foment suspicion until the police took him seriously.[2] Local gossip was swift to condemn Charlotte Bryant thanks to her affair with Leonard Parsons and when Harold Greenwood remarried less than twelve months after his wife's death, tongues began to wag in the deeply conservative small town where he had made his home. Greenwood himself wrote after his acquittal that he had been a victim of gossip and slander, stating his conviction that had he not offended Kidwelly public opinion by remarrying – partly to provide a mother for his children – there would have been no trial.[3]

The worst example of third party influence, however, occurred in respect of the case against Herbert Armstrong.[4] Armstrong had practised as a solicitor in Hay-on-Wye for a number of years by the time Oswald Martin took over the other legal practice in the little town. Martin married the only daughter of a local chemist, Fred Davies, and it was Mr Davies who would feature prominently in the eventual prosecution of Herbert Armstrong.

Davies began his campaign against Armstrong by approaching the local doctor to suggest that a stomach upset his son-in-law had suffered, following a visit to Armstrong's house for afternoon tea, might have been the result of arsenical poisoning. When the local doctor disagreed, saying that the symptoms had not been indicative of this, Davies continued to press the point, citing professional rivalry between Armstrong and Martin as a motive, and claiming that Armstrong had been behaving oddly.

Davies then produced a box of chocolates which he said had been sent anonymously to his daughter and son-in-law several weeks before, and which had made a guest who ate one ill. On examination, it was obvious that several of the chocolates had been clumsily drilled and adulterated with a substance which Davies suggested might be white arsenic.

Confronted with the chocolates, the local doctor was finally convinced that there might be grounds for suspicion, and suggested that Oswald Martin provide a sample of urine to be tested for arsenic. Fred Davies assisted by supplying the bottle for the test and later taking responsibility for parcelling up both the urine sample and the contaminated chocolates, before sending them off for analysis. When the urine sample arrived with John Webster at St Mary's Hospital, he found the 17½fl oz of urine contained ⅓₃ grain of arsenic – an amount massively above the normal level. Unfortunately, what no one at the time knew – including the team who would go on to defend Herbert Armstrong on the charges of murdering his wife and attempting to murder Oswald Martin – was that non-fatal overdoses of arsenic have a relatively rapid rate of clearance from both the bloodstream and urine.[5] Thus the arsenic found in Martin's urine sample was not indicative of a dose of arsenic received at the hands of a would-be poisoner at a tea party some five days before the sample was taken, but was clear evidence that the sample had been either accidentally or deliberately contaminated with arsenic at some point between Martin's passing it and its arrival in Webster's laboratory.

When the substance found in the chocolates turned out to be white arsenic, and white arsenic was subsequently discovered in Armstrong's possession, the police considered it strong evidence against him. Although it was perfectly legal to purchase arsenic, it was illegal to sell white arsenic over the counter without adding a dye of some kind, and the white arsenic discovered in Armstrong's possession was still in a packet bearing a label from Davies's shop. Although the chemist claimed that selling it in that condition could only have been a mistake, the coincidence has the feel of a plant. Moreover, the type of chocolates sent to the Martins were not available for purchase in Hay-on-Wye and from the batch number on the box, detectives quickly established that a relatively short period of time had elapsed between their manufacture and arrival at the Martins' home. Armstrong had not travelled beyond Hay during the period in question, and nor had he received any goods through the post. In spite of intensive investigations, all attempts to connect Armstrong with the purchase of the chocolates failed – unfortunately it did not occur to the police to investigate the movements or purchases of Fred Davies over the same period.

Without the persistent machinations of Fred Davies, there would never have been any suggestion that Herbert Armstrong was a poisoner: the body of his late wife would not have been exhumed and he would not have been wrongly executed[6] in 1922.

Of course the most obvious point of commonality which led to criminal charges was the fact that one or more bodies had been discovered containing an abnormal amount of arsenic – yet the presence of an unexplained overdose of arsenic did not invariably lead to a police investigation or attempted prosecution.

In July 1929, while the Croydon Arsenic inquests filled acres of newsprint, another inquest involving arsenic scarcely attracted a flicker of interest. Laura Benson, an eighteen-year-old assistant in a Liverpool fruit shop, had been admitted to hospital suffering from an enlarged goitre in her neck. During her stay she developed vomiting and diarrhoea and after eight days in hospital she died. Although vomiting and diarrhoea are not unusual in a patient suffering from hyperthyroidism, Laura Benson had not been expected to die and thus there was a post-mortem. Professor Roberts, the county analyst, detected 0.141 grain of arsenic in the girl's stomach and other organs, from which he calculated that at death her whole body must have contained about half a grain. By the time Laura Benson died, she was extremely emaciated and since the hospital were confident that she had not taken any arsenic in the eight days she had been a patient, Roberts decided that the arsenic must have been taken at least a week prior to her death, and therefore that most of it would have been expelled from Laura Benson's body by the time she died – thus he concluded that Laura Benson had died from acute arsenical poisoning.

The coroner questioned whether the girl might have been dosing herself with 'a quack' remedy, but her parents denied this and the girl's father pointed out that there had been no symptoms of poisoning until after his daughter was admitted to hospital. Nothing was found in the family home to explain the mystery, apart from traces of arsenic in the bedroom wallpaper, which Roberts said were so minute that they could not possibly have been involved. The coroner strongly advised the jury to bring in an open verdict, which they did.[7]

It is tempting to speculate that the lack of police interest in Laura Benson's strange death was in some way connected with the fact that her father was a retired police inspector, but Laura Benson's was not an isolated case. In October 1928 a similarly mysterious arsenic death had come before the Westminster coroner and by coincidence it was again a woman patient who had died in hospital. Alice Straigh was a fifty-year-old nurse who had been suffering from liver disease, which was considered to be the primary cause of death. However, her organs had yielded up ¹⁄₅₀ grain of arsenic, indicating that a much higher amount must have been present in the whole body. Alice Straigh had been in Westminster Hospital for a full month before her death and the hospital was insistent that she had not taken any arsenic during that time, while her family doctor testified that he had never prescribed any prior to her hospital admission and Miss Straigh's sister was also ready to confirm that Alice had never knowingly taken arsenic. The jury returned an open verdict in that case too.[8]

There is no suggestion that Miss Straigh's family had police connections – but there is an obvious similarity in that both deaths took place in hospital. When summing up for the jury at the Laura Benson inquest, the Liverpool coroner said, 'I think you will agree we can rule the hospital out of it.'[9] The question inevitably arises as to what sort of position the relatives might have found themselves in if either woman had not died in hospital.

The deaths of Laura Benson and Alice Straigh made such tiny ripples on the public stage that most people probably missed their stories altogether. Anyone who did read the paragraph or so devoted to such a death would be forgiven for assuming that it was a one-off – an isolated blip on the radar which bore no relationship to the high profile cases which were sometimes being reported in the same week's editions. Yet they would have been wrong. In 1930 Elsie Duckett died suddenly and arsenic was found in her organs. She was a seventeen-year-old domestic servant and had no apparent motive to commit suicide. She too had spent the last twelve days of her life in hospital, and the inquest resulted in another open verdict.[10]

Sixty-three-year-old Ellen Richardson died of acute arsenical poisoning in the Mayday Hospital in Croydon in 1926 – again there was no evidence of how she could have come by the arsenic.[11] Then there was Charles Allen of Addlestone in Surrey, who returned home from a Masonic dinner in 1931, became ill and died the same night: the provenance of the arsenic discovered in his body was a complete mystery.[12]

The most immediately obvious difference between these deaths – all attributed to acute arsenical poisoning – and the deaths of Mabel Greenwood, Katharine Armstrong, Frederick Bryant *et al* was that the circumstances surrounding their last days did not offer up a convenient coincidental suspect or suspects. Had Charles Allen not attended a Masonic dinner on the night he died, but rather eaten supper with his wife, would she have ended up in the dock like Beatrice Pace? For as Norman Birkett pointed out when defending Mrs Pace in 1928, 'every wife in the country has opportunity' and if one followed the line taken by those seeking to prosecute the case against Mrs Pace, 'every innocent thing the ordinary person may do becomes some evidence of guilt.'[13] If Alice Straigh had expired at home, would her sister have fallen under suspicion as did Annie Hearn? How perilously close was Alfred Richardson, the husband of Ellen, to following in the footsteps of Herbert Armstrong? Yet surely the difference between an open verdict and a verdict of murder had to rely on more than the availability of a suspect to pin it on?

'Many, many people have been poisoned with arsenic,' Mr Justice Darling opined at the trial of Herbert Armstrong in 1922.[14] Although this statement as it stands is broadly correct, when Darling uttered those words he was reflecting a widespread myth which had gripped the imagination of his own and earlier generations: the notion that arsenic was frequently employed as a murder weapon, not least because it was supposedly difficult to detect. Of course, when taken cumulatively across the centuries, arsenical poisoning had accounted for numerous deaths, but the vast majority of these were due to the accidental effects of acute or chronic exposure. Yet arsenic had become synonymous with murder, an instantly recognisable motif, reinforced via the popular culture of detective novels and ultimately in the title of the 1941 play *Arsenic and Old Lace* by Joseph Kesselring.

In a pamphlet published in 1938 Sir William Willcox continued to push the myth, writing, 'Arsenic produces symptoms so like those of natural disease, that it has been for all time the most commonly chosen for criminal purposes.'[15] Not only is such a statement a huge leap in the dark without hard figures to back it up, but what figures do exist imply that Sir William's contention was wrong. For example, between 1900 and 1928, out of more than 300 people who had been executed for murder in England and Wales, a mere dozen had employed poison as their weapon and of these only three had used arsenic – the same number as had employed prussic acid.[16] The suspicion about arsenic was not founded on hard figures, however, but on a widespread belief that people were regularly getting away with arsenical murder because their crimes went undetected. In a classic example of turning logic on its head, Spilsbury's biographers summed up the position when they wrote, 'The argument for undiscovered crimes in this genre is supported by the fact that … notwithstanding the popularity of arsenic among poisoners, these three cases [Seddon, Armstrong and the Croydon trio] stand isolated by long periods of time…'[17] In other words, the lack of hard evidence that such cases existed in any number was somehow proof that they did! Essentially this mindset would inform most of the investigations into alleged arsenic murders for the first thirty or so years of the twentieth century, leading in some cases to a situation which bore more resemblance to a medieval trial for witchcraft than a modern murder investigation.

The supposed popularity of arsenic was partly rooted in the idea that it was a difficult poison to trace – but this too flew in the face of solid fact. Reasonably reliable methods of testing for arsenic had existed from the eighteenth century onwards, and as far back as 1836 a test had been developed which would identify and provide lasting evidence of the presence of arsenic in a dead body. This was the Marsh test, which the London chemist James Marsh formulated in specific response to the problems facing a court in an arsenic-related murder trial.[18]

In simple terms, when using the formula and apparatus devised by Marsh, the suspect samples were heated with strong acids to render them into a solution, which was then heated to produce a gas. If arsenic was present, it would leave a silvery black deposit on a ceramic tile, known as an 'arsenic mirror'. The Marsh test (subsequently improved upon by Egar Reinsch in 1842) could be utilised not only to demonstrate the presence of arsenic, but also to determine the quantity. In order to measure the amount of arsenic detected, a chemist would first produce a series of arsenic mirrors by running known quantities of arsenic through the apparatus, and would then compare these mirrors with the results obtained from the unknown quantity.

The originator of the Marsh test had himself appeared as a medical witness and throughout the eighteenth and nineteenth centuries the value of expert medical testimony had increasingly come to be recognised. Marsh genuinely was an expert, but alas many of the doctors who gave evidence in poison trials during this period were experts in name only, sometimes offering testimony on subjects in which they had no actual practical experience.[19]

A prime example of this occurred in 1815, when the Turner family of London became ill after consuming a meal of steak and dumplings prepared by their cook, Elizabeth Fenning.[20] Fenning had also partaken of the meal and she too fell victim to the symptoms, which prostrated her to the extent that she was unable to clear up in the kitchen. Thus the saucepan in which the dumplings had been boiled was still unwashed the following day when John Marshall, a local surgeon, attended the family. Marshall examined the saucepan and noticed a quantity of white residue in it, which he pronounced to be arsenic. Elizabeth Fenning was carted off to prison and charged with administering poison with intent to murder her employers – intent to murder then being a capital offence. During the subsequent trial, the family gave evidence that the dumplings had been heavy and black inside and that the cutlery had become black on contact with them. Marshall testified not only that he had discovered arsenic in the saucepan, but also that arsenic would have turned the dumplings black inside and discoloured the cutlery as described – neither of these contentions is remotely accurate. Fenning was found guilty and executed.

Eleven years later a Sussex farmer called Benjamin Russell collapsed and died while in the act of carrying stolen corn home from a neighbour's barn.[21] Not wishing the theft to be discovered, his panic-stricken accomplices moved the body to nearby woods, where its discovery naturally initiated enquiries. The local surgeon on the scene this time was a Dr Evans, who performed an autopsy during which he claimed he had found 60 grains of white powder in Russell's stomach. Evans analysed the substance and decided it was arsenic – a conclusion which led to the arrest and trial of Russell's wife Hannah and a farm labourer, Daniel Leany, who were both found guilty of murder and sentenced to death.

The case came to the notice of a London surgeon, Dr Gideon Marshall, who at once pointed out the absurdity of the notion that Russell could have consumed enough arsenic to kill a couple of dozen men, then set out on his criminal mission, managing to walk over three miles, encumbered for part of that distance by a hefty sack of grain, before suddenly dropping dead – never having exhibited any signs of a man suffering from poisoning of any kind. Marshall also established that Russell was already known to have a weak heart – the obvious inference being that the strenuous work of the robbery itself had caused Russell's death, rather than the substance found in his stomach.

Thanks to Marshall's persistent intervention, Hannah Russell was pardoned – alas it was too late for Leany, whose execution had already been carried out. It might have been supposed that after this debacle medical men would be more cautious before jumping to a conclusion which could cost an innocent person their life – but not a bit of it.

In 1859 Dr Thomas Smethurst was charged with murdering a lady called Isabella Bankes.[22] Although aware of the existence of another Mrs Smethurst, Isabella had willingly entered into a bigamous marriage with Thomas Smethurst in order to achieve a semblance of respectability, but soon after the wedding Isabella became ill, suffering from nausea, vomiting and faintness; so Smethurst, who no longer actively practised medicine, called in a doctor. When Isabella became worse, a second opinion was sought and eventually a trio of local doctors were treating and prescribing for her, but the unfortunate woman still sickened and died. The doctors concluded that Smethurst – who in common with many married men stood to gain under his 'wife's' will – had poisoned Isabella.

They called in Professor Alfred Swaine Taylor, then the foremost toxicologist in the country, who, using the Marsh test, discovered arsenic in the deceased woman's kidneys. Smethurst was arrested and charged with murder. During the trial, however, Professor Taylor made a dramatic admission – the equipment he had used when making his analysis had been contaminated with arsenic before the test began and thus his results were absolutely meaningless. Moreover, it emerged in evidence that some of the medicines prescribed by the doctors attending Isabella had contained arsenic and thus it would be a surprise if Isabella's kidneys had not contained some trace of the substance.

In theory the case should have collapsed at that point, because there was absolutely no scientific evidence to underpin the theory that Isabella Bankes had been

criminally poisoned. One medical witness for the defence drew the jury's attention to the fact that Isabella's symptoms were entirely consistent with dysentery
– a disease which then accounted for on average 5,000 deaths a year. Furthermore,
it had been discovered after Isabella's death that she was six weeks pregnant –
a possibility not apparently considered by any of her medical attendants – but
which could easily have accounted for her original symptoms. Her failure to
recover may indeed have been due in part to the cocktail of medications prescribed during the course of her illness – the ingredients included quinine, ether,
sulphuric acid, prussic acid, opium, antimony and arsenic, to name but a few. Yet
in spite of all these factors, the three medical men who had attended the unfortunate woman in her last illness continued to assert that she had been poisoned.
The jury believed them. Like Elizabeth Fenning, Hannah Russell and Daniel
Leany, Thomas Smethurst was pronounced guilty of murder. Petitions were raised
against the verdict (signatories included the real Mrs Smethurst) and the conviction was eventually overturned.

In the meantime, Professor Taylor was publicly criticised, his professional reputation seriously damaged. In one sense this was fair comment – when giving
evidence at the magistrates' court, Taylor had originally stated on oath that his
equipment had been tested in advance of the analysis and found free from arsenic
– but in the long term this criticism would have a detrimental effect on much
more than Taylor's own career, because after what happened to Taylor, no medical
witness would be quick to put his hand up to a mistake again. The Smethurst case
cast such a long shadow that even half a century later, some medical experts felt
obliged to portray themselves as infallible.[23]

By the beginning of the twentieth century, what would come to be known as
forensic science was effectively still in its infancy; until 1935 there was no dedicated forensic science laboratory at the disposal of the police, who were reliant on
the work of either local county analysts, or the appointed Home Office analyst
and his assistants.[24] The Home Office Analyst was not a single discipline specialist working exclusively on criminal cases, but a practising doctor who fitted
in whatever criminal cases were referred to him around his other professional
commitments. Thus Sir William Willcox, who was appointed senior analyst to the
Home Office in 1904, was a working consultant on the staff of St Mary's Hospital
London, where he not only saw patients, but also taught in the medical school,
holding the position of Dean of Pathology. This was in addition to a thriving private practice run from his home in Welbeck Street, various outside lecture work,
writing and research.[25] While there can be no doubting the breadth of Willcox's
experience, or the various contributions he made to medical practice, it is also
possible to see that in this enormously wide portfolio of activity, Willcox cannot
possibly have had the opportunity to make a detailed study of every aspect of the
various subjects on which he would be required to supply expertise in his Home
Office role.

Just as Willcox had succeeded another St Mary's man (Dr A P Luff) in his
Home Office role, so he would in due course recommend other St Mary's staff to

become his assistants and successors as official Home Office analysts and pathologists – John Webster, Bernard Spilsbury and Gerard Roche Lynch were all St Mary's men – some of them had been students of Willcox, all were recommended to the Home Office by him. They knew one another, worked as a team and invariably spoke with one voice. When acting for the Home Office in a murder trial, they travelled together and stayed at the same hotel as the prosecuting counsel, discussing the case and preparing their testimony together.[26]

Between them they appeared at every murder trial for arsenical poisoning which took place in England and Wales between 1911 and 1936[27] and the frequency of their court appearances, coupled with their attitude of infallibility, had a significant impact on the proceedings. Harold Greenwood wrote of his trial, 'I cannot forget the deadly effects of the evidence of the Home Office experts. These men seemed so sure, so terribly sure, so calm and detached.'[28]

The formidable reputation of Sir William Willcox went before him. Juries were immediately impressed by Willcox's presence in the witness box, the practised assurance with which he delivered his answers and no doubt by the way every newspaper covering the case repeatedly referred to him as 'the expert, Sir William Willcox'. The defence had no hope of finding a medical witness with anything like Willcox's stature or reputation and the prosecuting counsel knew how to use this to their best advantage – often asking the medical experts who were appearing for the defence a series of questions which forced them to acknowledge that Willcox and his Home Office colleagues were leading authorities, thereby weakening the impact of their own dissenting opinions.[29]

When judges summed up the evidence for the jury, they not infrequently described Willcox and his cohorts as 'disinterested' and 'impartial'[30] – yet these descriptions were very far from painting an accurate picture. Willcox and co. appeared for the prosecution, whose sole aim was to bring about a guilty verdict, and as prosecution experts they gave their evidence with that specific end in view. It would not be an overstatement to say that Willcox, and later Spilsbury, perfected a technique for giving evidence in such a way that even points which should have told for the man or woman in the dock, were presented to their disadvantage. Forced to concede anything under cross-examination, rather than making a straightforward assent, both Willcox and Spilsbury invariably used the words: 'It is possible' – thereby offering only qualified agreement, tempered with an unspoken suggestion that such a contention was highly unlikely. During the trial of Frederick Seddon, Willcox employed this phrase so often during his examination by Marshall-Hall, that the famous KC was moved to remark, 'Everything is possible, apparently – or nearly so.'[31]

The difficulties presented by the role of the expert witness in an adversarial legal system have been recognised for many years. Expert witnesses are often essential to explain the nature of specialist evidence to the court, but the proper role of the expert witness has often been misunderstood. In a speech delivered in 2007, the Attorney General, Lord Goldsmith, pointed out that an expert witness is supposed to be impartial – irrespective of which side he appears for, 'the expert must not write his opinion to suit his paymaster and must be objective and unbiased ... the key point is that the expert is not a hired gun'.[32] Unfortunately there have been numerous examples of expert witnesses throughout the last two centuries who have tailored their evidence to suit the case of whichever side was retaining their services – indeed Willcox, Spilsbury and many who followed them, appear to have been recruited into a culture which tended to assume that Home Office experts existed solely to support the police in pursuance of a prosecution.

The position was well illustrated as recently as 1981, when the Home Office forensic scientist, Dr Alan Clift, testified during an enquiry undertaken into cases at which he had provided expert testimony, that 'police officers are our customers, and it is the view of some senior police officers that our job is to find evidence that may contribute to police enquiries.'[33] An investigation into Dr Clift's professional conduct began after it emerged that he withheld vital information which did not support the prosecution case during the trial of John Preece for the murder of Helen Wills in 1973, an episode which ultimately led to his suspension, and early retirement.[34]

Dr Clift was by no means alone in his approach. The Court of Appeal and a subsequent public enquiry uncovered the fact that forensic scientists Elliott and Higgs had both suppressed evidence and lied during the trials of the Maguire Seven and Judith Ward in the 1970s, in order to help secure convictions. The enquiry found that Elliott's witness statement both exaggerated his findings and was deliberately couched in language 'calculated to make it more difficult for defence experts to probe the matter'. Higgs had similarly 'overstated' his results, and misled the court about the efficacy of the test he was using.[35] More recently Professor Roy Meadow's confident, but seriously flawed, assertions on the subject of sudden infant death have resulted in the wrongful conviction of a number of innocent women.

Juries in the first third of the twentieth century not only failed to appreciate the biased nature of the expert testimony they were hearing, but were also misled on the point by judges who repeatedly emphasised the theoretically superior credentials and supposed impartiality of Home Office experts. The widespread assumption that experts appearing for the Crown were impartial, whereas those called in by the defence were merely hired guns, is illustrated by a letter which appeared in *The Times* as long ago as 1889, with the correspondent stating indignantly that the medical evidence called by the defence was 'rendered almost valueless ... these medical men were called in and paid for the express purpose of giving such evidence.'[36] It does not appear to have occurred to this correspondent (who signed himself An Old Schoolmaster) that experts who appeared for the prosecution were also paid. (One of the first documents a researcher encounters in the Croydon poisoning file is a bill from Sir Bernard Spilsbury.)

Expert witnesses who appeared regularly for the Crown acquired a level of fame and acknowledged expertise, which their professional colleagues with fewer court appearances found difficult to match. The impact of this is well illustrated by the remarks of one Tom Hopkins, the jury foreman at the Armstrong trial, who broke with the usual conventions by giving an interview to a local newspaper, in which he candidly admitted that after the evidence from the Home Office experts 'there was no chance of a not guilty verdict.'[37]

William Willcox's involvement with arsenic trials began in 1911, when he was invited to give expert evidence at the trial of Edith Bingham. At this stage in his career, Willcox had yet to attract quite the level of reverence he would inspire later and the jury were perhaps less than impressed once they realised that Willcox had not been involved in any of the post-mortem or analysis work himself, but was merely offering opinions based on reading the reports compiled by the doctor and analyst who had carried out the work.

Within twelve months, Willcox would be offering his expertise on arsenic again – this time at the trial of Frederick Seddon. In this case Willcox had been present at the exhumation and post-mortem of Eliza Barrow and he had performed the analysis on her organs himself, detecting a fatal dose of arsenic by means of the Marsh test. Although the Marsh test had featured in murder trials before, until the Seddon case it had only been used to prove the presence of arsenic: now it was also used to demonstrate the quantity of arsenic found and this set the pattern for the arsenic trials which would follow.

Supporting Willcox's testimony at the Seddon trial was his young protégé Dr Bernard Spilsbury, who would go on to become perhaps the most famous medical witness of all time. Spilsbury did not appear in the majority of the famous arsenic cases, but his involvement in the Croydon case had a double-edged significance which few appear to have appreciated at the time or since.

To understand the importance of the Croydon case to Spilsbury and vice versa, it is necessary to briefly consider his career up to that point.[38] At the turn of the century, pathology was still an extremely unfashionable branch of medicine and thus one in which it was easier to rise.[39] Appointed to the post of Resident Assistant Pathologist at St Mary's Hospital in 1905, Spilsbury – a workaholic – swiftly built up a reputation as a clear, concise inquest witness, which led to so much work being referred his way from the local coroners' courts that within three years his coroners' fees were doubling his income. Spilsbury did not appear as a witness in a murder trial until 1910, but as chance would have it one of the first trials at which he gave evidence was Rex v. Crippen and Le Neve – the criminal sensation of the year.

The saga of Crippen and his mistress had dominated the headlines for weeks and provided the perfect stage for Spilsbury, with his immaculate turn out and matinee idol looks.[40] Although only called to support the evidence of his superior, Dr A.J. Pepper, Spilsbury stole the show, introducing a microscope into the court room, through which members of the jury were invited to view the piece of tissue by which Spilsbury claimed to have identified Cora Crippen's remains. The impact of this evidence has been much exaggerated. Dr Crippen's wife had vanished without trace. Partial human remains had been discovered in Crippen's cellar, wrapped in his old pyjamas and prior to this discovery, he had fled the country with his mistress in tow – she disguised as a boy.[41] Men had been convicted of murder on considerably less and Spilsbury's evidence probably made very little difference one way or the other, but from then onwards, his reputation as an expert medical witness was made. And not just as an expert medical witness – Spilsbury quickly came to be regarded as a medical detective, a kind of Sherlock Holmes figure, who could see things other men could not see.[42]

It is easy to see what a dangerous situation this kind of adulation could create. As Katherine Watson writes in *Medical and Chemical Expertise in English Trials for Criminal Poisoning 1750-1914*, 'by the end of his career Spilsbury had become so influential that his mere reported interest in a case was said to have a very substantial psychological effect on the minds of the jury'.[43]

Spilsbury's involvement in another high profile trial in 1915 further enhanced his reputation as a 'star turn'. Although, just as in the Crippen case, when Spilsbury gave evidence against George 'Brides in the Bath' Smith, it probably had little quantifiable effect on the fate of the accused, whose pattern of marrying, then insuring the lives of a series of women who were subsequently found drowned in their own bathwater, spoke for itself; yet this too would come to be cited as one of the cases which made Spilsbury's name.

Bernard Spilsbury married in 1908 and as the years went by his financial responsibilities increased – four children to be educated, a house in the suburbs, a flat to be nearer his work, school fees followed by a university education for his three sons … Spilsbury had a reputation as a driven workaholic, a man with an obsessive fascination and zeal for his work, but towards the end of his long career there was a glimmer of another possible motivation: in the last years of his life with his health failing, Spilsbury privately told some friends that he could not afford to give up, or even undertake a long convalescence following a stroke, lest some other man usurp his position, because he needed the financial recompense it brought.[44] Whether Spilsbury really needed the money is a moot point, the fact is that he believed he did – and if this had always been a factor in his career then he must have been particularly hostile to any potential interlopers in the field.

Within England there was only a limited chance of anyone emerging to steal his crown. St Mary's led the pack in forensic medicine and dictated the Home Office succession, thus hardly anyone who appeared against Spilsbury could hope to match his reputation or experience – but in 1922 a challenger appeared from an unexpected quarter. Dr Robert Matthew Bronte, a virtual contemporary of Spilsbury, qualified in Ireland where he had risen to the position of Crown Analyst, but following the establishment of the Irish Free State in 1922 Bronte moved to London, where he was appointed pathologist at Harrow Hospital and soon began to get post-mortem work from the London Coroners' courts.[45] Defence teams were not slow to seize on Bronte's potential as an experienced expert witness and, within three years of arriving in London, his services were in demand as a medical expert with the potential to rebut evidence provided by Spilsbury.

Their first major courtroom clash occurred at the trial of Norman Thorne in 1925, when not just Bronte, but seven other doctors appeared in the witness box to directly contradict Spilsbury's assertion that marks on the victim's neck were natural creases rather than the results of a rope having been tied around it. (Thorne claimed that the victim had hung herself, Spilsbury claimed she had been beaten to death.) In spite of the numerical superiority of the defence's medical team and a considerable degree of implausibility in Spilsbury's testimony, the judge eulogised Spilsbury in his summing up and the jury brought in a verdict of murder against Thorne.[46]

Bronte's testimony and the telling points he made against Spilsbury were not lost on the thinking public, however, and for the first time Spilsbury's reputation for infallibility and the dangerous influence this had on juries was publicly called into question. Letters appeared both in the national press and specialist legal and medical journals complaining that judges and juries now accepted Spilsbury's every utterance without question, even where there was strong conflicting testimony from other well qualified witnesses.[47]

That the fleeting period of criticism which followed the Thorne case temporarily damaged Spilsbury is evidenced by the fact that rather less work came his way in 1926.[48] His biographers refer to this period as a 'campaign'[49] against him, which is perhaps overstating the issue somewhat, although any campaign would have been entirely justified, given that Spilsbury was directly or indirectly responsible for several miscarriages of justice – one of which took place in 1927 when Spilsbury made a rare appearance in the Scottish courts, in order to support the defence of John Donald Merrett who was standing trial accused of matricide. Two eminent experts, respectively Professors of Forensic Medicine at Edinburgh and Glasgow Universities, gave evidence for the prosecution, but Spilsbury made the better impression in the witness box and the verdict of Not Proven was considered largely due to his participation in the trial. Very few people today believe that Merrett was not responsible for his mother's murder – not least because he went on to murder his wife and his mother-in-law.[50] Since Spilsbury usually appeared for the Crown, however, his evidence generally presented a threat to the innocent, rather than a reprieve for the guilty.

Spilsbury undoubtedly 'saw things which others did not'. In the Crippen case, it was Spilsbury who would decisively identify a tiny remnant of skin as definitely belonging to the late Cora Crippen, insisting that where others saw only a fold, he could see a distinctive scar. In the Thorne case, where others saw marks of a rope consistent with strangulation, Spilsbury insisted the marks were no more than the natural creases which he claimed were present on the necks of every young woman – thereby destroying Norman Thorne's line of defence. In the case of Mrs Rosaline Fox, Spilsbury claimed that he had seen a bruise on the victim's larynx. Both Professor Sydney Smith and Dr Bronte would deny seeing any such mark – a mark which was particularly significant from the prosecution point of view. When viewing the larynx in the laboratory with the other pathologists, Spilsbury agreed that the mark was no longer visible, but insisted that it had been there when he initially examined the body: the inference being that it had now been lost thanks to post-mortem changes.[51]

Alas, when confronted with these conflicting testimonies, juries merely assumed that Sir Bernard (a knighthood in 1923 had further enhanced his reputation) was the more observant pathologist: the great medical detective. Similarly, when Bronte stated honestly that this or that matter was outside his knowledge, or was impossible to quantify, juries assumed that 'the oracle', as Sir Sydney Smith would sarcastically refer to Spilsbury in his memoirs, was in possession of superior knowledge. Bronte was honest enough to admit that he did not know everything: Spilsbury affected the opposite and juries tended to believe him. As P.D. James would write, 'Juries hate scientific evidence ... What they want is certainty.'[52]

At the trial of Norman Thorne in 1925, Spilsbury not only claimed to have observed post-mortem bruising, which had conveniently disappeared by the time Bronte viewed the corpse, but also went on to explain in precise detail how long before death these bruises had been inflicted and in which order. Tactfully ridiculing this evidence in court, Bronte said, 'It is impossible for me to say, six weeks after a body is dead, lying in clay soil, exposed to water and organisms, whether these bruises were made three minutes, two minutes, one minute or ten minutes later or earlier than a bruise here.'

'You mean,' asked defence counsel, 'It is impossible in your opinion to express that view?'

'Not impossible to express the view,' said Bronte, 'but impossible to substantiate it.'[53]

This attempt to expose Spilsbury's bombast appears to have been lost on the jury, who alas interpreted Bronte's truthful acknowledgement of the limitations of current medical science as an admission that he was the man who knew the lesser of the two. Again and again, when asked to choose between two opinions, juries opted for Spilsbury.

In truth Spilsbury was neither infallible nor even necessarily thorough, and occasionally the truth of this shone through. For example, when he carried out the post-mortem on Pamela Coventry, a child murdered in Hornchurch, Essex, in January 1939, he failed to take a routine blood sample from the body. This made it impossible to compare her blood to the bloodstains subsequently found on a mackintosh belonging to the chief suspect, Leonard Richardson. It appears that when a genuine opportunity to use forensic science came along, Spilsbury failed to take advantage of it. Richardson's trial collapsed when the jury indicated that there was insufficient evidence to bring in a guilty verdict.[54]

The most charitable view might be that Spilsbury was merely capable of self delusion on a grand scale, but alas the exaggerations and untruths which sometimes emerged in his evidence suggest otherwise. When it came to cases of poisoning, Spilsbury wilfully misled courts about the level of experience he possessed in this highly specialised field. At the trial of Herbert Armstrong, for example, Spilsbury stated that he had 'considerable experience of poisoning cases', which were 'an almost weekly, certainly monthly occurrence.'[55] Since the question was posed in the context of arsenic poisoning, this answer would obviously be taken to imply experience of that specific kind of poison – but in order to make his answer 'true' Spilsbury can only have been referring to poisoning cases in their very widest sense. Poisoning covered a multitude of sins – the most frequent type of poisoning recorded in Spilsbury's own index cards is carbon monoxide.[56] There were also accidental overdoses of sleeping drugs, cyanide, morphine, strychnine, cocaine and deaths under anaesthetic – all of which crossed Spilsbury's mortuary slabs. But among the hundreds of post-mortems Spilsbury carried out every week of every year, he might encounter arsenic once in a blue moon – but this was not the impression he intended the Armstrong jury to receive.

Out of the estimated 25,000 post-mortems Spilsbury performed during his career, a mere 250 are thought to have been murder cases and of these only a minute proportion involved poisoning. At the trial of Frederick Seddon in 1912 Spilsbury would similarly answer that he had experience of other cases of arsenical poisoning; what he did not add was that these cases were few and far between, were not murder cases and did not involve the exhumation of a body which had been buried for two months. By April 1912 Spilsbury had been qualified and working in the field for just over seven years, during which time there had only been one alleged murder with arsenic: the Edith Bingham case, in which Spilsbury had played no part. Thus, any deaths by acute arsenical poisoning which had come Spilsbury's way must have been accidental ingestion or suicide, both of which were relatively rare. Moreover, by the time Spilsbury informed the court that the body of Seddon's alleged victim was surprisingly well preserved and that he considered this due to arsenic, Spilsbury had virtually no experience of exhumations and none which involved the alleged use of arsenic.[57]

Unfortunately it took many years for the truth about Spilsbury to emerge and, by the mid-1920s, his position as a pre-eminent expert medical witness appeared all but unassailable – until the arrival of Dr Bronte. Spilsbury undoubtedly perceived Robert Bronte as a professional threat and after the Thorne trial, he attempted to hurt Bronte's reputation as much as possible.[58] Even much later in his career, with his own reputation assured and his status as 'the greatest pathologist of the day' firmly established, Spilsbury appears to have jealously guarded his position. Professor Keith Simpson recalled that as his own career advanced in the mid-1930s, 'I had the sneaking feeling that he wasn't pleased to see me appear increasingly frequently at court to give evidence.'[59]

Rumbles of discontent about Spilsbury[60] were loudest during the years when Bronte regularly stood against him,[61] but ultimately Robert Bronte would only trouble Spilsbury for a matter of half a dozen years: his premature death in 1932 cut short their rivalry. This left Bronte a largely forgotten figure, although his obituaries leave no doubt about the threat he once posed to the 'infallibility' of the great Sir Bernard. *The Times* described him as 'well known to the general public' thanks to his participation as an expert witness in a number of murder trials, saying, 'he was an excellent witness, able to make highly technical evidence clear to any jury and he spared no trouble in preparing it'.[62] The *Medical Times* went as far as they tactfully dared, stating, 'We shall miss him as an opponent of Sir Bernard's,' going on to say that Bronte provided an example and a warning against 'being too cocksure … it is for this reason that we especially regret the death of Dr Bronte, who might always be counted on to weigh the force of other men's evidence.'[63]

In 1929 Sir Bernard Spilsbury had no way of foreseeing that his principal rival would be removed so soon. When he realised that the original post-mortem on Edmund Duff had been carried out by none other than Dr Robert Bronte, he must have perceived it as a heaven-sent opportunity to show Bronte up for a fool and an incompetent, by suggesting not only that Bronte had apparently missed a clear case of arsenical poisoning, but also that he had managed to dispatch the wrong set of organs for testing, thereby ensuring that the analyst failed to identify the cause of death either. If the case came to court, it would surely present a very public humiliation for Dr Bronte and perhaps set the final seal of valediction on the superiority of Sir Bernard.

CHAPTER TWELVE

'NO MAN'S LIFE SHOULD DEPEND ON A COMPARISON BETWEEN ONE SHADOW AND ANOTHER'

There is a legend that when the first coffin was raised at the Croydon exhumations in March 1929, Sir Bernard Spilsbury stepped forward, bent over the coffin and, having inhaled deeply, stepped back, straightened up and pronounced, 'Arsenic, gentlemen.'[1] Possibly the story is apocryphal, although the theatrical gesture and its acceptance by a credulous group of mere mortals rapt in the presence of the great Sir Bernard, cannot be entirely ruled out. A similar story emanated from Dr Binning, who was present at the exhumation of Edmund Duff's body. This time Spilsbury's powers of detection were brought to bear in the mortuary, when immediately prior to the coffin lid being raised, Spilsbury allegedly invited Binning to blow his nose, preparatory to taking a sniff as the lid was lifted. As the lid was raised, Spilsbury leant over and inhaled, before straightening up to announce: 'Arsenic.'[2]

If the Home Office pathologist did indulge in such antics, then it certainly reinforces the view that he had already made up his mind what he was going to find, before actually embarking on the post-mortem examination he had been detailed to carry out. In the coroner's court, of course, there would be no mention of sniffing this telltale odour – not least because any cross-examination about odours risked revealing the fact that by the end of the 1920s, Spilsbury had almost entirely lost his sense of smell.[3]

The points Spilsbury did major on when giving his evidence were observations of a more concrete nature: fatty degeneration of the organs, and the mysteriously good state of preservation in which he had found each body. However when it came to the actual conclusion that death had been due to arsenical poisoning, Spilsbury would explain that he relied almost entirely on the reports of the analysts who had tested the organs and found arsenic therein.[4] Yet by the time Spilsbury left the mortuary, long before the results of the analyst were in, he had already given a definite impression of the presence of arsenic to everyone involved. This was corroborated by Hedges' reports which speak confidently of the presence of arsenic in the bodies, well before the analyst's results were in, and by Tom Sidney, who testified that when the bodies of his mother and sister arrived in the Mayday Hospital mortuary, the word 'arsenic' was whispered all around. Since Tom Sidney did not wait to see the autopsies performed, this again reinforces the suggestion that premature conclusions were being drawn.

What of these telltales signs of poisoning which Spilsbury detected? Fatty degeneration of the organs is indicative of numerous conditions, not just arsenical poisoning. Moreover, at the trial of Frederick Seddon, where the alleged victim's organs were free from fatty degeneration, Spilsbury testified that fatty degeneration would only be expected in cases of chronic, rather than acute arsenical poisoning.[5] What hope is there for a defendant, when the presence of fatty degeneration is apparently evidence of their guilt, but its absence is no indicator of their innocence?

The worst piece of skulduggery, however, was Spilsbury's emphasis on the abnormal preservation of the bodies. This had been cited so often in arsenic-related exhumations that a well preserved body had become a by-word for the presence of arsenic, not least because Spilsbury and his allies were seldom challenged in court about the factors which actually dictated post-mortem decomposition. (It is worth noting that when the coroner challenged Tom Sidney about how he knew that arsenic impaired decomposition, Tom replied, 'Surely it is general knowledge?' adding that he had read about 'several cases' in the newspapers.[6])

Contrary to the myth perpetuated in one arsenic case after another, the principal factors which advance or delay decomposition are temperature, access by insects, burial and depth – the most important being temperature.[7] It is fair to say that less information was available concerning rates of decomposition when Spilsbury was working in the field, but enough was known to appreciate that temperature was the single most important issue.[8] We can be sure that Spilsbury was well aware of this, because in a non-poisoning case in 1925, he gave evidence that if a body was buried in December, the chilly conditions would delay putrefaction.[9]

When Vera Sidney's body was raised some four weeks after burial, even the hyacinths in her hand were virtually unchanged, but Spilsbury affected to believe that the state of the corpse was almost entirely due to the presence of arsenic therein. It was a shameless attempt to mislead. What Spilsbury must have suspected – nay, known – was that all of the bodies buried in the Queen's Road Cemetery during the preceding months would have been in an equally fine state of preservation. During the first three months of 1929 the country was in the grip of one of the worst winters in years. It was so cold that Windermere froze, a phenomenon which requires such a sustained period of low temperatures, that it only occurs on average once in every seventy years. Temperature records show that during the thirty days between Vera's burial and exhumation, the night time temperature fell to below freezing point on all but seven days, and for a third of the period in question, the maximum daytime temperature never got above 5C degrees.[10] Effectively Vera's body had been in the next best thing to a deep freeze.

The effects of the cool weather would also have been a factor in the preservation of Edmund Duff's body. He had been buried for just over a year, but the long cold winter of 1928-9, coupled with a cool summer in 1928, meant that the temperature was 5C degrees or below for more than half that time and only exceeded 20C degrees on a mere sixty-eight days.[11] The effects of temperature are particularly well illustrated by comparison between the autopsy reports on the remains of Edmund Duff and those of another alleged arsenic victim, Katharine Armstrong, who was exhumed on 31 December 1921, having been buried for just over ten months. Duff's remains were comparatively well preserved, but Mrs Armstrong's body was in an advanced state of putrefaction, with much of the soft tissue already rotted away.[12] The very noticeable difference between the condition of Katharine Armstrong's body and the condition of Edmund Duff's coincides with the different climatic conditions during the periods between their burials and exhumations. In the ten months following Katharine Armstrong's death, the temperature only failed to rise above 5C degrees on eleven days, but there were more than seventy days on which the temperature rose to 20C degrees or higher, including a sustained period in July 1921 when daytime temperatures regularly hit 25C degrees and above.[13] (In spite of the contents of his own report detailing the state of Mrs Armstrong's remains, Spilsbury still testified that the body was 'remarkably well preserved' at the Armstrong trial![14])

Mrs Armstrong's remains supposedly contained in excess of 2 grains of arsenic, more than double the quantity said to have been found in Edmund Duff's – and yet the corpse was in a much more advanced state of decomposition, although it had been buried for a slightly shorter period. In failing to draw the obvious conclusion that factors other than arsenic must have been at play, Spilsbury demonstrates either a remarkable lack of intelligence or a complete absence of professional integrity.

Juries might have been forgiven for believing that death by acute arsenical poisoning left no more sign for a pathologist than a good state of preservation and a stain on a ceramic tile, but according to the text books of the time, there were other distinctive post-mortem signs of death by arsenic. One of these was the presence of yellow staining in the stomach and intestines, occasionally accompanied by a yellowish fluid or residue in the stomach, due to the chemical change by which arsenic is converted into yellow sulphide in the body.[15] This was not only described in text books of the period, but Spilsbury himself had encountered it at least once, when performing a post-mortem on a known arsenic victim, who committed suicide in 1913;[16] yet in spite of having first-hand experience and a personal record of an autopsy displaying these classic symptoms in a known case of arsenical poisoning, Spilsbury failed to remark on the absence of this yellow staining in the bodies of the three alleged victims in the Croydon case.

Then there were the other possible post-mortem indicators: the extreme inflammation of the mucous membrane in the stomach, with perhaps groups of petechiae[17] and sometimes larger haemorrhages, ulcerations and erosions.[18] All of these had been present in the body of Spilsbury's 1913 suicide, but none of them were present in the well preserved remains of Vera Sidney.[19] (The situation is somewhat clouded in the cases of Violet Sidney, where Spilsbury's surviving post-mortem report is rather less detailed and in the case of Edmund Duff, where it was impossible for Spilsbury to make any observations on the condition of the stomach and various other internal organs, as they had been removed at the original post-mortem.)

In spite of the existence of clear physical signs which could indicate cases of acute arsenical poisoning, Spilsbury allowed juries to believe that a diagnosis depended on chemical analysis alone. Asked to confirm during the Seddon trial that aside from the results of Willcox's analysis, there was essentially nothing found in Miss Barrow's body to indicate arsenical poisoning, Spilsbury typically fended off the actual admission of a point which might have told for the defence by responding, 'With the exception of the preservation of the body.'[20] The reliance on the chemical analysis – a sort of modern magic trick, by which the 'undetectable' could be revealed to the world, fell neatly into line with the perception that without the aid of the 'modern-day Sherlock Holmes' folk might be getting away with murdering their relatives all the time. Yet according to *Glaister's Medical Jurisprudence and Toxicology*, arsenic is frequently retained in the stomach for a considerable time after ingestion because of its 'tenacious association with the gastric mucosa;'[21] so far from requiring minute chemical analysis, in cases where death had genuinely occurred following a large dose of arsenic, there was an expectation that some remnants of that arsenic should have been found in the stomach.

The lack of these obvious physical indicators does not alter the fact that analysts detected arsenic in the bodies of Vera and Violet Sidney and Edmund Duff. However, arsenic is a natural element, traces of which occur in all of us, so in itself the detection of arsenic was not sinister. In 1929 the technology did not exist to enable minute quantities of arsenic to be weighed, so instead its weight had to be estimated by comparing one arsenic mirror to another.

This was not as straightforward as it might sound. The deposits made by the arsenic were irregular in shape, so comparison of the mirrors was somewhat akin to matching one ink blot to another. At the trial of Frederick Seddon in 1911, the arsenic mirrors produced by testing samples derived from Miss Barrow's body were brought into courts as exhibits, enabling Sir Edward Marshall-Hall, who was defending, to question their role in the evidence closely.[22]

'It is a question of eyesight,' Marshall-Hall suggested, when asking Willcox to produce the mirror which was his standard for ⅕₀mg, followed by the mirror he had obtained by analysing a sample from Eliza Barrow's lung which, according to his report, also equated to ⅕₀mg.

Marshall-Hall then asked Willcox to produce the mirrors which provided his standard for ¼₀mg and ⅙₀mg and to pass them, together with the 'lung' mirror, for examination by the jury, pointing out that depending on which way you looked at it, the mirror produced from the sample of lung might equally be either ¼₀mg or ⅙₀mg. Indicating the ⅕₀mg mirror, Willcox said, 'I judged that one to be a match,' but Marshall-Hall had made an important point. The process was one of approximation not certainty.

Marshall-Hall had not finished: 'Now would you agree with me as to the importance of accuracy – absolute accuracy, not relative accuracy, with regard to whether it is ⅟40, ⅟50, or ⅟60?'

'It is most important to be as accurate as possible,' Willcox agreed.

'But the minute difference makes a very great deal of difference in the result of arsenic calculated in the body, does it not?'

Willcox admitted that it did, because the samples from which he obtained his results represented only part of each organ. When initially explaining how he did the test, Willcox stated that he 'took a sample of an organ, for example one quarter…' but Marshall-Hall soon extracted the information that in practice these samples were very much smaller. The sample of lung Willcox had actually tested for arsenic represented such a small part of the total lung tissue, that in order to arrive at his assessment of the amount of arsenic present in the whole of both lungs, Willcox then had to multiply his sample result by 60.

'Therefore any error in the diagnosis of the mirror is multiplied by 50 or 60 times in the calculation of the arsenic,' said Marshall-Hall. When Willcox conceded the point, Marshall-Hall forced him to admit that the multiplying factor for the stomach was 200, for the kidneys 60, the spleen 13, the hair 50 and the blood 11½. 'The actual quantities found were minute, were they not?'

Marshall-Hall moved his attention to the total amount of poison supposedly present in the muscles. According to Willcox's report, more than half the total amount of arsenic discovered in Miss Barrow's body had been located in the muscles. The original sample of muscle he tested had weighed a mere 6g, and in order to arrive at the amount Willcox claimed had been present in all the muscle tissue in the body, he had multiplied the result obtained from those 6g by a factor of 2,000. Marshall-Hall wanted to now how the factor of 2,000 had been arrived at: was the weight of the dead woman known? Willcox said it was not. The calculation had been based on the average weight for a woman of her height, which he claimed was 10½ stone. As Miss Barrow was known to have been only 5ft 4in tall and of medium build, that sounds like something of an over estimate, but Marshall-Hall did not pursue the point.

This exchange between Willcox and Marshall-Hall makes it clear that a considerable amount of approximation was involved, in order to determine the quantities of arsenic which Willcox and his fellow analysts so confidently claimed to have discovered in the bodies of the various victims. A further problem with this method lay in the fact that arsenic was not necessarily distributed evenly throughout any part of the body: a point inadvertently demonstrated by Willcox himself, when he produced the two mirrors which had been obtained from separate samples taken from Miss Barrow's stomach, and the judge observed that one mirror contained noticeably more black deposit than another.

'Different proportions from the same sample,' Willcox replied, adding as he passed the mirror showing the larger stain across to the jury, 'This is from the stomach, there is a large quantity there.'

The vital question which surely arises here, was which result had been multiplied by 200 in order to arrive at the amount of arsenic 'found' in the stomach as a whole?

At the trial of Edward Black, the accuracy of this method of determining the amount of arsenic in the deceased's body was again called into question, but in vain did Edward Black's defence counsel, Mr Pratt, ask whether the jury considered, 'that no man's life should depend on some calculation that was based on a comparison between one shadow and another.' In summing up, Mr Justice Rowlett said the court had had: '…the best scientific evidence they could get. Scientific people can reach extraordinarily accurate results which those without scientific knowledge cannot appreciate. The experts from whom you have heard are satisfied that their methods were safe and proper methods on which to base their conclusions.'[23]

Alas these methods were neither safe nor proper, not least because again and again the Home Office experts who testified in arsenic poisoning cases exaggerated everything which told against an accused person, while attempting to diminish, or dismiss altogether, the significance of any points which told in their favour.

At the Black trial, Webster and Willcox arrived at their conclusions by analysing the small number of organs available, then multiplying the results they achieved by 2¼ – which they deposed to be 'an acceptable formula' for determining the amount of arsenic which would have been present in the whole body at death – and even this only produced a grand total of ⅙ grain of arsenic.

When asked how this formula had been arrived at, Webster was forced to admit that he did not know, but Willcox elucidated the matter further, explaining that he had devised the formula himself, basing it on an analysis he had carried out on one whole body. It was, he said, 'an accepted formula'.[24] While the formula may have been accepted by Willcox and Webster, the present author can find no evidence that it was utilised by anyone else – or indeed that either man employed it in any other criminal cases.

At the Greenwood trial in 1920, Willcox tried to suggest that Mabel Greenwood's symptoms had not been consistent which the heart disease from which she was known to have suffered, stating that when he attended the autopsy on Mabel Greenwood's exhumed remains he had not observed any evidence of valvular heart disease. This was one of many statements made in evidence by Willcox and his Home Office colleagues which, while not actively untruthful, was exceedingly misleading: the defence counsel eventually prised out of Willcox that the reason he had not observed any heart disease was because Mrs Greenwood's heart was too decomposed to make any pronouncement about its state one way or the other.[25]

When appearing at the inquest into the death of Harry Pace in 1928, Willcox did his best to sway the inquest jury by trotting out alleged similarities between the amount of arsenic discovered in Pace's body with a whole list of famous criminal poisoning cases; these included Madeleine Smith and Florence Maybrick, cases with which he had no personal connection whatever, but mention of whose names sent out a clear and wholly inappropriate message to the jury.[26] At Edward Black's trial, he opined that Mrs Black's symptoms indicated that the fatal dose of arsenic must have been given several days before her death and that no arsenic had been administered in the days immediately before her demise – a very convenient opinion from the point of view of the Crown, since Black had not been in the district for the final days of his wife's life – but an opinion based on no specific medical indicators whatever. Willcox similarly concluded that although Mrs Black was suffering from a kidney disease, it had not been sufficiently serious to kill her.[27]

Occasionally the Home Office experts' testimony was not just misleading but completely inaccurate. When asked at the Black inquest whether taking arsenic accidentally could account for a fatal amount being found in a body, John Webster answered in the negative – which was sheer nonsense, as accidental ingestion regularly accounted for arsenic deaths.[28] At the Greenwood trial in 1920 Webster would make an equally remarkable statement. When asked by Marshall-Hall (again called in to defend), 'Do you suggest that there is no arsenic in the human body constantly?' Webster replied, 'No, not detectable … in very minute cases in some, in others none at all.'

Other medical experts appeared at the trial to point out that detectable levels of arsenic did occur naturally in humans, who could sometimes tolerate several grains without fatal effect; but the stock response to counter any opposing opinions was for the Home Office man to disagree, saying that 'was not his experience' or 'not his opinion'. Thus when Marshall-Hall asked Willcox to comment on the statement in a standard medical text book, which said that in a case of fatal poisoning, a pathologist would be liable to find at least 1 grain of arsenic in the stomach, Willcox simply disagreed, saying that his experience was otherwise.[29]

In a similar vein, while testifying before the magistrates in the Greenwood case, Willcox expressed an opinion which directly contradicted evidence given by Spilsbury in the Seddon case; but when the defence pounced, Willcox neatly sidestepped by claiming, 'There are absolutely no constant symptoms of arsenic poisoning.'[30]

In 1934 two doctors based at the University of Edinburgh who had been conducting research on arsenic in the human body published their findings in the *British Medical Journal,* noting that almost identical discoveries in the Seddon and Hearn cases had led to opposite deductions being put forward by the Crown – to the detriment of the accused in both cases.[31]

To the dispassionate observer, there is something horrifying in the lack of scruples displayed by these expert witnesses. How could any man of conscience set out to mislead a court of law, when a man or woman's life was at stake? The answer may be that they did not consciously do so. Following the enquiry into the conduct of Dr Alan Clift in 1981, the Home Office report stated: 'He does not seem to have turned his mind to the possibilities of his evidence incriminating innocent people – trusting that the police were always right in their initial suspicions.'[32]

Bizarre as such a contention may sound, it does appear to explain the behaviour of both Willcox and Spilsbury: each time they were called in to perform an autopsy or analysis on a suspected arsenic case, their approach seems to have been to provide proof of poisoning, rather than to confirm or deny that mere suspicions were correct. They may have imagined that a considerable body of evidence already existed in order for the police to have called them in. No one likes the idea of a murderer evading justice through lack of evidence. The experts, having been called in to help prosecute a case of poisoning would help the case along as much as they could, short of actual perjury.

Imagine then the position of the analyst, Webster, Roche Lynch or Ryffel, on receiving the organs extracted at an 'arsenic' post-mortem conducted in such a climate. Consider in particular the position of Gerard Roche Lynch, confronted with samples from the body of the late Edmund Duff. The great Spilsbury had already given his opinion – arsenical poisoning. Who was going to go against Spilsbury? Certainly not an analyst who doesn't want his reputation ruined. Candy and Bronte had already made fools of themselves and Dr Lynch wasn't going to follow suit. There *was* arsenic in the body and he would damn well find it. The police and Spilsbury had already made their minds up that Edmund Duff had been poisoned and it only remained for him to produce a figure to demonstrate how much arsenic was still present in the body.

There is more than a suggestion that Professor Candy recognised the position Lynch was in, when he made that telling remark at the conclusion of the Duff inquest, that if he had 'examined the organs on the understanding that arsenic must be there and that I had got to find it if possible, I should have pegged away until I did find it.'[33]

Each of the experts who deposed that arsenic had been the cause of death during the Croydon inquests invariably mentioned that they based their opinion on not only their own findings, but also on those of their respective colleagues. This round robin of agreement formed part of a fatal circle of misplaced trust, in which everyone's suspicions reinforced everyone else's. The police felt their suspicions were confirmed by the medical experts, the experts were encouraged to believe they were on the right lines by the increasing certainty of the police. But as Curtis Bennett, who conducted the defence of Herbert Rowse Armstrong, put it, these were cases 'based on a falsehood and developed backwards'.[34]

The Croydon case began with the death of one elderly lady and developed into an unstoppable bandwagon of exhumations and rumours of exhumations, all based on the belief that three members of a single family had been murdered with arsenic – but had they?

CHAPTER THIRTEEN

THE GREAT POST-MORTEM
BLUNDER

One of the mysteries surrounding Edmund Duff's death was the fact that the pathologist and analyst who reported to the original inquest in 1928 had failed to detect any signs of death by arsenical poisoning. In order to explain this it was intimated that Bronte's original autopsy was less than thorough and that the unfortunate Professor Candy was sent the wrong set of organs for analysis. In the highly fictionalised reconstruction *A Most Mysterious Murder*,[1] narrator Julian Fellowes refers to Dr Bronte as 'the hopeless Dr Bronte', while Richard Whittington-Egan, although implying that Bronte and the mortuary assistant Baker were lying about the manner in which they carried out post-mortem procedures at the Mayday Hospital, tends to the theory that it was the analyst Professor Candy who made what he describes as 'the great post-mortem blunder'.[2] However this free and easy dismissal of Bronte and Candy tends to ignore their stature and experience as pathologist and analyst. A man does not usually rise to be Crown Analyst in Ireland by being 'hopeless'. By 1929 Hugh Candy was a senior lecturer at London Hospital Medical College and had considerably more years of analytical experience than Gerard Roche Lynch, who provided the second analysis.[3]

Whittington-Egan tells us that when one or more post-mortems are carried out in quick succession, the first body is not always sewn up before the second is opened,[4] but even if that was the way things operated in the Mayday Hospital mortuary (something which both Bronte and Baker denied on oath) this still does not explain how one patient's body parts could become confused with another's. The other body to be examined on 29 April 1928 was that of Rose Ellen Walker, an eighty-four-year-old woman who had died as a result of chronic heart and kidney disease.[5] It was not deemed necessary to submit Rose Walker's organs for analysis, so there is no question of two sets of organs being placed in jars and wrongly labelled.

Moreover, when Edmund Duff's body was exhumed, all the organs which had been submitted to Candy for analysis were found to be missing: thus if Rose Walker's organs had been mistakenly sent in place of Edmund Duff's, we would have to assume that when Duff's organs were removed, a matching set of organs belonging to Rose Walker were somehow packed up and labelled as Edmund Duff's, while his corresponding organs were placed in Rose Walker's body prior to its being stitched up for burial. The mortuary in question was not full of people rushing about, moving body parts from one place to another. Only Bronte and the mortuary assistant were present and the chances of such a mix up occurring would appear remote in the extreme.

There was a minor mistake in Baker's labelling of the jars sent to Professor Candy, because Candy noted that in addition to the items listed on the labels, one of the jars contained a piece of lung. (Bronte's notebook included the lung in his list of organs submitted for analysis, but Baker evidently missed it off the label.) This was something of a gift to the mixed-up-organs theory, because on discovering the section of lung, Candy had noted it as 'lung with trachea attached'. During his evidence, Spilsbury made a point of emphasising that Edmund Duff's trachea was intact at the exhumation; Candy responded that when he wrote 'trachea' he did not specifically mean that it was trachea – it might equally have been a piece of bronchus.

In spite of Spilsbury's insinuations, there is strong evidence that the items Candy received for testing had come from Edmund Duff, because Candy's original analysis picked up the presence of both quinine and mercury,[6] consistent with medicinal doses. In the last hours of his life, Edmund Duff is known to have dosed himself with both quinine and Calomel, which is a mercury preparation.[7] The odds against Rose Walker having coincidentally taken both quinine and mercury are surely enormous. The fall-back position was that Candy did test Duff's organs, but only tested one sample for arsenic and that sample did not reveal a strong enough concentration for him to pick it up. Like Bronte, Candy was an honest enough witness to admit himself capable of error, saying rather bitterly that he 'did not claim to be infallible'.[8] Unfortunately this sort of candour merely encouraged juries to follow the evidence of witnesses who did affect an air of infallibility.

However, in addition to Candy's failure to find arsenic, it is essential to remember that Robert Bronte found no indicators of arsenical poisoning during his physical examination of the corpse – no ulceration or inflammation of the stomach, no petechiae, no yellow staining. Can the fact that two experienced professionals failed to detect the slightest indication that this man met his death by acute arsenical poisoning merely be dismissed as sheer incompetence? After all, the diagnosis of death by arsenic was entirely reliant on the opinions of two other experts – and why should we accept the word of any one pair of experts over another?

When Spilsbury undertook his examination almost a year after Edmund's death, he was unable to examine the stomach – possibly the most important organ in the detection of arsenical poisoning – because it had already been removed, as had the heart, kidneys and liver. The intestines were mostly intact and showed 'slight reddening in parts'. The conclusion of Spilsbury's report is worth reproducing in full:

In the absence of so many organs, it is impossible to state the cause of death from the post-mortem examination alone. The history of the last illness points to some form of acute gastro-intestinal irritation, and this is corroborated by the empty condition of the parts of the intestines which remain in the body and the reddening of their inner surfaces. A remarkable feature of the examination is the degree of preservation of the body and the organs which remain, in view of the fact that death occurred more than one year previously.[9]

During his appearances in the witness chair at Edmund Duff's inquest, Spilsbury would opine that death was due to arsenical poisoning and enter into all manner of speculative ruminations on just when and how Edmund Duff might have received a fatal dose of arsenic – but the hard fact of the matter is that Spilsbury's own examination of Edmund Duff threw up nothing conclusive about the cause of his death at all.

In evidence, Spilsbury said he relied not only on the analysis provided by Dr Lynch, but also the symptoms exhibited during Edmund's last illness. It is therefore important to revisit those symptoms in some detail. At the inquest on 6 August 1929, Spilsbury claimed that Edmund's case was compatible with his having taken arsenic in his beer during the early evening because he commenced vomiting several hours later and, during the lengthy interrogation of Grace Duff, there was an attempt to establish that Edmund first began to be sick shortly after retiring to bed and continued to be sick throughout the night and into the next day. Grace denied this, saying that she believed her husband had not been sick until the following morning – although she candidly admitted that she could no longer be sure of the details, after an interval of almost eighteen months.

Another witness who could not be sure of things was Dr John Binning. Like Dr Elwell, he had not kept any notes about the consultations involving Edmund Duff, so when testifying at the inquest on 16 July 1929, although he said he thought that he had been told Edmund had an attack of diarrhoea on the evening of his death, he could not be sure. Nor could he remember what he had been told by the patient about when the first onset of vomiting had occurred. In the light of these extremely vague recollections about key symptoms it is little short of astonishing that during his evidence on this occasion he said, 'the symptoms I found on my second visit were typical of acute arsenical poisoning ... I took a very grave view of these symptoms.'[10]

The sense of confusion increased when Binning's statement about his visit during the afternoon of 27 April 1928, a visit during which he now claimed that he had suspected arsenic and 'took a grave view' of Edmund's condition, was read alongside Dr Elwell's testimony on 11 July 1929, when he was asked to recall Edmund's last day. According to Dr Elwell, when he visited during the afternoon, he experienced no great alarm over his patient's condition, and he was not seriously worried until his final visit during which Edmund actually died. Moreover, if Dr Binning had suspected arsenical poisoning back in April 1928, surely he would have mentioned it when he and Elwell conferred about the case at the time? According to the various statements made by both doctors, Binning discussed the case with Elwell at least once during the afternoon of 27 April, but apparently Binning expressed no great anxiety about the patient's condition and made no mention whatever of arsenic.

Throughout the course of the 1929 inquests on Edmund Duff, the coroner attempted to gain some sort of consensus about the onset and relative severity of the vomiting and diarrhoea which had afflicted Edmund Duff during the last twenty-four hours of his life. As neither of the doctors who attended him in those last hours had made any notes, conclusions were drawn from their hit and miss recollections, coupled with suppositions advanced by Spilsbury, and the fact that Grace said she had heard Edmund moving about in the night and flushing the lavatory on a couple of occasions; yet all the time there existed a much more reliable source of evidence. The testimony given at the original inquest enquiring into the cause of Edmund Duff's death was all still on record. The proceedings had been concluded within five weeks of the event, when memories were fresh enough to be reasonably reliable and every recollection had not been overshadowed by theories about criminal poisoning. Astonishingly, the prevalent attitude of the proceedings was typified by Home Office Analyst Lynch, who said, 'Ignoring the evidence given at the first inquest on E.C. Duff in 1928, but taking into account in place thereof, the evidence given at this inquest, I am of the opinion that deceased died from acute arsenical poisoning.'[11]

The accounts given at the first inquest on 1 June 1928 contain several crucial differences to those given at the second, while various points which would become sources of doubt and confusion later on emerge with clarity.[12] For example, by mid 1929, Dr Elwell had become confused about the precise timing of his first house call on the evening of Edmund's return from Hampshire, but in 1928 his memory was crystal clear. He recalled arriving at about 8 o'clock, mentioning that Edmund's supper had already been consumed and cleared away. Elwell found his patient smoking in the drawing room. Edmund appeared cheerful, but was complaining of a sore throat and feared the onset of a bout of malaria. His temperature was about 100, and his throat slightly injected. Elwell prescribed quinine, aspirin and bed rest.

Before they retired to bed that evening, Edmund had commented to Grace that he intended to take some Calomel. Calomel was a popular purgative[13] in an age when many people turned to laxatives and emetics to rid themselves of almost any internal upset. According to both his brother and his wife, Edmund Duff placed particular reliance on Calomel, which he said 'affected him fore and aft'. It would be surprising, therefore, if after taking some Calomel, Edmund Duff had *not* exhibited signs of diarrhoea, or vomiting, or both.

According to both Grace and Dr Elwell, it was at around 7 o'clock the following morning when Edmund vomited for the first time, and as he was still worried about his condition, Dr Binning attended in lieu of Dr Elwell. Dr Binning could not find anything more wrong with the patient than had his partner, but as Edmund Duff had not had a bowel movement, Binning prescribed Calomel – something he surely would not have done if diarrhoea was already a symptom of the case. Edmund took this second dose of Calomel and later attempted to follow it with a third, which he vomited back almost immediately. From then onwards he appears to have suffered from intermittent vomiting throughout the day, and managed to take nothing but several whisky and sodas, some neat whisky and a bicarbonate mixture prescribed by Dr Elwell 'to wash his stomach out'.

When Dr Elwell arrived again at 6 p.m. Edmund was suffering from stomach cramps, which the doctor attributed to loss of fluid due to persistent vomiting – prior to this Elwell said that Edmund had not complained of any particular localised pain, but rather that he was feeling very unwell generally. At that stage, Elwell was absolutely sure that Edmund had suffered only two loose motions – presumably helped by Calomel, Epsom Salts and bicarbonate of soda, which he had taken throughout the preceding twelve hours – and he had only one more bowel movement thereafter, which occurred when Dr Binning was in the house at around 9 p.m: the occasion on which Edmund tried to get out of bed and collapsed. Although the two doctors collectively called to see Edmund at least half a dozen times between 8 o'clock on the evening of 26 June and his death the following night, neither actually observed Edmund being sick. It was Grace who said he had been excessively sick, saying that she could only remember him being that sick once before – when he had been suffering from measles.

According to Grace,[14] by about 8 o'clock on 27 June Edmund had become so anxious about his condition that he told her he thought his number might be up. Throughout the whole episode, it would appear that almost until the moments of his final collapse, only Edmund fully appreciated the true seriousness of his condition.

Neither doctor came to any definite diagnosis, either immediately before or after death. Binning ruled out appendicitis, but suggested it might be 'a bad liver attack'. Elwell suspected ptomaine poisoning, but felt it could be ruled out because no one else had been affected. There were question marks over a recurrence of malaria, or a form of heatstroke, after it became known that Edmund had spent the whole of Tuesday standing in very cold water, wearing waders but no hat, while the sun beat down on the back of his bare head. Grace mentioned that Edmund was not accustomed to going without a hat and one of the minor mysteries of the case is why he did so on that particular day.

After death, Edmund's organs were analysed for a variety of poisons, or any evidence of food poisoning, but none was found. Dr Bronte found no signs of poisoning, but did consider that Edmund's death was due to heart failure.[15] He felt that the vomiting and diarrhoea were due either to the various purgatives taken during Edmund's last hours, or to the effects of heatstroke incurred in Hampshire, and he considered that both the heatstroke and the strain of severe vomiting could have helped contribute to the heart failure.

On the face of it this appears to be a perfectly reasonable diagnosis. Edmund was fifty-nine years old, stockily built, a moderate drinker and a very heavy smoker. After standing in the sun all day on 24 April, he felt unwell all the next day and decided to return home, where on arrival, according to the evidence of his wife and son, he felt giddy and was on the point of collapse. He had little appetite for his meal, but did drink one, or possibly two, bottles of beer. In spite of remaining outwardly cheerful – when Grace telephoned the doctor, Elwell heard Edmund call cheerfully from the drawing room, 'Tell him I've got bubonic plague'[16] – he must have been fairly concerned about his condition on 26 April to take the unusual step of calling in the doctor. Although Grace frequently solicited medical aid for the children, Edmund very rarely summoned the doctor; by April 1928 he had been a patient of Dr Elwell for almost eight years, but had consulted him on fewer than half a dozen occasions.[17]

Far from exhibiting any signs of arsenical poisoning, Edmund does indeed appear to have been suffering the effects of the heat, perhaps allied with some other throat infection, or even a recurrence of malaria (as he himself initially believed). From bedtime on 26 April he employed a series of medications calculated to produce vomiting and diarrhoea, coupled with alcohol, which would worsen the dehydrating effects of his other symptoms. He also became acutely anxious, and anxiety is known to exacerbate the effects of heart failure. Ultimately, Edmund's death may have been accelerated by his own conviction that he was about to die and the terror that this induced in him – such cases are far from unknown. There is also a hint that during the post-mortem examination, Dr Bronte observed an underlying problem with Edmund Duff's heart. Bronte's deposition at the original inquest does not specifically mention this, but according to young John Duff, after the inquest Dr Bronte had told the family that 'Daddy ... may have dropped down at any time from his heart.'[18]

Certainly, in the light of the evidence given at the original inquest, the theory that Edmund Duff drank a solution containing enough arsenic to kill him at around 7 o'clock on the evening of 26 April, but suffered no vomiting until twelve hours later (after taking a dose of Calomel) and had no bowel movements until several hours after that (after taking a second dose of Calomel) begins to appear at best somewhat fanciful.

Yet by the time Edmund Duff's body was exhumed in May 1929, even Dr Bronte was willing to testify that he believed the death to be the result of acute arsenical poisoning.[19] The dramatic about face was the result of the analysis performed by Gerard Roche Lynch, which Spilsbury also cited at the inquest as his primary reason for concluding that death was due to arsenical poisoning. Nor was Bronte the only one to have experienced a change of heart:

> I was present at the inquest when the widow of the deceased gave her evidence and she was very distressed and I very boldly say that I was very much convinced and I feel that I could not point a finger of suspicion to her in con-

nection with the death of her husband ...The deceased and his wife were very much devoted to one another ... by the death of the deceased, the widow is reduced almost to penury...

The sympathetic hand which penned this report on 3 May 1928, confidently assuring his superiors that there were no suspicious circumstances surrounding the death of Edmund Duff, belonged to none other than Inspector Fred Hedges.[20] Hedges was called in after Edmund's death to initiate routine enquiries by Coroner Jackson, who, according to Hedges' report, did not consider there were any suspicious circumstances either. The entire tone of this report could hardly be more different to that of a report submitted by Hedges eleven months later, clamouring for the exhumation of Edmund Duff, vilifying Grace, and stating his personal conviction that if exhumed, 'a considerable amount of arsenic would be found in the body of Edmund Duff.'[21]

In the sense of actual hard evidence, absolutely nothing had changed between the submission of those two reports – except the suspicion that two other members of Edmund Duff's family had been poisoned. It was the classic operation of the principle Curtis Bennett had described – a case 'based on a falsehood and developed backwards'.

By the time Dr Lynch took away his samples for analysis in May 1929, he was already well aware of the investigating officer's belief that 'a considerable quantity of arsenic' would be found in them and he had also been present in the mortuary during Spilsbury's examination of Edmund Duff's remains. Indeed his preliminary report[22] states that he partly based his conclusions on what he had observed in the mortuary, although in reality there was little aside from whispers and the usual nonsense about a 'remarkably' well preserved corpse, which could possibly lead to any conclusions about the presence of arsenic.

It is a known fact that arsenic exists – even if only in minute traces – in all human bodies, and that its concentration varies from one body part to another.[23] Indeed, as Willcox had inadvertently demonstrated in the Seddon case, the quantity can vary from one sample of the same body part to another. Candy's remark that if he had 'pegged away hard enough' he would have found some arsenic, is therefore no more than the truth. We have no way of knowing how hard Dr Gerard Roche Lynch 'pegged away' in order to get a set of results worth talking about, but close scrutiny of his evidence implies the distinct possibility that he 'pegged away' very hard indeed.

Dr Lynch presented the results of his analysis as a table. In the first column was a list of the samples tested; in the second, the amount of arsenic actually found in a whole sample; in the third column the amount he deemed to be present where he had not had an entire sample, but had to multiply the amount found by the assumed weight of a whole body part.[24]

Column 1	Column 2	Column 3
Large intestine 13.1oz	0.014 grain	
Small intestine 18.3oz	0.040 grain	
Rectum 7.0oz	0.003 grain	
Pancreas 5.8oz	0.002 grain	
Omentum 18.6oz	0.004 grain	
Bladder 3.2oz	0.001 grain	
Lung		0.016 grain
Fluid from chest 6.5floz	0.005 grain	
Brain		0.027 grain
Toenails 0.09oz	0.0001 grain	
Fingernails	0.0001 grain	
Muscle		0.654 grain
Bone		0.049 grain
Total	0.069 grain	0.746 grain
Total column 2 0.069 grain		
Total column 3 <u>0.746</u> grain		
Total <u>0.815</u> grain		

The most obvious point about this table is that the majority of the arsenic which made up the grand total came from column 3; the figures arrived at by testing a small sample and then multiplying the result in order to estimate how much arsenic would have been in that part of the body as a whole. In order to decide what factor to multiply by, Lynch first had to estimate the total bodyweight and then estimate what proportion of bodyweight would be accounted for by the areas of the body to which his sample related (for example the muscles, or skeleton). These estimates introduced an element of uncertainty into his findings which was not in the least evident when he presented them to coroner and jury.

In his report, Lynch admits that:

> The total weights of the organs and tissues are not known. For the muscles and bones, average weights have been calculated on the basis of a normal man whose weight was 10 stone. The late E.C. Duff, although short of stature, was a muscular, thick set and fat man, and I am of the opinion that his weight was over 11 stone…

Lynch goes on to say that in spite of this he has based his calculations on a man weighing 10 stone, the implication being that if Lynch had based his calculations on Duff's actual weight, the levels of arsenic would have been even higher.

Due to post-mortem changes, it was impossible to accurately gauge what the weight of a person whose body had been buried for any period of time would have been in life. Lynch mentioned in court that Edmund Duff was short, but not how short. In fact, at 5ft 1in, Edmund was exceptionally short[25] and although remembered by various witnesses as muscular, thickset, or stocky, is never described as fat anywhere but in Lynch's report. Estimating weight is extremely difficult and bodyweight can vary enormously between individuals of the same height, but according to the standard body mass index calculation, even 10 stone is categorised as obese for a man of 5ft 1in, the top end of normal being a mere 8½ stone.[26] Repeated medical studies, on the subject of average weight to height, place the average for a man of Duff's height at around 8½-9 stone and a 1929 study of fifty-year-old men who were 5ft 8in tall, found their average weight to be 160lbs – allowing 5lbs for clothing and shoes.[27] This strongly suggests that far from underestimating Edmund's bodyweight, Lynch may have been considerably overestimating it and thereby artificially inflating his figures.

Having started out with a figure which is too high, Lynch then decided that the skeleton represents 20 per cent of human bodyweight, which he claims is the 'usually accepted basis of calculation'. Lynch may have 'usually accepted' this himself, but he appears to have been somewhat singular in doing so, because the figure given in Professor Sydney Smith's standard 1920s hand-book *Forensic Medicine* is 15 per cent and more modern sources place the figure lower than that.[28]

Lynch's claim that muscle represents 40 per cent of bodyweight is on target, but given that the distribution of arsenic is not uniform and that its presence in, say, an abdominal muscle is absolutely no guarantee whatsoever of a similar amount existing in a calf muscle, any conclusions based on a single sample multiplied up to represent almost half a person's bodyweight is self evidently far from a safe basis on which to proceed.

At this point, however, we find Lynch engaged in another misleading little game – because having wrongly stated that the skeleton is accepted to represent 20 per cent of bodyweight, he then says that he will base his calculation on the much lower proportion of 15 per cent, and the muscles at the lower proportion of 30 per cent. Again we see the coroner and jury hoodwinked into assuming that Lynch's figures are conservative, rather than the opposite. To further talk up his results, Lynch adds that the stomach and other missing organs would normally 'contain a considerable quantity of arsenic in cases of poisoning by this substance' – which while true as it stands, tends to presuppose the fact that this *was* a case of poisoning and ignore the inconvenient truth that Professor Candy found no trace of the stuff when he tested for it.

While it is impossible to know the accuracy with which Dr Lynch compared the results produced from his samples with the his standard arsenic mirrors, the underlying tendency to exaggeration which can be detected throughout his report does not inspire confidence in the integrity of this critical part of the process, and as Willcox was forced to admit when cross-examined at the Seddon trial, any mistake in interpreting the mirrors would result in a huge over estima-tion when multiplying by factors of several hundred, as Lynch was in respect of his two largest figures, the bone and the muscle, which between them represent 0.703 of his total of 0.815 grain.

Not only is there a significant risk that Lynch's calculations were wrong, but throughout the report the conscious or sub-conscious desire on his part to exaggerate the amount of arsenic found in Edmund Duff's body is so apparent, that it is difficult to believe him either an honest or objective witness. In spite of this, Lynch's findings became the pivotal part of the entire proceedings, with every single medical witness who appeared at the inquest accepting that death was due to arsenical poisoning, essentially because Lynch's report said so. Long before the conclusion of the inquest, the verdict had been pre-empted: the proceedings ceased to be about determining how Edmund Duff had died, but instead became an enquiry into when and how arsenic had been administered to him. In Coroner Jackson's summing up, he never once questioned the cause of death as such, but instead invited the jury to consider whether death had been due to accident, suicide, or criminal poisoning, majoring of course on the latter. It was as if a strange form of collective blindness afflicted everyone involved, whereby only evidence which told in one particular direction – arsenical poisoning – could be seen.

Yet there was a good deal of evidence to suggest that Edmund Duff had not died of arsenical poisoning at all. The original symptoms, post-mortem and analysis had not indicated it. Duff was not suicidal, apparently had no opportunity to imbibe a fatal dose by accident and no one appeared to have had a motive to murder him. In addition there was one other important factor which no one bothered to raise at all.

CHAPTER FOURTEEN

RIDDLED WITH ARSENIC

In 1931, during the trial of Annie Hearn, the judge queried with Dr Roche Lynch whether it was not the case that arsenic was always found in the human body. 'I regard arsenic as practically always found in the body,' the analyst replied. 'The figure is something like 0.01 parts per million.'

If one thing is invariably calculated to confuse the layman, it is the use of mathematical formulae. Mr Justice Roche (no relation) pursued the point: 'Can you give us any idea of the arsenical contents of the human body?'

'I have never worked it out,' the analyst said. 'But it is probably 100 times less.'[1]

Here, then, is a somewhat astonishing confession from a man who had by then appeared as an expert in several cases of alleged arsenical poisoning – Lynch did not know exactly what constituted a normal level of arsenic in a human body.

Norman Birkett, who was defending Mrs Hearn, drew further interesting admissions from Dr Lynch, including the fact that he had no experience whatsoever of any living persons who had been suffering from arsenical poisoning, and that he had never before been involved in a case where the soil was heavily impregnated with arsenic, as was the soil in the churchyard where the exhumations of Mrs Thomas and Miss Everard had taken place. Some of the soil in the churchyard contained 125 parts to the million of arsenic, while other samples had tested much lower. Birkett wanted to know why some of the soil samples apparently contained more than 200 times the levels of arsenic found in the supposed victims' organs and why the sample of soil taken from above the coffin contained more than twice the level of arsenic than did the sample taken from immediately below it. Lynch was unable to give any sort of sensible answer and by the end of Birkett's cross-examination, the court may well have been left with the impression that the things Gerard Roche Lynch did not know about arsenic would have made a substantial essay.

Birkett asked whether it did not logically follow that in an area where there was obviously a high concentration of arsenic in the soil, the drinking water would also contain a lot of arsenic.

'Traces, I have no doubt,' replied Roche Lynch – following the Willcox-Spilsbury protocol for minimising any concession which might have told in favour of the accused.

Birkett then forced the witness to admit that the samples he had taken from both bodies had been obtained under such conditions that incidental contamination with the soil was almost inevitable, thereby casting serious doubt on the veracity of his results.[2]

The most important truth which had been wrung from this so-called expert, however, was that neither he, nor presumably his colleagues, John Webster and John Ryffel, both of whom featured prominently in the prosecutions of men and women accused of arsenical poisoning, actually knew the levels of arsenic which constituted the norm in a human body. This is hardly surprising given that most of the detailed research on the subject was only undertaken long after all three had retired. In 1968 Bäumler, Obersteg and Shafer tested the bodies of twenty recently deceased citizens of Basle in an attempt to establish the levels of arsenic in a human body and in April 2000 Kraus, Quidenus and Schaller performed a similar experiment in Germany, using a larger sample of fifty dead bodies.[3] Yet even now it is extremely difficult to pin down exactly how much is too much. Chemistry researcher and lecturer John Emsley writes that the average normal level in a person weighing 70kgs would be around 7mg of arsenic,[4] whereas Dr Elson M. Haas places the normal level at between 10-20mg.[5]

In spite of the huge difference of opinion represented by these two figures, neither can be condemned as incorrect, because just as knowledge about levels of arsenic in the human body has increased, so has an understanding of its extreme variability from one person to another. It has now been established beyond doubt that arsenic levels in humans are dependent on a variety of environmental factors, including geographical location and diet. Birkett was right on target when he suggested a possible connection between the level of arsenic in the local water supply and that found in the bodies of Mrs Thomas and Miss Everard. Diet also plays a part, because some foods are naturally much higher in arsenic than others, in particular seafood, which virtually guarantees that the average citizen of Japan will register a higher level of arsenic in his or her body than a citizen of any land-locked district in Western Europe.[6]

On the United States Government Agency for Toxic Substances website,[7] the advice on evaluating a clinical diagnosis of acute arsenical poisoning warns that clinical diagnosis is 'often difficult' and 'the medical history should include: occupational history, diet, residential history (proximity to smelters, other industry and hazardous waste sites), smoking history, condition of household pets, hobbies (including use of pesticides or herbicides in farming and gardening), medications, source of drinking water, and home heating methods (wood burning stoves and fireplaces).' When Dr Lynch so confidently deposed that Edmund Duff died as a result of arsenical poisoning, he was clearly unaware of the need to consider any of these factors, just as he was unaware of what level of arsenic he might normally expect to find in the body of a fifty-nine-year-old man living in Croydon in 1928.

Lynch claimed to have discovered 0.815 of a grain of arsenic in Edmund's remains, which equates to 51mg – more than twice the upper limit mentioned by Dr Haas. However, Lynch's findings were suspect for a number of reasons and their value diminishes still further when another point is brought to bear. Lynch's results include arsenic found in finger and toenails and bone. This arsenic was supposedly all part of a fatal dose Edmund Duff received within thirty hours of his death, but as Dr Bronte rightly pointed out in 1929, it takes several days for arsenic to permeate either nail or bone. One of the many authorities which points this out is *Glaister's Dictionary of Medical Jurisprudence and Toxicology*, which also includes the telling information: 'In order to establish that death resulted from arsenical poisoning, the history of the symptomatology prior to death must receive careful consideration, and there must be a sensible amount of arsenic isolated.'[8] This 'sensible amount' is later quantified as 'three to four times' the usual trace amounts.[9] Thus even taking the arsenic found in the nails and bones (which might arguably have been the result of post-mortem permeation of the arsenic from elsewhere in the body) and accepting the results of Roche Lynch's analysis at face value, it is rather difficult to accept them as representing a conclusive argument for death by arsenical poisoning.

The greatest problem with all the conclusions drawn in the various arsenic cases which arose during the first half of the twentieth century, is that they were based on inadequate information. No one really knew what sort of arsenic levels were normally found in the body of the average British citizen in 1929. The vast majority of deaths were put down to natural causes and therefore did not involve any sort of autopsy, while only a small proportion of those where an autopsy did take place would include chemical tests for arsenic.[10] Whenever 'high' levels of arsenic were thrown up but no immediate explanation for its presence could be found, for example in the cases of Alice Straigh and Laura Benson (the women whose deaths in 1928 and 1929 were not thought to be suspicious because they had occurred in hospital), the Home Office experts were apparently content to accept these deaths as unsolved mysteries, without bothering to consider what the results might be telling them about the other arsenic cases in which they became involved.

In more recent times, numerous articles about arsenic have included speculation that it may have been employed to poison Napoleon Bonaparte: a theory which arose following the discovery of high levels of arsenic in a sample of the ex-emperor's hair, obtained just after his death. Suggestions about Bourbon agents and green wallpaper inevitably follow, but hardly any of these writers include the two most important points in respect of the story: firstly that samples of Napoleon's hair, taken as keepsakes at various different times of his life, have also tested higher than 'normal' levels of arsenic. Secondly, as Ronald Bentley and Thomas Chasteen point out in their *Arsenic Curiosa and Humanity*,[11] the interpretation of what was 'normal' in this particular case is impossible without access to samples from Napoleon's contemporaries and associates for comparison.

Resistance to the toxic effects of arsenic is built up by exposure to it. Peasants in the Styrian Alps on the Austro-Hungarian border were for several centuries in the habit of consuming quantities of arsenic which would have been lethal to almost anyone else, believing it to be beneficial to their health.[12] Today it is generally recognised that if someone lives in an environment where they are routinely exposed to slightly higher concentrations of arsenic than is the norm, the levels found in their body will be higher than those found in people living elsewhere, without their health necessarily being affected. Moreover, there is good reason for believing that the average British citizen in 1928-9 would have come into contact with arsenic a good deal more frequently than would the average British citizen today.

Arsenic does not just enter our bodies by mouth. It can also be breathed in and absorbed through the skin. Arsenic occurs naturally in coal and when coal was burned in a million grates, the invisible gases given off in the process invaded everything in their path, from the food on the table to the soft furnishings of the drawing room.

The presence of arsenic in coal became an important issue in the prosecution of Charlotte Bryant in 1936,[13] because part of the case against her was the allegation that she had attempted to destroy the tin of weedkiller she had used to poison her husband by burning it. Roche Lynch testified at her trial that the level of arsenic he found in the ashes from the Bryants' stove was so excessive that it proved some arsenic had been burned in the stove. During his summing up the judge in the case told the jury that this was important evidence, because it corroborated the otherwise unsubstantiated testimony of another prosecution witness.

When Professor Bone of the Imperial College of Science and Technology read an account of this evidence, he was so appalled that he wrote urgently to point out that the arsenic content of coal varies enormously from one sample to another, and that its natural content could be up to six or seven times higher than the amount Roche Lynch had isolated in the ashes. In spite of Professor Bone's experience and reputation, the judges sitting at Charlotte Bryant's appeal refused to hear this corrective evidence, with the Lord Chief Justice saying, 'It would be intolerable if the court were to listen to the afterthoughts of a scientific gentleman in a capital case or any other case.' Presumably His Lordship thought it far more tolerable to see a woman executed on the basis of evidence from a 'scientific gentleman' who did not know what he was talking about.

It was a common feature of every arsenic trial to find that the household of the accused person contained some sort of lethal product involving arsenic. The Seddons had fly papers; the Paces and the Bryants sheep dip; worming tablets made with arsenic were discovered in the Thomas's farmhouse; Armstrong, Black, Greenwood and Tom Sidney all employed some form of arsenical rat poison. Weedkiller was found on or near to the premises of Edith Bingham, Tom Sidney, Grace Duff, Violet and Vera Sidney, Annie Hearn, Herbert Armstrong and Harold Greenwood. Three separate brands, Eureka, Noble's and Acme were involved, to say nothing of Major Armstrong's personal preference – neat arsenic – which he found most efficacious in keeping down the dandelions. The sinister implications of this list are somewhat diluted by the realisation that keen gardeners the length and breadth of the land kept arsenic-based weedkiller in their sheds, that in 1911 everyone's fly papers were impregnated with arsenic and that not only sheep dip, but a variety of other agricultural products in regular daily use were also arsenic based.

Nor was it just these obviously poisonous household and agricultural preparations which brought people into constant routine contact with arsenic. In his
book *Endangered Lives – Public Health in Victorian Britain*, Anthony Wohl writes:

> In 1899 the Medical Society of London discovered arsenic was used in paper,
> labels, advertisement cards, playing cards, sweet wrappers, book jackets, wallpa-
> per, lampshades, artificial leaves and flowers, wax ornaments, fabrics intended
> for clothes, curtains, children's toys, including rubber balls, dolls, rocking horses;
> distemper, household paint, decoration on tin plates, japanned goods, blinds,
> American and oil cloths, printed table baizes, carpets, floorcloths, linoleum,
> book covers, coloured soaps, wafers, sweetmeats and false malachite.

Nor were these mere traces. An experiment on twenty yards of fabric yielded
up 100 grains of arsenic. [14] To this list Ronald Bentley and Thomas Chasteen
in their *Arsenic Curiosa and Humanity* add wrapping paper, paint used on
kitchenware, artificial and dried flowers, stuffed animals (arsenic was used as a
preservative in taxidermy), candles and as a colorant in a variety of foodstuffs
and their packagings. [15]

Although the Medical Society's findings were made at the very end of Victoria's
reign, neither the objects themselves, nor their methods of manufacture, had conveniently vanished thirty years later. Violet Sidney's home was cluttered with the
furniture and ornaments she had acquired on her marriage and tenaciously clung
to thereafter. The first decades of the twentieth century were not a throw-away
era. Many people born long after 1929 can recall childhood visits to the homes
of grandparents, in which the handling and usage of objects which derived from
before the turn of the twentieth century formed a daily event. Violet could afford
to replace things but she did not, preferring for example to have her saucepans
and soup tureen extensively mended.

Industry was another source from which arsenic seeped invisibly into everyday
lives. In Cornwall the connection between arsenic and industry was fairly obvious.
Here, where arsenic had been mined for generations, the arsenic was extracted by
roasting the ore in furnaces, with the residual arsenic trioxide, which accumulated
in the flues, regularly removed and thrown onto open waste tips. [16] However, other
areas of Britain had their share of industrial processes which involved arsenic. It was
used in tanneries, as a wood preservative, in the manufacture of glass, and was a by-
product of smelting lead, zinc, cobalt and nickel. It was given off to some degree in
just about every process which involved the burning of fossil fuels.

The extent to which invisible gases could contaminate their surroundings, and
the idea that living in proximity to such operations was harmful, was little understood. In 1901 a serious outbreak of arsenical poisoning occurred in the north
of England, which was eventually traced back to contaminated beer. The Royal
Commission set up to investigate the matter found that the glucose used in the
manufacture of the beer had been made using sulphuric acid which contained
high concentrations of arsenic. In a further complication, the Commission found

that hops had sometimes been dried using coke which had higher than average arsenic levels, and in other cases malt kilns had not been cleaned out regularly enough to prevent large build ups of arsenic in the soot. The Commission noted that as sulphuric acid was also extensively used in the production of treacle and vinegar, the potential for problems was presumably not confined to beer.[17]

As Britain approached the 1930s little headway had been made. The Clean Air Acts were still many years away and in 1926 Neville Chamberlain pointed out to the House of Commons that the wording of the proposed Smoke Abatement Bill was something of a nonsense in that a prohibition on factories discharging 'black smoke' would do nothing whatsoever to prevent them from discharging white smoke 'containing lead, arsenic and all manner of noxious fumes'.[18]

The dangers of arsenic in wallpaper had been recognised as early as 1815, by a German chemist Leopold Gmelin,[19] but the popularity of William Morris's designs, which were heavily reliant on the deep green dyes which derived from arsenic, and were widely imitated by all British manufacturers of domestic wall coverings, ensured that an arsenic-based dye was introduced into one or more rooms in many homes during the late nineteenth or early twentieth century. A gradual appreciation that this might not be a good idea led to increasing numbers of papers being manufactured with arsenic-free dyes, but this did not entirely solve the problem, because the practice of putting successive layers of wallpaper one on top of another created the perfect conditions to give off lethal arsenious oxide, when the layers of mouldering paper reacted with rising damp. Not until the deaths of two children in 1931 did it come to be generally accepted that arsenic in wallpaper dyes might still be a serious problem.[20]

Even after death there was no escaping arsenic. Enquiries at Croydon's Queen's Road Cemetery in 1929 elicited the information that arsenic-based weedkiller had been in regular use there for at least twenty years. According to the superintendent of the cemetery, John Bird,[21] their original preference had been for liquid weedkiller, but latterly they had used Eureka powder, which was stored in the belfry of the Chapel of Rest. Hedges was happy to accept John Bird's opinion that none of the weedkiller could have found its way into the soil of the Duff and Sidney graves, as it was never used on the grass, only on the paths, with the nearest point treated at least 10-12ft away from the Duff and Sidney graves. Cemetery keeper and policeman were both blissfully unaware of the principal of run-off, by which rain would wash the weedkiller into the surrounding earth. John Bird had also tried out the Eureka as a means of ridding the cemetery of wasps' nests, but to his disappointment, found it not efficacious for this purpose.

In spite of the scare over arsenic in beer, food and drink (including beer) continued to contain arsenic – either by accident or design – well into the twentieth century.[22] In January 1904 *The Times* was again reporting higher than permissible levels of arsenic in beer and during the same week, that some arsenic-contaminated sugar had been discovered. In 1911 a bakery on the Isle of Arran was unable to account for the presence of non-fatal levels of arsenic in its scones. In 1920 residents of Haslemere in Surrey became ill after consuming sugar purchased from a shipment which had been contaminated when liquid weedkiller, which it had travelled next to in the train, seeped into the sugar barrel. Newspapers regularly recorded cases of arsenic-related food adulteration brought against individual retailers, and sometimes against household names such as Rowntrees and Nestlé, who were at different times both accused of selling arsenic-adulterated cocoa. Sweets and confectionery provided a regular source of complaints to the local county analysts: in 1931 alone there were eighteen reported cases. Even medicinal bismuth and meat juice, which were regularly prescribed for invalids, were subject to arsenic contamination.

One particular scare centred around apples. Arsenic crop sprays were widely used in the USA and during the second half of the 1920s, arsenic was regularly discovered in imported apples. A few people actually became ill after eating them, but most consumers suffered no ill effects at all and the official line was that any risk could be negated by washing the fruit at home before consuming it.[23] In fact the advice concerning the apples was a typical over-simplification. The arsenic was not just on the skin of the fruit, but present throughout the apple, introduced not just via the spraying of the current crop, but via the root system of the trees, which stood in orchards where the soil had become impregnated with arsenic – because once introduced into soil, arsenic stayed put.

As far back as 1902, Arthur Angell, the Public Analyst for Hampshire, had proved by experiment that crops grown in soil which had a high concentration of arsenic, took up arsenic via their root systems,[24] but scarcely anyone appears to have taken on board the implications of the fact that amateur and professional vegetable growers alike regularly treated their patch with a poisonous chemical which would then reappear in their own food chain. The tin of carrot seeds found in an empty Eureka Weed Killer tin in Violet Sidney's shed was symbolic of a much wider, but generally unacknowledged, association between the diet of the average person and arsenical weedkillers.

One product in particular became almost irretrievably associated with arsenic – tobacco – a crop which, in common with apples, was routinely sprayed with arsenic to remove pests, and which gradually became so charged with poison from built-up arsenic levels in the soil, that the average American cigarette contained 40mg of arsenic.[25] Once lit, the arsenic from the tobacco entered both the atmosphere of the room and the lungs of the smoker.

Edmund Duff was universally acknowledged to be a very heavy smoker.[26] He lived in a house heated by coal fires and enjoyed a diet in which arsenic would have been present in much greater quantities than it is today. He lived in an environment where the average person had, in all likelihood, a far greater exposure and therefore a far higher tolerance to arsenic, than would generally be the case by the end of the twentieth century. The theory that it was Grace Duff who murdered her mother and sister relied heavily on the fact that she had the greatest motive and opportunity to murder her husband Edmund – but the balance of probabilities is that Edmund was not murdered at all. Bronte and Candy were right and Roche Lynch and Spilsbury were wrong.

CHAPTER FIFTEEN

ROUNDING UP

The solicitors who had acted for the Metropolitan Police, Wontner & Sons, describe the Croydon case in a letter to the Commissioner, as 'for all practical purposes, three verdicts of murder'.[1] In point of fact the verdict on Violet Sidney was not murder, but death by arsenical poisoning, with the jury refusing to rule out the possibility that it had been self-administered. While the point may appear somewhat pedantic, Wonter's casual rounding up of two murder verdicts into three is worth noting as emblematic of almost everyone's approach to the case.

In Hedges' report to Sir Archibald Bodkin on 12 August, he casually throws in a reference to Edmund Duff being twenty years older than Grace;[2] this enormous gulf apparently representing one of Grace's motives for disposing of her husband, but the age difference was actually seventeen years, which was obviously known to Hedges as he mentions both their ages elsewhere on the same page of the report. If Hedges seriously believed that a large age difference between a married couple constituted a motive for murder, then the difference between seventeen years and twenty must have seemed fairly academic, but if looking to express it in round figures, why not say fifteen, which was actually closer?

The tendency to exaggerate a position by apparently casual use of speech was a trick well known to Sir Bernard Spilsbury. One of the best possible examples occurs in the Armstrong case when Spilsbury was invited by the prosecuting counsel, while on oath in the witness box, to state how often he saw a poisoning case. Such cases were 'an almost weekly, certainly monthly occurrence,' Spilsbury said.[3] Almost weekly equates to around fifty per year, whereas monthly is four times less.

Perhaps the most blatant and astonishing example of rounding up in the Croydon story, however, comes from Dr John Ryffel, who performed the analysis on samples from Vera Sidney's body. Like his colleague Dr Lynch, Ryffel presented his report to the inquest in the form of a table, showing how much arsenic (expressed in grains) he calculated to be present in each part tested:[4]

Liver	0.255
Spleen	0.0014
Kidneys	0.012
Heart	0.019
Stomach	0.012
Stomach contents	0.0005
Small intestine	0.019
Large intestine	0.025
Rectum	0.0094
Brain	0.009
Pleural & peritoneal fluids	0.003
Bones	0.019 (assuming total weight 5,000g)
Muscles	0.93 (assuming total weight 20,000g)
Total	1.48

It does not appear to have occurred to anyone to check Ryffel's addition – perhaps it was assumed that a man who worked in complex calculations involving multiples of millionths on an almost daily basis would be capable of adding a column of figures. Possibly it was the 'expert factor' kicking in again: the feeling that these marvellous 'independent' Home Office men could never make a mistake. Whatever the reason, no one in court pointed out that Ryffel's total was wrong. The figures do not add up to 1.48 grain of arsenic, but to 1.3143.

Having given this total, Ryffel goes on to state that he found 'slight traces' of arsenic in the hair, finger and toenails. 'The skin and lungs were not supplied, but may be assumed to contain an additional 0.05 grain…' In the next paragraph, when summarising his findings, Ryffel rounds up the amount of arsenic to '1.5 grains'. The amount of error, assumption and rounding up which appear on this single page of Ryffel's report are hardly consistent with the sort of precise and detailed analysis one would hope to encounter in evidence which might eventually form part of a case against someone standing trial for their life.

Ryffel's 1.5 grain was of course taken up by Spilsbury in his evidence, which consistently refers to 'one and a half grains'.[5] Even assuming Ryffel's analysis was correct, this is exaggerating the position by almost 20 per cent and with the whole diagnosis of arsenical poisoning relying on this analysis, its accuracy in every respect was absolutely crucial, because just as in Edmund's case, there was little or nothing else to indicate arsenical poisoning in Vera Sidney's remains.

According to Spilsbury's autopsy report,[6] her stomach wall showed no signs of inflammation and although there was some reddening of the intestines, there was no sign of ulceration anywhere. What Spilsbury did identify were clear indications of various other problems which had troubled Vera in the period before her death. He found confirmation of the cold she had been suffering from, with mucus in her air passages and congestion in her lungs; but there was also evidence that Vera may have been suffering from other debilitating conditions of an entirely different nature.

On examination, Spilsbury found that her uterus was enlarged and the walls thickened, while her right ovary was also enlarged and contained several cysts. Both conditions can result in heavy menstrual bleeding and physical discomfort, which can be extremely debilitating. In the 1920s and '30s there was a considerable reticence in discussing 'women's problems' or consulting one's doctor about them, but Spilsbury's findings are highly suggestive in the light of Grace's statement to Inspector Hedges that, 'I think it is only right to mention that Vera had been very anaemic and latterly very much so.'[7] It is reasonably safe to assume that Grace was not referring to a clinical diagnosis of anaemia by Dr Elwell (which he would presumably have mentioned when questioned about Vera) but rather the 'anaemia' which was assumed to occur as a result of heavy menstrual bleeding.

According to the contemporary *Wheeler's Handbook of Medicine*[8] the most effective treatment for anaemia was arsenic, and Fowler's Solution[9] was recommended. There is of course absolutely no hard evidence that Vera ever took this or any other arsenic-based tonic, but this kind of self-medication cannot be entirely ruled out. In a statement on the 18 April, Grace mentioned that Vera had been rather worried about her health lately, coupling this with the opinion that Vera had been overdoing it,[10] and when Vera's own diary entries were read out in court, they confirmed her constant feelings of tiredness and periodic colds and stomach upsets. We know that Vera had not consulted her general practitioner about this, because Dr Elwell had no record of treating her between a bout of flu in February 1928 and her final illness in February 1929;[11] so, if Vera had been taking anything, then it was not a remedy obtained via Dr Elwell.

According to Kathleen Noakes, both Violet and Vera habitually took their medicines in private and kept the bottles in their own bedrooms. 'There were a great many bottles' in both rooms, according to Mrs Noakes, but she never touched any of them and had no idea what they contained.[12] This evidence of Vera and Violet taking and keeping medicines privately in their own bedrooms was confirmed by Kathleen Noakes' predecessor, Clara Collett, when she gave a statement to Inspector Hedges.[13] If this hypothetical bottle of arsenic-based tonic existed, there is no reason why anyone but Vera would have been aware of its presence in the house, although one might hope that Grace, Tom, the letting agents who eventually assisted in the clearance of the house, or even Inspector Hedges might have noticed it and appreciated its significance at some stage.

Returning to Spilsbury's post-mortem report, his conclusions as to the cause of death are distinctly vague: 'Syncope due to fatty degeneration of the heart, liver and kidneys ... the small amount of material in the stomach and intestines ... suggest ... a gastro intestinal irritant...' and of course his old favourite, 'a comparative absence of post-mortem degeneration or putrefaction, remarkable in a body exhumed five weeks after death.'[14] To his original autopsy, however, Spilsbury would add a supplementary report, which opens with the words: 'The cause of death was syncope due to acute arsenical poisoning, as is shown by the presence of approximately 1½ grains of arsenic...'[15]

Again Spilsbury based his eventual conclusion not on anything he had discovered in his own examination, but on the analysis provided by a colleague. This supplementary report is remarkable if only as one of the most acute examples of developing an argument along the lines of wishful thinking. It commences with a list of Vera's symptoms, explaining that they are all indicative of arsenical poisoning, without troubling to qualify this by adding that they are all equally indicative of a whole variety of other conditions, and altogether omitting to mention that various accepted post-mortem signs of arsenical poisoning were notably absent from Vera Sidney's body. Spilsbury goes on to claim that Vera's symptoms are consistent with having received an earlier dose of poison on Monday night, and 'the fact that Mrs Noakes and the cat were sick after taking soup which had been served at the evening meal on Monday points to the presence of arsenic in the soup.' Surely a preposterous assumption for anyone to make, since the fact that someone happens to be sick after consuming some soup is statistically most unlikely to be due to the fact that it contains arsenic!

Taking the sickness of the cook and the cat as proof positive of his theory, Spilsbury continues as if the presence of arsenic in Monday's soup is now a proven fact, explaining that because Vera's heart was damaged by the dose on Monday, this would explain the marked dilation of the heart, noted by Dr Elwell when he examined her on Wednesday. The report concludes with the following piece of contorted logic:

> If arsenic had been taken in medicinal doses for any appreciable period of time,
> I should have expected the hair to show more than slight traces of arsenic,
> though this would not exclude the previous administration of a poisonous dose,
> if the effects passed off quickly.

In other words, the relative absence of arsenic in Vera's hair precludes any medicinal doses, but not any previous criminal attempts on her life.

The description of Vera's heart in Spilsbury's autopsy report is extremely significant. He described the heart as enlarged and covered in fat, with the right cavities somewhat dilated, the left auricle slightly dilated and the left ventricle more so. Spilsbury affected to believe that these changes had been brought about by a preliminary brush with arsenic a couple of days before Vera died, but these clear abnormalities were almost certainly of a longstanding nature and indicative that Vera was probably suffering from a form of dilated cardiomyopathy.[16]

Hidden away in a statement to the police given on 7 March 1929, Grace Duff had made a surprising remark about her sister. Vera has generally emerged as a sporty, outdoor type, who played golf and went for long walks, but according to Grace, 'her heart had received a strain during the war. She was really more delicate than most people knew.'[17] It has been suggested that if Grace Duff killed her relatives, she would have been keen to play up or invent alternative explanations for their demises, but this remark about Vera is potentially significant inasmuch that the autopsy indicated there was a problem with Vera's heart – something Grace could not possibly have foreseen at that point, as the exhumation had yet to take place. Like the evidence that Vera may have been suffering from gynaecological problems, this suggests that Grace was no more than honest in her evidence about her sister's state of health.

Today it would be simple enough for an investigating officer to test this comment about some sort of previous 'heart problems' against Vera's medical records. Since the inception of the NHS, it has been customary for the records of each patient to follow them from practice to practice, but prior to 1948 any patient records belonged to the general practitioners themselves, and were retained by them when the patient moved on. In addition, there was no statutory duty for a general practitioner to keep detailed records of patient consultations and most did not.[18] Neither of the general practitioners involved in the Croydon case kept any notes aside from their account and prescription books and nor would they necessarily have known anything about a patient's past medical history, unless it happened to emerge during a discussion of some current condition. Thus if Vera had suffered from some 'heart trouble' during the war, we cannot assume that Dr Elwell would have known about it, or that Vera would ever have volunteered this information during his previous professional dealings with her. Unfortunately, although Inspector Hedges went to endless lengths to chase up the medical histories of Grace Duff's two dead children, he never bothered to follow up this possible clue about Vera.

With or without Grace's recollections, it is clear that Vera Sidney had been unwell during the first weeks of 1929. The secretary of Croham Golf Club told the press that when they played a round of golf together in the week before she died, although he thought her much better, he understood that she had recently been suffering from influenza.[19] Her own diary refers to feeling both specifically and generally unwell for some time and all the surviving members of the family, together with Kathleen Noakes and Gwendoline Greenwell, recalled that at the very least she had been suffering from a cold.

To a modern audience, the contention that an apparently healthy, forty-year-old woman could die of influenza appears farfetched. Moreover, we now associate influenza with symptoms of the common cold, not the vomiting and diarrhoea with which Vera Sidney was afflicted. In February 1929, however, this scenario was not only possible, but a reasonably frequent occurrence, because the country was in the grip of what was then known as gastric influenza. The epidemic was so bad that on 2 February 1929 *The Times* reported that nearly 500 schools across the Greater London area had applied for temporary teachers to fill the places of those who were away from work. The day before, the same paper reported that between 4-5 per cent of London Transport staff had gone down with the disease, and throughout the first three months of the year, the newspapers carried grim statistics of the influenza death rate, not only in Britain, but also in Europe and

North America. On 16 February (the same week that Vera Sidney died) *The Times* reported that there had been 331 influenza deaths in the Greater London area alone and that doctors believed the true figure was much higher as many death certificates recorded fatal illnesses such as pneumonia and bronchitis, which had been initially brought on by catching influenza. Gastric influenza did not discriminate by age: one of the notable factors of the epidemic was the number of young victims it claimed.

The illness was well known, although it did not usually reach such epidemic proportions. During 1929 it would start to lose its 'gastric influenza' tag, when an American, Dr John Zahorsky, coined the term 'winter vomiting disease' and it is now thought that the 1929 epidemic may have been a form of non-bacterial enteritis transmitted from person to person, in all probability the illness we now know as Norovirus.[20] The symptoms of Norovirus are nausea, vomiting, diarrhoea, weakness, muscle ache, headache and fever. These were also the symptoms of gastric influenza and Vera Sidney suffered from all of them during the last hours of her life. Even today Norovirus is life threatening if the dehydration suffered as a result of vomiting and diarrhoea is not adequately treated. Ultimately, dehydration leads to heart failure – the likelihood of which is vastly increased in patients with pre-existing cardiac problems.

In 1929 there were fewer weapons at a doctor's disposal to combat severe dehydration. Moreover, some of the treatments then in vogue had an unfortunate tendency to compound the problem. Alcohol – which featured in Edmund's treatment – would also be offered to Vera in the form of both brandy and champagne, allied with the inevitable purgatives upon which 1920s medicine was so reliant, including castor oil.

With little available in the way of medical intervention, even seriously ill patients who could afford it were nursed privately at home. The level of attention Vera received from Dr Elwell could not be faulted. From being called in at around 9 o'clock on the evening of 13 February until Vera's death just over twenty-four hours later, Elwell called at the house on ten occasions, solicited the advice of both his partner and a specialist, Dr Bolton, and organised the services of two professional nurses, collecting each of them in his car and conveying them to 29 Birdhurst Rise himself.[21]

Dr Elwell's own recollections of Vera's last twenty-four hours match every symptom of gastric influenza and remarkably few which were consistent with arsenical poisoning.[22] In spite of spending a considerable amount of time with his dying patient, according to Elwell, at no stage did Vera suggest to him that she thought her illness might have been the result of something she had eaten. Moreover Elwell stated, 'in my opinion the symptoms were not consistent with poisoning,' although he did consider them consistent with gastric influenza, an illness with which it is reasonable to suppose he was familiar, as he added, 'there was a lot of gastric influenza about.'

Dr Binning was first called in to assist with the case at 4 p.m. on the last afternoon of Vera's life.[23] He stayed with her until 7.30, when he left for a couple of hours, returning at around 9.30, after which he remained with her until she died. According to the evidence he gave in 1929, during all that time he did not observe Vera passing any motions or straining to do so, vomiting or experiencing the urge to vomit – all of which are classic signs of arsenical poisoning. He did observe that she was acutely ill, in a collapsed state, with her heart dilated and her pulse feeble. Aware that Dr Elwell had already diagnosed gastric influenza, Binning readily concurred at the time, saying that he 'had no suspicion that death was other than due to natural causes.'

Norovirus can be passed on by a person who does not themselves exhibit any symptoms of the illness. It is therefore entirely possible that Vera could have contracted the illness from someone she met when she left the house on Tuesday, from a member of her own family, or from Kathleen Noakes, who prepared all the food she ate. It is also possible that what finally killed Vera was a combination of her pre-existing heart condition and food poisoning. The reheated soup must be considered suspect, particularly since Mrs Greenwell became ill soon after eating it. Whether food poisoning or gastric influenza, the dehydrating effects of either were capable of killing Vera, particularly if she was already in a debilitated condition, or suffered from a weak heart.

Vera's post-mortem threw up one more interesting possibility. Spilsbury's report refers to 'an enlarged gland at the end of the mesentery,'[24] which contained an encapsulated and partly calcified mass.'[25] Spilsbury made no attempt to elaborate on this point and was never questioned about it, but this calcified mass may have been another important indicator of Vera's general state of health. It would later be suggested that Vera's tiredness and recurrent unexplained symptoms of illness could have been due to someone progressively feeding her tiny doses of arsenic, in the weeks leading up to her death. However, the calcified mass may have been a metastatic node from a carcinoma, possibly ovarian. If Vera was suffering from some form of cancer, her constant tiredness and general weakness fall into place.

What of the arsenic found in her body? Like her brother-in-law Edmund, Vera lived in an environment filled with opportunities for arsenical encounters. During her last illness, she was prescribed both bismuth and meat juice,[26] which were among the numerous products which had a history of arsenic contamination. The deaths of Miss Barrow, Mrs Armstrong, Mrs Black and Mrs Morgan all involved bismuth and in both the latter cases, the bottles were analysed and tested positive for arsenic. When the Black case came to court, Sir William Willcox ridiculed the idea that the minute quantities of arsenic found in the bismuth could have constituted a fatal dose.[27] Typically, this statement was correct and yet misleading, for while there was insufficient arsenic in the bismuth mixture to kill Mrs Black, the fact that she was taking a mixture infused with arsenic must surely have contributed to the total amount of arsenic found in her body after death. (Mrs Black's tooth-whitening powder was also found to contain arsenic, but Dr Webster similarly assured the court that this would not have contributed to the arsenic isolated in her body.)

In Vera's case we are also faced with the involvement of Dr Ryffel, whose report not only betrays a desire to exaggerate his findings, but who was demonstrably inaccurate in his basic addition, which hardly fosters confidence in the much more complex mathematics involved in arriving at some of his figures. Just as in the case of Edmund Duff, the vast majority of the calculated total of arsenic originated in areas which required a huge multiplier, thereby vastly distorting the picture in the event that the initial reading of the arsenic mirror was incorrect. According to Ryffel, 0.93 of the 1.31 grain of arsenic he calculated to be present was in Vera's muscles. Nowhere in his evidence does Ryffel ever tell us the actual size of the muscle sample he worked on, what the factor of multiplication was, or how he determined what that figure should be – but the eventual total can only have been arrived at by multiplying his actual result by several hundred and the multiplier may have been as high as 2,000.

That Ryffel was slipshod and cavalier when examining the samples supplied to him in the Croydon case emerged particularly clearly during the evidence he gave in connection with Violet Sidney's death. When testing the residual liquid in the Metatone bottle, Ryffel used the entire sample in one go, thereby negating any possibility of checking his result. He did not measure the contents of the bottle before analysis and nor did he attempt to quantify the amount of material present in the wine glass, or even the amount of arsenic he claimed to have isolated in the wine glass, merely describing it as 'rich in arsenic', a phrase suggestive of wilful exaggeration and effectively meaningless.[28]

Another question mark over Ryffel's competency arose in respect of the arsenic found in both Vera and Violet's fingernails. By 1929 it was well known that arsenic takes several days after ingestion to arrive in a person's fingernails, so its presence or absence in the nails was crucially important in determining at what point a person had first been exposed to the poison. Ryffel's findings were useless in this respect, because he had not detached the nails from the surrounding skin before running his tests.[29] Nor was Ryffel able to say exactly how much arsenic he had detected – there was 'more in the nails than the hair', but 'I cannot give a figure for the amounts'.[30]

Alone among the medical witnesses, Dr Bronte attempted to focus attention on the potential significance of this, pointing out that there was always a delay between arsenic's arrival in the body and its absorption into the nails and hair,[31] but hardly anyone appears to have been much interested in the point and in his next report to his superiors, Inspector Hedges grumbled that, 'Dr Bronte has not assisted us in this case and if I may say so, his evidence has somewhat complicated the matter…' going on to add, 'No doubt other evidence will be forthcoming which will negate his opinion.'[32]

If Dr Bronte did not help the police case, Ryffel was not much better. He fared badly under the cross-examination of Mr Fearnley-Whittingstall and it was perhaps for this reason that he was not called upon to undertake the analysis of Edmund Duff's organs, when that body was exhumed, two days after Ryffel's first court appearance in connection with the Violet Sidney enquiry.

When he appeared at the Croydon inquests, Dr Ryffel appears to have been at the start of his career with the Home Office and described himself as the Junior Home Office Analyst – he never made it to Senior Home Office Analyst.[33] At the Sidney inquests in 1929, he told the court that he had been undertaking the analysis of human tissue for coroners' courts for two years, and this had included 'several cases of poisoning.'[34] As already discussed, a claim from a Home Office expert to have handled cases of 'poisoning' was not necessarily the same as their having had experience of arsenical poisoning and although such experience cannot be discounted, there is no surviving evidence that, prior to the Croydon cases, Ryffel had ever been involved in detailed analyses to calculate the amount of arsenic in a body.[35] Moreover, his elementary error over the fingernails implies a lack of experience or understanding of this particular kind of case. After Croydon, the Home Office did not call on Ryffel for their big arsenic cases again, preferring to rely on Roche Lynch.[36]

Essentially, the assumption that Vera Sidney met her death at the hand of a poisoner relied on the evidence of a man whose casual methods would have horrified the average chemistry student, and who was so slipshod about his evidence that he would present, as sworn testimony, a report in which the figures did not add up.

CHAPTER SIXTEEN

A COLOSSAL ERROR?

In July 1929 the *Sunday Express* was running a series 'Famous Miscarriages of Justice' which included the case of Benjamin Russell, whose farm labourer, Daniel Leany, had been hanged on the mistaken assumption that he had poisoned his employer in 1826. Thus by pure coincidence, in an edition of the paper which included the latest report of the Croydon inquests, another page carried the headline 'Doctor's Colossal Error in Murder Trial' and in the text beneath it appeared the telling line: 'the doctor was sufficiently important and wise looking to impress the majority of his audience.'[1]

In a similar coincidence of timing, the *Sunday People* happened to be running a series devoted to the great barrister Sir Edward Marshall-Hall and three weeks before the aforementioned item in the *Express*, the *People* had devoted a double-page spread to his unsuccessful defence of Frederick Seddon, hanged for poisoning Eliza Barrow in 1911, which quoted Sir William Willcox admitting of Marshall-Hall's cross-examination, 'He very nearly tied me up. I don't think I've ever been so nearly trapped as I was then … it was extraordinarily clever of him.'[2] Trapped? Surely trapped is a rather strange way of putting it if one's evidence is merely a factual report, without embellishment, concealment or any attempt at misrepresentation?

Did any citizen of Britain read the reports coming out of the Croydon inquest side by side with these features and begin to wonder if there was something to be learned? For those with slightly longer memories, there had been a report in 1924 of a French chemist, whose original life sentence had been quashed, now that doctors had discovered that the 2mg of arsenic found in his wife's body at the post-mortem conducted in 1878, far from being indicative of murder, were lower than the amount which might normally be expected.[3]

Another story which had contextual bearing on the events in Croydon surfaced in April 1929, during newspaper coverage of a Royal Commission report on various aspects of policing, which had included, among its criticisms of the police, the allegation that they forced witnesses into making incriminating statements. An anonymous Scotland Yard detective responded to this in terms which could have been drafted by Fred Hedges, complaining that the police were being asked to 'exercise ridiculous caution' when interviewing witnesses, coupled with the claim that there would be a lot more unsolved murders, 'unless there is an end to the recent tendency to criticise police methods ... It is often impossible to bring a murderer to justice, unless a certain amount of pressure is brought to bear on witnesses to reveal what they know.'[4]

From the moment the local police were alerted in the immediate aftermath of Violet Sidney's death, the Croydon case developed into an unstoppable bandwagon. Already convinced he was dealing with a big murder enquiry, Hedges' suspicions escalated into certainties following the results of the post-mortems conducted on Vera and Violet's remains. Unfortunately, the doctors who produced those results had already made up their minds what they were going to find, based on the suspicions of the police. Hedges reinforced the experts, who in turn reinforced Hedges, to the degree that long before Edmund Duff's body was exhumed, Hedges would repeatedly write that he was sure arsenic would be found in it.

Although Dr Jackson endeavoured to be fair and objective, it simply did not occur to him to encourage the jury to question the actual cause of death, because once Spilsbury mentioned the word 'arsenic' and the analysts had produced their figures to back him up, it was universally accepted that death had been due to arsenic and, in the fashion of the Emperor's New Clothes, everyone else simply fell into line, adding their voices to the unanimous chorus of agreement. This attitude was particularly apparent on the occasion when Ryffel demonstrated his Metatone experiments in court, and Dr Jackson was overheard remarking to Mr Fearnley-Whittingstall, 'We don't know exactly what was done and we have to assume things.'[5] Needless to say, no court of any kind should merely 'assume things' but the problem with the Croydon case was that it rested on one assumption after another.

Most accounts of the Croydon poisonings begin with Edmund Duff's return home from Hampshire in April 1928, but the true story has its genesis almost a year later, when Violet Sidney sat alone in the dining room of 29 Birdhurst Rise, mourning the death of her daughter Vera. The Sidney family were unusually devoted to one another; this was not just their own assessment, but much to Inspector Hedges' irritation, it was without exception the opinion of everyone he approached who knew them well or had worked for them. The closest of these relationships was the one between Violet and her younger daughter Vera. Clara Collett, who lived and worked at 29 Birdhurst Rise for fifteen months, remarked that on the rare occasions when Violet and Vera exchanged 'sharp words' it 'would be only momentary and the next moment they would be loving [hugging] one another.'[6]

Might Violet Sidney have become sufficiently downhearted that she took her own life? She was undoubtedly depressed by Vera's death. The letter she wrote on the last morning of her life was a sad letter, essentially full of misery and tinged with self pity. Indeed when Amy Sidney received it, she assumed on hearing of Violet's death that she *had* killed herself – so the idea of Violet's suicide was not all that fantastic to some members of her family.[7] Tom mentioned during one court appearance that Violet had stated an intention to kill herself if the Germans invaded, and in spite of strongly protesting that her mother's religious convictions precluded any possibility of her committing suicide, Grace did concede that the idea had gone through her mind on the night of Vera's death, when her mother had been 'beside herself' with grief.[8]

In Violet Sidney's world, ladies did not live lonely lives. Until Vera's death, Violet had never lived alone. She had been raised in a large family and when she first married there were a handful of servants living on the premises to minister to her needs. When Thomas Sidney deserted her, she still had her three young children, together with a posse of live-in domestics,[9] and even with Tom and Grace gone she still had Vera. It was a common practice for the youngest daughter to stay at home – often unmarried – to be with her widowed mother; Violet would never have foreseen the possibility of being left by herself, until Vera suddenly predeceased her.

Even Kate Noakes was not going to be there much longer. Mrs Noakes was working her notice; indeed, on the morning of her death, Violet had asked Grace to enquire at the Registry for another servant.[10] This question of Mrs Noakes' departure had hovered around the inquest without Coroner Jackson ever looking very deeply into it. Presumably he saw little to be gained from pursuing the point, but it is possible that he should have done.

Kathleen Noakes had definitely given notice on 14 or 15 February, but for some reason Violet made no attempt to replace her until 5 March, when the month's notice had a mere ten days left to run. This is a curious omission for a woman who was normally well organised. Had Violet assumed the notice withdrawn? Kate Noakes had given notice on a previous occasion,[11] then changed her mind and Violet believed her to be a homeless widow, rather than a woman who had never intended to work at no.29 on anything other than a temporary basis, so perhaps Violet thought this latest threat to leave had been made in the heat of the moment and was not seriously meant.

Maybe at some point on the morning of 5 March there had been a conversation between mistress and maid, during which Violet realised that her general servant really was leaving – and that her departure was imminent. If this conversation had taken place, it would be entirely in character for Kathleen Noakes – who was always extremely touchy and evasive about the whole question of her notice – not to mention it later, particularly if Violet had appeared in any way surprised or upset by the exchange. Such a conversation can only ever be conjecture, but what evidence there is supports it, and if Violet suddenly discovered that she had barely a week and a half to replace her cook-general, it may have helped plunge her deeper into despair.

By the end of the 1920s, it was becoming increasingly difficult to get 'good help.' Other employment opportunities were opening up for young women and 'the servant problem' was a middle class preoccupation. Violet had never lived without servants and the possibility of being unable to find someone satisfactory to fill the vacancy was, at the very least, another dark cloud on the horizon. Even filling the vacancy meant training someone else into the ways of the household, instructing her on where things were kept and what was required.

Without Vera, Violet had become terribly isolated. Her last close friend had died at the end of 1928 – apart from her immediate family, the only callers were those who came out of duty, such as the curate's wife.[12] Margaret came a couple of times each week and Tom and Grace popped in every day – but never for more than twenty minutes or half an hour at a time. For the past three weeks Violet had not been well enough to leave the house: apart from her own weakness, the terrible cold was a huge deterrent – the papers were reporting cases of old ladies collapsing in the streets on account of it.[13] The long lonely hours must have dragged interminably, with nothing to do, no one to talk to and this constant feeling of ill health, the dizziness, the problems with her bowels.

Violet's unhappy state during the last fortnight of her life was a repeated theme among the various witnesses. In his statement on 11 March, Dr Elwell explained that Mrs Sidney had been too ill to attend her daughter's funeral, and that a professional nurse had been engaged to stay in the house with her for the first week after Vera's death.[14] Her loss of appetite and consequent loss of weight were remarked upon by both Grace Duff and Kathleen Noakes, who suggested to her mistress that she might like to take breakfast in bed, only to be told by Violet that if she started taking her meals in bed, she was afraid she 'might never get up again.'[15]

In a letter written on 24th February, breaking the news of Vera's death, she wrote, *I hardly have the courage to tell you my terrible news. I have lost my darling Vera – the one I love most in the world. I don't know how I can live without her.* To Grace, Violet had said that she did not know how she would go on living, to Tom, 'I can't go on without Vera,' and to Kathleen Noakes, 'however shall I live without my daughter?'[16]

On the morning of her death, after she had written declining her sister-in-law's invitation to stay, Dr Elwell popped in and said she was looking a bit better. After he had gone, did Violet ponder the question: better for what exactly? What was left to her now but more waiting, listening to the tick of the clock, marking the hours until it was time to face the next meal for which she had no appetite, the next brief visit from Tom, or Margaret, or Grace. During his visit, Dr Elwell reminded her about the tonic[17] – and perhaps this suggested something: a way out.

Did Violet poison her own medicine? She probably did not know much about poisons – a little knowledge garnered from theatre and opera perhaps – which would have suggested to her that any effects would be dramatic and immediate. But after taking the medicine, apart from experiencing a moment's revulsion at the unaccustomed taste, nothing happened at all. Soon afterwards Mrs Noakes brought in the lunch, which Violet ate as usual, perhaps wondering why she had not dropped down dead.

Shortly after lunch the arsenic did take effect, its symptoms painful and embarrassing. Grace's arrival coincided with their onset and, entering the dining room, she immediately asked Violet what was the matter.[18] Violet at once replied that she thought she had taken poison – in spite of which she tried to tell Grace that she did not want a doctor called, which was slightly odd in itself, given that Violet was not generally averse to calling a doctor.

Up until the 1960s and beyond, many people would habitually say they had been 'poisoned' merely on having eaten something which violently disagreed with them, but throughout the afternoon, Violet Sidney appeared to go further, persistently trying to tell everyone that she has been poisoned – even pointing them all in the direction of the medicine. Had she changed her mind – seen the anguished reactions of her family and remembered after all how much she was loved?

It would be entirely understandable if Violet could not bring herself to tell them what she had done; suicide was a sin and in the past she herself had criticised others for taking the coward's way out. It could be argued that when Violet realised she was dying, she would not have kept silent on the source of the poison, knowing the terrible position in which her family would be placed if she should die and traces of poison were subsequently found in the medicine bottle. But this is to grant her the benefit of foresight – Violet was not to know that the bottle would be sent for analysis, that it was possible to extract arsenic from an apparently empty bottle, or even that there would be an inquest into her death. If she gave the matter any thought at all, Violet may have assumed that her death would be attributed to natural causes, the certificate issued by obliging Dr Elwell, to save the family any public embarrassment of an inquest. According to Margaret Sidney, her mother-in-law had been somewhat irritated by Dr Elwell's refusal to issue a death certificate when Edmund Duff died, as she felt it was the business of the family doctor to ensure that the family did not have to endure a public inquest.[19]

There is an interesting glimmer of support for the theory of self administration in the description of the events given by Grace Duff when she appeared in court on 22 April 1929. In the first statement Grace made to the police on 7 March, she said that when she arrived and asked her mother what was wrong, Violet said, 'I think I have had some poison.' Tom, Dr Binning and Dr Elwell all variously describe Violet using similar words, but in her evidence on 22 April, Grace describes the scene slightly differently.[20] It is in fact an altogether more thorough description of events, which begins with her arriving in the dining room and finding her mother seated in an attitude which suggested to Grace that she might have had a stroke. When Grace asked her mother what was the matter, 'she looked up at me and she said "I have had some poison." Then she sat back.' There is something in the tone of this description which has a ring of genuine remembrance – Grace remembering her mother lifting her head, then looking down again. Were those Violet's exact words? Not that she 'thought' or 'believed' she had 'been poisoned' but the definite knowledge that she *had* had some poison: a confident statement, made because she had administered it to herself?

There was certainly something very odd about Violet's final dose of medicine, and it wasn't just the taste. During the speculations about the medicine, everyone appears to have operated on the premise that Violet was down to her last two teaspoonfuls and that her killer slipped some arsenic into this final dose – but the evidence about the medicine does not necessarily support this. According to Dr Elwell's testimony,[21] when he called to see Violet on 27 February, she told him she had not started taking the medicine. When he made another routine visit on the final morning of Violet's life, she said that she had 'not been very regular with it', at which he jokingly pointed out that it wouldn't do her much good if she did not take it. According to Grace Duff,[22] during her first visit to the house on 5 March, Violet mentioned that she had not taken her medicine that day – implying that she had been dosing herself, but had forgotten to do so that morning.

From the evidence of both Dr Elwell and the chemist Fredrick Rose, we know that if Violet had taken the Metatone as directed, it would have been finished well before 5 March, which at the very least supports the fact that Violet had not taken it regularly. It also seems odd that Violet would bother to tell her daughter and the doctor that she had not been taking the medicine, if in fact she had nearly finished it. All this evidence indicates that by lunchtime on 5 March, there might have been rather more than two teaspoons of mixture left in the bottle. However, this was definitely the point at which Violet finished the bottle, because Kathleen Noakes was always clear that when she entered the room and found Violet pulling faces, she could see that the dose had emptied the bottle. When Grace arrived a few minutes later, she too observed an empty bottle and from then onwards, every single observer confirms that the bottle was empty.

One scenario which no one ever seems to have allowed for was that Violet may have taken either a very large dose, or even the whole bottle at a single go, in order to disguise the ingestion of some other substance. If Violet had been in the habit of taking her medicine in a wine glass, even intermittently, then it is somewhat surprising that Kate Noakes had absolutely no recollection of washing one up. When specifically asked about this, she confirmed that she had not been aware of Mrs Sidney using a wine glass in the preceding few days and it may be significant that there had been no definite sightings of the medicine bottle or a wine glass until the day of Violet's death, when the bottle, teaspoon and wine glass all suddenly appeared in the dining room. An assumption was made that Violet had consistently obtained her own wine glass from the pantry, taken the medicine in her bedroom, then washed the glass and teaspoon herself. This is entirely possible, but if that had been Violet's habit, why did she change her routine on this one particular day? Moreover, if this last dose of medicine had suddenly developed a visible white sediment, it is somewhat curious that Violet took it at all and even more curious that she made no comment about its altered appearance later.

One of the arguments against Violet Sidney having poisoned herself was the question of procuring the arsenic with which to do it. Following the discovery of Eureka Weed Killer and Noble's Liquid Weed Killer at Tom and Grace's respective premises, Dr Ryffel embarked on a series of experiments to see whether adding either substance to Metatone would reproduce a liquid of identical colour and consistency to that observed in the Metatone bottle after Violet's death. The fact that he was unable to achieve this, even after trying a variety of different permutations and leaving mixtures to stand for several days, leads to the glaringly obvious conclusion that the arsenic present in Violet's tonic did not derive from either of the weedkillers, but had been obtained from some completely different source.

In spite of Hedges' initial claim that he had searched the house from top to bottom, the cursory nature of his search became increasingly apparent as the weeks went by, with even the agents charged with preparing Violet's house for a tenant producing a substantial quantity of bottles and jars from various nooks and crannies, months after her death. The statements of her servants and surviving children all point to the fact that Violet's home was overflowing with part-used and empty bottles and jars and that Hedges' selective haul was merely the tip of a very large iceberg. Throughout the enquiry the police focussed on the usual arsenic-based suspects – weedkiller and rat poison – but there was another possible source of arsenic which was apparently never considered by those investigating the Croydon case.

Today we associate the use of arsenic for cosmetic purposes with the Victorian era, when many women routinely used arsenic in small quantities to whiten their complexions. Two of the best known arsenic *causes célèbres*, Madeleine Smith and Florence Maybrick, freely admitted that they used arsenic for this purpose. It is too easy to perceive the 1920s as part of the modern age, quite separate from the century which had preceded it – but every Victorian lady did not die *en masse* with the passing of the old queen and nor did their habits and ideas. As late as 1897 prosecutions were still being brought against chemists selling arsenical beauty soap, not because it was toxic, but because it did not contain enough arsenic.[23] Arsenic continued to be a popular cosmetic throughout the Edwardian era and well into the 1920s, particularly with older women, who still favoured a pale complexion.

As arsenic became more difficult to obtain and its dangers better known, there was a public perception that such usage was dying out, but for many women who had been using homemade arsenical preparations for years, any suggestion of prohibition must have appeared no more than so much namby pamby nonsense. Violet Sidney was a Victorian through and through – a direct contemporary of Florence Maybrick, who was in fact three years younger than Violet and outlived her by more than a decade. The use of arsenic cosmetics was not confined to women who became involved in high profile murder enquiries or even particularly exceptional – at the inquest into the death of forty-four-year-old Hilda Bagwell in 1911,[24] her regular use of cosmetic arsenical preparations was mentioned. Here, then, is another almost exact contemporary of Violet's, still using arsenic long after the first flush of girlhood had departed.

Having settled on a beauty routine in their teens, many women never modified it, irrespective of changing fashions. Was Violet still using arsenic, perhaps mixed with face powder? In evidence, Grace Duff said her mother was 'old-fashioned and secretive' and the secrets of a lady's dressing table are generally hers alone. Violet's cosmetic preparations may have lasted her for years. She was 'careful' with everything and her face powder would have been no exception. When the police searched 29 Birdhurst Rise, how much attention did they pay to the contents of Violet's dressing table? Face powder does not appear among the lists of items passed on for analysis at any stage in the enquiry.[25]

CHAPTER SEVENTEEN

'DO YOU READ STORIES...?'

In August 1929 a general practitioner in Kent sent a urine sample belonging to one of his patients, Mrs Annie Maria Luck, for analysis at St Bartholomew's Hospital in London.[1] The sample tested positive for arsenic, a result which coincided with Annie Luck's death. Her vigilant GP, Dr Hepper, promptly informed the local police and refused to issue a death certificate. However, at the post-mortem there were no obvious signs of poisoning and the local pathologist concluded that seventy-three-year-old Mrs Luck had succumbed to a longstanding kidney complaint. As a precaution, organ samples were sent to Dr Roche Lynch for analysis, but he failed to detect any arsenic. In spite of this, when Dr Hepper appeared at the inquest, possibly inspired by the recent events in Croydon, he stuck to his guns, insisting that the unfortunate woman had been poisoned.

In the face of what had the potential to become a serious situation, the deceased's relatives had retained professional counsel, who, clearly exasperated with Dr Hepper, asked, 'Do you read stories where the police are always wrong and the amateur detective always right?' Hepper admitted that he did.

Owing to Dr Hepper's statement to the police and his continued intransigence at the inquest, the coroner felt obliged to adjourn proceedings until Dr Roche Lynch could appear in person. At the resumed inquest, Roche Lynch explained that there was nothing out of the ordinary in the urine analysis, as it was 'quite common to detect traces of arsenic in normal people.' The jury belatedly returned a verdict of death by natural causes.

Mrs Luck's relatives had cause to count themselves fortunate. Had circumstances been slightly different – had Mrs Luck for example not been elderly and already suffering from an obviously fatal condition, had another relative coincidentally died in the recent past, or the Kent police called upon the services of a different pathologist, they might have found themselves cast in the leading roles of yet another arsenic drama.

Many of the alleged murders discussed in these pages originated as a direct result of unsubstantiated suspicion, rumour or gossip, often traceable to a single individual. Herbert Armstrong would never have stood trial, but for the obsessive machinations of Fred Davies. Annie Hearn owed her time in the dock to the spite of her dead friend's brother. Harold Greenwood's swift remarriage offended the village busybodies and rumours began to fly. Beatrice Pace became the victim of her mother-in-law's persistent accusations. In the Croydon case too, a single individual appears to have been responsible for planting the seeds of suspicion which drove a loving family apart. By the end the Sidneys were openly accusing one another of the crime – even Grace's uncle told her at one stage that he had come to the conclusion that she must be the guilty party,[2] because once everyone accepted that Edmund Duff had been poisoned, the finger of suspicion pointed inexorably to Grace; but the whole notion that Edmund had been poisoned was almost certainly incorrect, as was the theory that Vera's death was brought about as a result of arsenic administration.

The death of Violet Sidney is generally perceived as the one which finally aroused suspicions, but several weeks before Violet's death, one man was already whispering in someone's ear. In statements to the police and sworn depositions in court, Tom Sidney claimed that on the day after his sister Vera's death, Dr Binning remarked that 'if he had not known the family better, he would have suspected arsenic.'[3] Tom does not appear to have initially taken this seriously – perhaps dismissing it as rather black humour – but significantly, it was again Binning who first put to him the similarity between Edmund's death and that of his mother and sister.[4]

When he appeared in court on 16 July 1929, Dr Binning was questioned about his alleged remark on the day after Vera's death, but claimed that he could not remember making it. He admitted that he 'might' have said it, but was at pains to assure the coroner that whatever he had or had not said, he had not in fact suspected arsenical poisoning in Vera's case until after Mrs Sidney's death.[5] This lack of genuine suspicion is borne out by his witness statement, made on 7 March, when he said that at the time of Vera's death, he considered it due to heart failure following gastric influenza and, 'I had not the slightest suspicion of poisoning.'

So was the initial remark about arsenic some kind of joke? It seems a strange thing to say to a sick patient who has just lost his sister. We know that Binning called on Tom Sidney that day, because not only did the doctor and his patient mention it, but Margaret Sidney and the daily help also confirmed the visit in their statements. There were no witnesses to this or any of the conversations in which Tom alleges that his family doctor was pushing the idea that his relatives had been poisoned – but it is difficult to see why Tom would invent these conversations, and circumstantial support for their existence can be found elsewhere.

When under oath or providing a signed witness statement, Dr Binning was invariably at pains to deny that he had entertained any suspicions whatsoever about poisoning prior to Violet's death, but when Inspector Hedges made his first report on the case,[6] he mentions that in a 'confidential conversation', Dr Binning had informed him that he and Dr Elwell were 'strongly suspicious about the similarity of the symptoms of Edmund Duff, Vera and Violet Sidney.' During this off-the-record chat, Binning told Hedges that ever since Edmund's death, both doctors had been 'extremely cautious' about their dealings with the

Duff and Sidney families – a claim which appears somewhat ridiculous in the light of the fact that Dr Elwell had no hesitation in issuing a death certificate for Vera and had made a lengthy statement to Hedges dated 11 March, which indicated that he had never entertained the slightest suspicions whatsoever about her death or Edmund's.[7]

John Binning's involvement in the Croydon case is often seen as marginal. In at least one television adaptation, he was cut out of the story altogether.[8] None of the three deceased were his patients, and he only became involved in Edmund and Violet's cases because his partner happened to be unavailable, and in Vera's because Dr Elwell invited him to give a second opinion; yet in the final analysis, John Binning may have been the most important player of all.

When Richard Whittington-Egan was researching his book on the Croydon arsenic case, he tracked John Binning to his retirement home in Cornwall,[9] where the doctor agreed not only to discuss the case, but also to produce a written report for inclusion in the finished book. Even making due allowance for the fact that Dr Binning was attempting to recall events which had taken place more than thirty years before, this report includes so many statements which contradict the original evidence given in 1929, that the motives of its author must be called into question.

According to Dr Binning, Edmund Duff was a 'beastly' man and he opens his report with a description of a consultation which allegedly took place between himself and Edmund Duff on the morning of Duff's departure for the Hampshire fishing trip in 1928, at which time Duff was supposedly complaining of diarrhoea and abdominal pain.[10] As this episode is never referred to in any of the witness statements made at the time (in fact all witnesses agreed that Edmund was in the best of health on the morning he left home and had specifically not been exhibiting any such symptoms) and, moreover, since Dr Binning was not actually Edmund Duff's medical practitioner, it is reasonable to assume that this episode never took place.

Binning then goes on to describe Edmund's last illness in completely different terms to that described at the original inquest in 1928, and follows this up with the claim that he knew the Duffs' married life together was unhappy, not least because he had examined Mrs Duff and observed bruises inflicted by her husband during forced sexual intercourse. Had such an event occurred, it is remarkable that Dr Binning (who had the ear of Inspector Hedges throughout the long investigation) never troubled to mention it at the time. This part of the account smacks suspiciously of a 'borrowed' memory from testimony provided by Dr Elwell who, as Grace's own doctor, was far more likely to be examining her and had indeed reported once seeing some bruises.

Another instance of Binning writing himself into the story comes with the allegation that he carried out chemistry experiments on behalf of the police, during which he succeeded in replicating the sediment in Violet's tonic – again there is no substantiating evidence for this and little reason why Binning should have been asked to undertake this when professional analysts were already involved.

Binning's account of Vera's death is similarly at variance with the details provided by contemporaneous witness accounts (including his own) while his description of the day of Violet's death includes even greater flights of fancy.

In Binning's 1962 description of the three deaths the presence of Dr Elwell scarcely registers on the reader, with Binning constantly allocating himself a starring role in the drama. He allegedly has a conversation with Sir Bernard Spilsbury (with whom he claims a close acquaintance) in which he explained that Edmund Duff's symptoms were identical to those of his mother and sister-in-law and, 'as a result of our conversations, Sir Bernard got permission to exhume Vera's body and later Duff's.' This is of course totally false. Spilsbury had no part in arranging exhumations, but within this falsehood there is an incidental truth. From the very first it appears to have been Dr Binning who encouraged Hedges to believe that Edmund Duff had been poisoned and to agitate for his exhumation.

Binning mentioned his suspicions about Edmund Duff in his first statement, made the day after Violet Sidney's death. Hedges alluded to these suspicions in the confidential report on the case which he wrote on 13 March. On 23 March Hedges recorded a further conversation with Binning, in which the latter had stated himself in favour of exhuming Edmund Duff's body, claiming that Duff's symptoms of poisoning had been even more marked than those of Violet or Vera.[11] By the time he wrote his next report, Hedges had engaged in 'another long conversation' with Dr Binning[12] who 'is still convinced that if Duff is exhumed, arsenic will be found in his organs.' This is particularly astonishing when viewed alongside the evidence Binning was actually prepared to give on oath before the coroner, which makes it abundantly obvious that he had no clear recollection of what Edmund Duff's symptoms actually were. In his July 1929 court appearance, Dr Binning 'could not recall' when vomiting and diarrhoea first occurred, but by the time he wrote his report in 1962 he could remember perfectly and added for good measure that he had observed all three victims suffering from tenesmus – a symptom singularly absent from anyone's recollections at the time.[13]

Equally suggestive is the fact that Dr Elwell is never on record as expressing any concerns about the death of Edmund Duff, until after the authorities decided to organise an exhumation – but then neither does Dr Elwell appear to have shared his one-time partner's fixation with the occult[14] or his evident desire to be at the centre of a thrilling criminal case. That Binning became a close confidante of Inspector Hedges is evidenced by Hedges' own reports, which more often than not refer to conversations he has been having with Dr Binning. Although Hedges initially ascribed his suspicions about the death of Miss Kelvey and the Duffs' two daughters to an anonymous tip off, the fact that Dr Binning's 1962 report includes the belief that it might still be possible to solve the case if Miss Kelvey's remains were to be exhumed tells its own story. Nor is it difficult to suggest an identity for the unnamed medical man who advised Hedges that the symptoms which Suzanne Duff exhibited before her death were not those of meningitis, but rather arsenical poisoning – in spite of assurances to the contrary from the two doctors (Elwell and Poynton) who actually attended the child.[15]

It was Binning who on his own initiative took samples of food and vomit from 29 Birdhurst Rise, to say nothing of the infamous Metatone bottle, all of which he retained at his premises overnight before handing them over to the police, and Binning who elected to attend both the exhumations, in spite of the fact that none of the three deceased had been his patients.

Binning appears to have struck up a close relationship with Hedges from the outset. Hedges was perhaps drawn to Binning, firstly because he was the only person closely involved who never really came under suspicion, but more importantly because Binning appeared to be 'on his side', constantly fuelling and reinforcing his suspicions, while taking an unusually active interest in the investigation. In various reports, Hedges freely quotes Binning's opinions on the case, at one point mentioning apropos of nothing in particular that 'Dr Binning is confident that Thomas Sidney is an innocent man'.[16] It is clear that Hedges frequently popped in to see Binning, both to pump him for further revelations and apparently to discuss the progress of the case with him – an involvement which Binning appears to have relished.

In 1932 a survey among Metropolitan police officers established that between 80-90 per cent of recruits had not gone beyond elementary education.[17] It was a time when promotion still relied principally on longevity of service and 'a good character'. Levels of efficiency were uncertain and morale was low; the situation was so serious that in 1933 the Home Office set up a committee to enquire into 'the whole field of detective work'.[18]

Hedges had worked his way up from the bottom and was acutely conscious of class and social issues – forever categorising witnesses as 'refined' or feeling it necessary to describe Tom Sidney as 'a high class entertainer' (as opposed to a 'low' music hall type). In 1929 a doctor's time was very obviously a valuable commodity and their social standing in the community rather greater than it is in today's less deferential society. The reader can almost sense Hedges mentally tugging his forelock as he writes in his first report 'Dr Elwell and Dr Binning are highly respected, medical gentlemen, and I may say that they have treated me throughout my enquiries with frankness…'[19] Accustomed to being patronised by people who thought they were his betters (stories of policemen being referred to the servants' entrance are far from apocryphal) Hedges would have warmed to Dr Binning's willingness to assist with the investigation, perhaps even been flattered by the level of attention he was receiving from the doctor.

Dr Binning's enthusiasm for active involvement in the case saw him leap to centre stage again, when during the preparation of Richard Whittington-Egan's book he not only provided his written account, but agreed to accompany Whittington-Egan on a second visit to Grace Duff (the first having ended in Mrs Duff shutting the door in the author's face).[20]

As the man whose unwarranted suspicions first encouraged a police investigation into the deaths of Vera Sidney and Edmund Duff, John Binning does indeed deserve a central place in the Croydon story. It is not a particularly creditable place – for here is someone who, while publicly admitting on oath that he had no clear recollection of observing any symptoms consistent with poisoning, was conniving behind the scenes to widen the scope of an investigation into the probable suicide of one elderly lady, until it became a multiple murder investigation involving up to half a dozen victims. Set against the extensive testimony which survives from 1928-9, Binning's 1962 report contains what can only be described as a disturbing level of falsehood and invention.

In an afterword written by Grace Duff's daughter Mary,[21] it is claimed that Dr Binning made romantic overtures to the widowed Grace – overtures which were rejected, not least because Binning was a married man. Intriguingly Mary also mentions that Dr Elwell not only stated that Binning was 'besotted' with her mother, but that Elwell actually suspected him of being the murderer – a suggestion Robert Elwell would go on to repeat to Richard Whittington-Egan some thirty years later.[22]

In common with everyone else, by the end of the enquiry Dr Elwell was under the impression that three murders had occurred and thus that someone among the small pool of suspects *had* to be responsible – and he considered the person most capable of committing the crime was his one-time partner. By 1961 Elwell and Binning had no good to say of one another. It is clear, however, that unlike his ex-partner, Elwell had little desire to discuss the case with Richard Whittington-Egan and was unshakeable in his belief that Grace Duff was completely innocent.[23] Robert Elwell emerges throughout as a conscientious man, objective in his assessments and generally well regarded, despite various allegations linking him romantically with Grace Duff. It is difficult to imagine him saying, as John Binning did, that Edmund Duff 'was a brute, who behaved like a beast and deserved to die'[24] – a strangely passionate comment to make about a man who was no more than a slight acquaintance.

Was Dr Binning obsessed or infatuated with Grace Duff? Grace was evidently something of a beauty, who emerges as a charming, intelligent woman. Her sister-in-law, Margaret, described her in 1929 as 'brilliant' and 'well read'[25] while her daughter tells us that Grace was a popular woman, who had many friends, had been Head Girl at her school and had passed the entrance exams for Oxford – although she did not go on to university.[26] Mary also described her mother as 'a happy-go-lucky person' and glimpses of this Grace emerge clearly from the police files: someone who did not worry about money or convention, who, unlike the careful Violet and Vera, did not keep accounts, and whose home 'always had an atmosphere of fun and laughter'.[27] According to her daughter, Grace was 'generous to a fault' and this is borne out by her impulsive gift of half a crown to her mother's housekeeper on Christmas Day and the survival of a letter to one of her ex-servants, in the police files.[28]

John Binning's role in the Croydon case may have owed its origins to his interest in, and rejection by, its leading lady, or else to a perverse desire for the second-hand excitement of playing detective. It is also entirely possible that he managed to convince himself that Edmund Duff and Vera Sidney had been poisoned – his initial suspicions apparently confirmed by the Home Office reports

– even if his actual recollections of their symptoms were vague. Nor is it difficult to see what put the idea of arsenic into his head in the first place. There had been a series of sensational poisoning trials throughout the 1920s. In the summer following Edmund Duff's death, the national papers carried reports of the now largely forgotten Llewellyn case;[29] in January 1929 the death of Harold Greenwood was widely reported, recalling his trial for the alleged poisoning of his wife;[30] and in the same month *The Times* reported that Sir William Willcox had delivered a lecture to the BMA in London on 'Secret Poisoning'. Binning may even have attended. If not, perhaps he read an account of the occasion, noting Willcox's confident assertion that there had been such great advances as to make it practically impossible for poisoners to evade detection in modern Britain, thanks to 'the careful investigation of the Home Office and other official authorities'.

Or perhaps there was another motive – a doctor who unmasked a murderer stood to become something of a local celebrity. Any doctor might guess this, but a doctor in Croydon had particular reason to be aware of it.

In October 1902 Robert Marsh of Longfellow Road, Croydon, was so worried about the condition of his recently married daughter, Maud, that he asked his own family practitioner, Dr Francis Grapel, to call on the young woman at her new home in Southwark.[31] Grapel duly visited and decided that Maud was suffering from some acute form of poisoning. He promised to return and see what he could do for her, but next day came news that Maud had died, prompting Grapel to send a telegram to the Southwark coroner, urgently suggesting that the body be tested for arsenic – which action was later commended as bringing a murderer to justice.

Thanks to Grapel's intervention the body was tested for various poisons, and although no arsenic was discovered, it was swiftly established that Maud Marsh had been poisoned with antimony, administered by her 'husband' George Chapman, a.k.a. Severin Klosowski. On further investigation it emerged that Mr Klosowski had not only 'married' then murdered Maud for her money, but had similarly disposed of two previous 'wives', Isabella Spink and Bessie Taylor.

Dr Grapel's part in apprehending a serial killer made headlines and it is inconceivable that Dr Binning was unaware of the story, because his famous colleague was still practising in Croydon when Binning arrived there and continued to do so for a number of years afterwards.[32] It is quite likely that the two men encountered one another and even if they did not, Dr Binning would surely have heard about the famous 'arsenic' telegram.

According to her daughter, when Grace Duff knew she was close to death, she said, 'Now I shall never know who did those terrible things.'[33] The 'terrible things' of which she spoke were the supposed murders of three members of her family – yet equally terrible were the other 'things' – the ordeal to which she and her family were subjected throughout 1929, the notoriety which accompanied it and the ultimate destruction of Grace's relationship with her brother Tom.

Until the deaths of Edmund, Vera and Violet, the Sidney-Duff clan had been a happy family. One ex-servant, Evelyn King, spoke for many others when she told the police: 'I never saw a more happy family than the Sidneys and the Duffs.'[34] This is indeed the picture that emerges, of Christmas parties and Sunday teas at Violet's, the adults discussing the books they had read and going off to the theatre together; the older children arriving to borrow the sledge from their grandmother's shed, watching tennis from the vantage point of her back garden, running upstairs to admire Aunt Vera's golf trophies, or into the kitchen to see a litter of kittens. The word most frequently used to describe them was 'devoted'.[35] Even with three of its key members gone, the households of Tom and Grace might have continued to enjoy this golden relationship, had it not been for the schism which arose out of misplaced allegations of murder.

In retirement Fred Hedges was wont to claim that Grace Duff was 'the luckiest woman alive'.[36] His lack of objectivity clearly remained strong until the end. Hedges never managed to uncover any real evidence that Grace Duff had poisoned her relatives, but rather a considerable amount of evidence to suggest that she did not, yet his prejudice against her remained strong. Grace was a particularly intelligent, attractive, slightly unconventional woman, who belonged to a social class above Fred Hedges. He developed a strong antipathy to her and, coupled with John Binning's constant whispering in his ear, quickly decided she was his prime suspect.

In his way Fred Hedges too became obsessed with Grace Duff. Probably forced to watch the pennies all his life, he clearly could not understand how 'an educated woman', as he frequently described her, could be so careless about money that she 'had only a hazy idea of what her mother was worth',[37] or 'didn't worry about money'.[38] (Hedges also appears to have been suspicious of, and possibly even threatened by, the very fact that Grace was such an obviously intelligent, educated woman.) There may also have been an element of resentment. Grace was in a sense typical of a middle class woman who lived comfortably, but 'never had any money'. Within a couple of miles of Birdhurst Rise, hardworking men and women were living hand-to-mouth in dreadful housing conditions, with families of as many as a dozen sharing one or two rooms according to the *Croydon Advertiser*, who reported that there were more than 7,000 families on the council's list, waiting to be rehoused.[39]

In fact Grace was not lucky. With Edmund gone, she swiftly ran through her money and eventually had to take a job, a big come-down from her more carefree Croydon days. Her beloved son John was killed during the Second World War, her daughter Mary never married and her younger son Alastair and his wife Lorna were childless. The woman who so loved children never became a grandmother and the Croydon affair haunted her to the end of her days.[40]

Tom Sidney was more fortunate, but he too had paid a heavy price. Confronted by the fact that three members of his family had apparently been murdered, and knowing himself to be innocent of the deed, Tom was reluctantly forced to conclude that Grace had to be the guilty party. In this his suspicions were undoubtedly fanned by Hedges, Binning and various others. Yet, although he penned an afterword to Whittington-Egan's book and in his own memoir *Echoes of the Past*[41] appears to accept Grace's guilt, there is an underlying sense that he never really came to terms with what appeared to be the obvious solution, and to the end of his life he agonised over what had really happened and who was responsible.[42]

Tom and Margaret moved away from Croydon, eventually making a new life on the other side of the Atlantic. From 1930 onwards Tom regularly returned from America in connection with his antiques business, but when in England he never made contact with his surviving sister,[43] nor was he able to pick up the threads of his once flourishing entertainment career.

The greatest responsibility for this tragedy lies with the so-called experts:

> For lawyers, jurors and judges, a forensic scientist conjures up the image of a man in a white coat working in a laboratory, approaching his task with cold neutrality, and dedicated only to the pursuit of scientific truth. It is a sombre thought that the reality is sometimes different. Forensic scientists may become partisan. The very fact that the police seek their assistance may create a relationship between the police and the forensic scientists – and the adversarial character of proceedings tend to promote this process. Forensic scientists employed by the government may come to see their function as helping the police. They may lose their objectivity.[44]

These words could have been written about any one of the arsenic *cause célèbres* which made headlines in the first half of the twentieth century, but in fact they were spoken in the Court of Appeal in 1992.

According to Fred Hedges, Grace Duff was lucky. By the standards of those who became caught in the web of an arsenic case, perhaps she was: Edward Black, Herbert Armstrong and Charlotte Bryant were all executed. Asked if there was anything they wished to say before sentence was pronounced, each of them chose a variation of the same words: 'I am innocent'.

NOTES ON THE TEXT

The following frequently used reference will be found in abbreviated form in the notes below:
'Wilful Murder by Poisoning by Person(s) unknown of Edmund Creighton Duff on 23/4/1928, Vera Sidney on 14-15/2/29 and Violet Emilia Sidney on 5/3/29 all at Croydon' MEPO 3/861 The National Archives.

Chapter 1

1 Various witness statements concur on the timing and agree about who was on the premises at the time. MEPO 3/861.

2 Letter from Mrs Estella Addis, 9 November 1936. MEPO 3/861.

3 Richard Whittington-Egan, *The Riddle of Birdhurst Rise* (London, George G. Harrap & Co. Ltd, 1975).

4 The episode devoted to the Sidney case in the occasional series *Julian Fellowes Investigates: A Most Mysterious Murder* first broadcast on BBC TV 16 October 2004.

5 No contemporary description of the house interior survives, but no.29 Birdhurst Rise was built to the same design as no.32 and no.3 and internal descriptions of these properties exist in CR/993 & CR/M/101, Croydon Local Studies.

6 The details of the Lendy, Sidney and Duff families which appear in this chapter have been confirmed by reference to the General Register Office of England records of births, deaths and marriages; Calendar of Wills held by the Principal Probate Registry; census returns held by the National Archives and statements made in MEPO 3/861.

7 Peter Dawson (1882–1961) was a bass baritone who enjoyed a long and successful concert career. It was said that most British households which owned a gramophone in the 1920s and 30s had at least one Peter Dawson recording in their collection.

8 Indices of Ships' Passenger Lists held at the National Archives.

9 The *Croydon Advertiser & Surrey County Reporter*, 23 March 1929.

10 1929 ledger entry, J.B. Shakespeare Ltd.

11 There are constant references to the severe weather conditions in newspapers of the period – see in particular the *Croydon Advertiser & Surrey County Reporter*, 12 January 1929 and *The Times*, 16 February 1929 which carry reports of standpipes in the streets. Also, statement of Elsie Anderson, 5 April 1929; statement of Kathleen Noakes, 16 April 1929 and report of Frederick Hedges, 30 April 1929. MEPO 3/861.

12 1929 ledger entry, J.B. Shakespeare Ltd.

13 Report by Dr R.M. Bronte, 6 April 1929. MEPO 3/861.

14 The *Croydon Advertiser & Surrey County Reporter*, 16 March 1929.

15 Report by Detective Inspector Hedges, 13 March 1929 and statement by Samuel Clarke, 14 March 1929. MEPO 3/861.

Chapter 2

1 The *Croydon Advertiser & Surrey County Reporter*, 23 March 1929.
2 The *Croydon Advertiser & Surrey County Reporter*, 30 March 1929.
3 The *Times*, 24 July 1919.
4 The *Croydon Advertiser & Surrey County Reporter*, 25 May 1907 and 18 May 1907.
5 Murder of Richard Beck by Richard Brinkley on 21 April 1907. MEPO 3/177, National Archives.
6 Numerous newspapers covered both the inquest and re-interment, including the *Croydon Advertiser & Surrey County Reporter*, 30 March 1929.
7 The *Croydon Times & Surrey County Mail*, 23 March 1929.
8 The *Croydon Times & Surrey County Mail*, 20 March 1929.
9 This account of the hearing held on 4 April 1929 is derived from deposition of Thomas Sidney, 4 April 1929 and deposition of John Archibald Binning, 4 April 1929. MEPO 3/861; and the *Croydon Advertiser & Surrey County Reporter*, 6 April 1929.
10 Viscera is a collective term used to describe internal organs.
11 Thomas Stafford Sidney died in 1917. General Register Office of England records of deaths.
12 An aperient is a general term for a mild laxative.
13 Tom Sidney had become confused about the dates. It is an incontrovertible fact that his mother died on Tuesday 5 March and that he had taken tea with her on Sunday 3 March – and this is consistent with his original statement made on 7 March. However, by time he gave evidence on 4 April he had 'lost a day' and appears to have believed his mother to have died on the day immediately after he visited for tea – hence his mistake over the days and dates. Grace also appears to have acquired this confusion, as she too implies in subsequent statements that her mother died on the Monday. Neither coroner nor police picked up the discrepancy, which appears to be the result of genuine confusion, rather than a deliberate attempt to mislead.
14 Ptomaine poisoning was the term then in use for food poisoning. Improved knowledge regarding the origins of food poisoning has rendered the term obsolete.
15 Emetics are substances given to induce vomiting, and were commonly used in cases of food or other accidental poisoning or drug overdose.
16 Letter from Cyril Herbert Kirby, dated 10 April 1929. COR/1 130, Croydon Local Studies.
17 This account of the hearing held on 12 April 1929 is derived from deposition of Thomas Sidney, 12 March 1929; deposition of Sydney Gardiner, 12 April 1929; deposition of Frederick Hedges, 12 April 1929; deposition of Samuel John Clarke 12 April 1929; deposition of John Henry Baker, 12 April 1929 and deposition of John Henry Ryffel, 12 April 1929. MEPO 3/861; the *Croydon Advertiser & Surrey County Reporter*, 13 April 1929 and the *Croydon Advertiser & Surrey County Reporter* 20 April 1929.
18 Statement of Samuel Clarke, 14 March 1929. MEPO 3/861.
19 A grain was a standard measurement equivalent to 64.8mg.
20 The *Croydon Times & Surrey County Mail*, 17 April 1929.
21 This account of the hearing held on 17 April 1929 is derived from deposition of Kathleen Noakes 17 April 1929. MEPO 3/861; the *Croydon Advertiser & Surrey County Reporter*, 20 April 1929 and the *Croydon Times & Surrey County Mail*, 20 April 1929.

Chapter 3

1 This account of the hearing held on 18 April 1929 is derived from deposition of Grace Duff, 18 April 1929; deposition of Robert Graham Elwell, 18 April 1929. MEPO 3/861 and the *Croydon Advertiser & Surrey County Reporter*, 20 April 1929.

2 This account of the hearing held on 22 April 1929 is derived from deposition of Grace Duff, 22 April 1929; deposition of Frederick Sandford Rose, 22 April 1929, and deposition of Robert Graham Elwell, 22 April 1929. MEPO 3/861; the *Croydon Advertiser & Surrey County Reporter*, 27 April 1929 and the *Croydon Times & Surrey County Mail*, 24 April 1929.

3 The average wage in 1929 was approximately £200 per annum. Domestic servants, agricultural workers and shop assistants were all in receipt of less than half that amount. Christopher Hibbert, *The English A Social History 1066-1945* (London, Grafton Publishing, 1987) Chapter 60. The eventual amount of Violet Sidney's estate was reckoned at £11,439 13s 10d according to the *Croydon Advertiser & Surrey County Reporter*, 15 June 1929.

4 For example in *The Sunday People*, 28 April 1929.

5 This account of the hearing held on 27 April is derived from deposition of Sydney Gardiner, 27 April 1929; deposition of John Henry Ryffel, 27 April 1929; report of Bernard Henry Spilsbury, 3 April 1929, and deposition of Thomas Sidney, 27 April 1929. MEPO 3/861; and the *Croydon Advertiser & Surrey County Reporter*, 4 May 1929.

6 Syncope is a medical term for collapse/fainting.

Chapter 4

1 This account of the hearing held on 1 May 1929 is derived from deposition of Thomas Sidney, 1 May 1929, MEPO 3/861 and the *Croydon Advertiser & Surrey County Reporter*, 4 May 1929.

2 This account of the hearing held on 6 May 1929 is derived from deposition of Thomas Sidney, 6 May 1929; deposition of Kathleen Noakes, 6 May 1929; deposition of John Henry Ryffel, 6 May 1929; deposition of John Archibald Binning, 6 May 1929, and deposition of Robert Matthew Bronte, 6 May 1929, MEPO 3/861 and the *Croydon Advertiser & Surrey County Reporter*, 11 May 1929.

3 Statement of Thomas Sidney, 4 April 1929. MEPO 3/861.

4 The story of Eric Neville of Chipstead, who received a 'nasty gash' to his left foot, which required dressing at Purley Hospital before he was sent home, was typical of these local stories. The *Croydon Advertiser & Surrey County Reporter*, 11 May 1929.

5 The *Croydon Advertiser & Surrey County Reporter*, 13 July 1929.

6 The *Croydon Advertiser & Surrey County Reporter*, 8 June 1929.

7 This account of the hearing on 9 May 1929 is derived from deposition of Kathleen Noakes, 9 May 1929 and deposition of John Archibald Binning, 9 May 1929, MEPO 3/861 and the *Croydon Advertiser & Surrey County Reporter*, 11 May 1929.

8 This account of the hearing held on 13 May 1929 is derived from deposition of Rupert Henry Fortnum, 13 May 1929, and deposition of Robert Matthew Bronte, 13 May 1929, MEPO 3/861; the *Croydon Times & Surrey County Mail*, 15 May 1929 and the *Croydon Advertiser & Surrey County Reporter*, 18 May 1929.

9 The general election was held on 30 May 1929.

Chapter 5

1 A number of newspapers had implied this, including, for example, the *Croydon Times & Surrey County Mail*, 20 March 1929.

2 The *Sunday People*, 19 May 1929.

3 *Sunday Express*, 19 May 1929.

4 A letter from the Home Office giving permission for the exhumation is dated 16 May 1929, MEPO 3/861. The *Croydon Times & Surrey County Mail*, 25 May 1929 and the *Croydon Advertiser & Surrey County Reporter*, 25 May 1929, both give full reports of the timing and circumstances of the exhumation. Further details have been derived from the *Croydon Advertiser & Surrey County Reporter*, 1 June 1929.

5 Myocarditis is inflammation of the heart muscle, usually caused by infection or disease.

6 'Where the court is satisfied that by reason of discovery of new facts or evidence it is necessary or desirable in the interests of justice that an inquisition on an inquest previously held concerning a death should be quashed and that another inquest should be held the High Court can exercise its powers.' Coroners' (Amendment) Act 1926.

7 The *Croydon Times & Surrey County Mail*, 25 May 1929.

8 This account of the hearing held on 1 June 1929 is derived from deposition of Gwendoline Mary Stafford Greenwell, 1 June 1929; deposition of Dorothy Winifred Gent, 1 June 1929, and deposition of Thomas Sidney, 1 June 1929, MEPO 3/861; the *Croydon Advertiser & Surrey County Reporter*, 8 June 1929 and the *Croydon Times & Surrey County Mail*, 5 June 1929.

9 The account of the hearing held on 6 June 1929 is derived from deposition of Kathleen Noakes 6 June 1929; deposition of Reginald Morrish, 6 June 1929; deposition of John Henry Ryffel, 6 June 1929, and deposition of Thomas Sidney, 6 June 1929, MEPO 3/861; the *Croydon Advertiser & Surrey County Reporter*, 8 June 1929 and the *Croydon Times & Surrey County Mail*, 8 June 1929.

10 Statement of Thomas Sidney, 12 June 1929. MEPO 3/861.

11 The *Croydon Advertiser & Surrey County Reporter*, 15 June 1929.

12 The *Croydon Advertiser & Surrey County Reporter*, 15 June 1929.

13 The *Croydon Times & Surrey County Mail*, 19 June 1929.

14 The *Croydon Advertiser & Surrey County Reporter*, 22 June 1929.

15 The *Sunday Express*, 23 June 1929.

16 The *Sunday People*, 23 June 1929.

17 This account of the hearing held on 22 June 1929 is derived from deposition of Thomas Sidney, 22 June 1929; deposition of Grace Duff, 22 June 1929, and deposition of Bernard Henry Spilsbury, 22 June 1929, MEPO 3/861; the *Croydon Times & Surrey County Mail*, 26 June 1929 and the *Croydon Advertiser & Surrey County Reporter*, 29 June 1929.

18 The Savage Club is a London gentlemen's club operating from 1857 to the present day, whose premises were then in Adelphi Terrace, The Strand.

19 It may be that this was prompted by the natural reticence of a diarist, but it is possible that Vera feared her mother could be upset by the contents. Although an attractive woman with a lively personality, Vera had never married. One anonymous letter in the police file suggests that Vera was having a love affair with Grace, (Metropolitan Police report 17 August 1929. MEPO 3/861) – this appears to have been a completely unfounded piece of malicious gossip, but it does imply that there were rumours about Vera's sexuality at the time. Years later, Kathleen Noakes, while at pains to stress how 'normal' and 'healthy' Vera was, also remembered her as uninterested in men. Richard Whittington-Egan, *The Riddle of Birdhurst Rise* (London, George G. Harrap & Co. Ltd, 1975) p. 215. Vera's niece, Mary Duff, recalled a story of the local vicar, Revd Deane, forbidding his wife to meet with Vera as he considered their friendship 'unhealthy'. Richard Whittington-Egan, *The Riddle of Birdhurst Rise* (George G. Harrap & Co. Ltd, 1975) p. 282. Against this Tom Sidney suggests in his memoir *Echoes of the Past – An Autobiography* (privately published in the USA by M.N. Sidney, 1977) that Vera's sweetheart had been killed in the First World War. Vera's diaries were ultimately reclaimed from the coroner by Tom Sidney according to a report written by Carl Hagen, 20 November 1930. MEPO 3/861.

20 This account of the hearing held on 27 June 1929 is derived from deposition of John Henry Ryffel, 27 June 1929; deposition of Clara Caroline Collett, 27 June 1929; deposition of Robert Matthew Bronte, 27 June 1929; deposition of Ivy Walker, 27 June 1929; deposition of Grace Duff, 27 June 1929; deposition of Thomas Sidney, 27 June 1929, and deposition of Kathleen Noakes, 27 June 1929, MEPO 3/861; the *Croydon Times & Surrey County Mail*, 29 June 1929 and the *Croydon Advertiser & Surrey County Reporter*, 29 June 1929.

Chapter 6

1 *The Croydon Advertiser & Surrey County Reporter*, 6 July 1929.

2 This account of the hearing held on 5 July 1929 is derived from deposition of Samuel John Clarke, 5 July 1929; deposition of Sydney Gardiner, 5 July 1929; deposition of John Henry Baker, 5 July 1929, and deposition of Robert Graham Elwell, 5 July 1929, MEPO 3/861 and the *Croydon Advertiser & Surrey County Reporter*, 6 July 1929 and 13 July 1929.

3 This account of the hearing held on 11 July 1929 is derived from deposition of Charles De Vertus Duff, 11 July 1929, and deposition of Robert Graham Elwell, 11 July 1929, MEPO 3/861; the *Croydon Advertiser & Surrey County Reporter*, 13 July 1929 and the *Croydon Times & Surrey County Mail*, 13 July 1929.

4 Over many years of geographical separation, some of the Duff siblings had evidently fallen out of touch with one another. One of Edmund's sisters only heard about the resumed enquiries into his death when she read about the case in her local newspaper, the *Geelong Advertiser*. Letter from Mrs L.A. Hopkins of Portarlington, Victoria, dated May 1929. MEPO 3/861.

5 Calomel is a chemical compound of mercury chloride which was a popular medicine for many years. It was particularly recommended as a purgative because it 'causes less discomfort than most other purgatives'. Arthur R. Cushny, *Pharmacology, Therapeutics and the Action of Drugs* (London, J.A. Churchill, 1928) p. 104.

6 This account of the hearing held on 12 July 1929 is derived from deposition of Amy Clarke 12 July 1929, and deposition of Thomas Sidney, 12 July 1929, MEPO 3/861 and the *Croydon Advertiser & Surrey County Reporter*, 20 July 1929.

7 This account of the hearing held on 13 July 1929 is derived from deposition of Thomas Sidney, 13 July 1929; deposition of Harold Stanley Whitfield Edwardes, 13 July 1929; deposition of Bernard Henry Spilsbury, 13 July 1929; deposition of Gerard Roche Lynch, 13 July 1929; deposition of Robert Matthew Bronte, 13 July 1929, and deposition of Hugh Charles Herbert Candy, 13 July 1929, MEPO 3/861; the *Sunday Express*, 14 July 1929; the *Croydon Times & Surrey County Mail*, 17 July 1929 and the *Croydon Advertiser & Surrey County Reporter*, 20 July 1929.

8 Trachea is the medical term for windpipe.

9 In simple terms the bronchus is the continuation of the trachea where it enters the lungs.

10 This account of the hearing held on 16 July 1929 is derived from deposition of John Archibald Binning, 16 July 1929 and deposition of Grace Duff, 16 July 1929, MEPO 3/861; the *Croydon Advertiser & Surrey County Reporter*, 20 July 1929 and the *Croydon Times & Surrey County Mail*, 20 July 1929.

11 The *Croydon Advertiser & Surrey County Reporter*, 20 July 1929. According to Tom Sidney, he received at least two packages containing rope nooses. Thomas Sidney, *Echoes of the Past- An Autobiography* (privately published in the USA by M.N. Sidney, 1977), p. 78.

12 Turpentine stupe – a hot cloth or flannel which has been wrung out in boiling water and onto which a few drops of turpentine have been sprinkled. Recommended to ease sprains and bruises and for rubbing on the chest during bronchitis. John D. Comrie, *Black's Medical Dictionary* (London, A. & C. Black, 1918), p. 777, p. 609.

13 Grace Duff's eyes were mentioned frequently by people who shared their recollections of her with Richard Whittington-Egan, according to his book *The Riddle of Birdhurst Rise*.

14 The postal service in 1929 was such that people routinely communicated information at short notice via postcard, rather than using the more expensive telephone system.

15 In 1929 Saturday morning was still part of the normal working week for many people, so scheduling an inquest for that day was not in itself particularly unusual – however, many workers did have Saturday afternoon off, so continuing proceedings late into the evening would definitely have been perceived as an imposition.

16 This account of the hearing held on 20 July 1929 is derived from deposition of Grace Duff, 20 July 1929, and deposition of Bernard Henry Spilsbury, 20 July 1929, MEPO 3/861; the *Croydon Advertiser & Surrey County Reporter*, 27 July 1929 and the *Croydon Times & Surrey County Mail*, 24 July 1929.

17 Edmund Duff was in the habit of augmenting his regular earnings by contributing articles and short stories, mostly about overseas and colonial issues, to various publications.

18 For example, 'Secret Enemy in Poison Drama' was the headline in the *Sunday Express*, 21 July 1929.

19 *Liverpool Echo*, 26 July 1929.

20 This account of the hearing held on 26 July 1929 is derived from deposition of John Edmund Sidney Duff, 26 July 1929; deposition of Grace Duff, 26 July 1929; deposition of Margaret Neilson McConnell Sidney, 26 July 1929; deposition of Percival Warren, 26 July 1929; deposition of Arthur Henry Lane, 26 July 1929, and deposition of Sam Atkinson Noble, 26 July 1929. MEPO 3/861.

Chapter 7

1 The *Croydon Times & Surrey County Mail*, 31 July 1929.

2 This account of the hearing held on 29 July 1929 is derived from COR/1 130, Croydon Local Studies; the *Croydon Times & Surrey County Mail*, 31 July 1929 and the *Croydon Advertiser & Surrey County Reporter*, 3 August 1929.

3 This account of the hearing held on 31 July 1929 is derived from COR/1 128, Croydon Local Studies and the *Croydon Advertiser & Surrey County Reporter*, 3 August 1929.

4 This account of the hearing held on 6 August 1929 is derived from COR/1 132 Croydon Local Studies; deposition of Grace Duff 6 August 1929, and deposition of Bernard Henry Spilsbury 6 August 1929, MEPO 3/861; the *Croydon Times & Surrey County Mail*, 10 August 1929 and the *Croydon Advertiser & Surrey County Reporter*, 10 August 1929.

5 This had been established in evidence at earlier hearings and is corroborated in various statements by Grace Duff, John Duff and Amy Clarke.

6 The *Croydon Advertiser & Surrey County Reporter*, 10 August 1929.

7 The *Sunday People*, 4 August 1929.

8 The *Croydon Times & Surrey County Mail*, 10 August 1929.

9 *The Times*, 23 August 1929 contains an example of one such letter from an Ernest Cook of Bristol.

10 The *Croydon Advertiser & Surrey County Reporter*, 10 August 1929.

11 The *Croydon Times & Surrey County Mail*, 10 August 1929.

12 The *Croydon Advertiser & Surrey County Reporter*, 24 August 1929.

13 The *Croydon Advertiser & Surrey County Reporter*, 17 August 1929.

14 The *Croydon Advertiser & Surrey County Reporter*, 7 September 1929.

15 The *Sunday Express*, 11 August 1929.

16 H.L. Adam, *Murder by Persons Unknown* (London, W. Collins, Sons & Co. Ltd, 1931), pp. 268–79.

17 Richard Whittington-Egan, *The Riddle of Birdhurst Rise* (London, George G. Harrap & Co. Ltd, 1975), pp. 234–5.

18 According to the dust jacket of the original edition 'For ten years the completed manuscript of this book has lain under lock and key in the publisher's safe, waiting for the death of the chief suspect...'

19 *Murder Casebook No.53* (Marshall Cavendish, 1991)

Chapter 8

1 Report of Frederick Hedges, 13 March 1929. MEPO 3/861.

2 Statement of Robert Graham Elwell, 11 March 1929. MEPO 3/861.

3 Report of Frederick Hedges, 23 March 1929. MEPO 3/861.

4 A number of the people interviewed by Richard Whittington-Egan made
   unsubstantiated claims that Grace Duff and Dr Elwell had an affair. Mary Duff stated that
   after her father's death, Elwell was a good friend to her mother and eventually proposed
   marriage to Grace but she declined. According to Mary Duff, Dr Binning hoped to have
   an affair with her mother but was firmly rebuffed. Richard Whittington-Egan, *The Riddle
   of Birdhurst Rise* (London, George G. Harrap & Co. Ltd, 1975), pp. 282–5.

5 Report of Frederick Hedges, 21 April 1929. MEPO 3/861.

6 Report of Frederick Hedges, 13 March 1929. MEPO 3/861.

7 Report of Frederick Hedges, 30 April 1929. MEPO 3/861.

8 Statement of Ivy Walter, 23 April 1929; statement of Amy Clarke, 24 April 1929 and statement
   of Jenny Fleming, 26 April 1929, MEPO 3/861, consistently support this point of view.

9 Report of Frederick Hedges, 11 May 1929. MEPO 3/861.

10 Statement of Robert Graham Elwell, 22 May 1929. MEPO 3/861.

11 Romping or play-fighting.

12 Statement of Jessie Bonfield, 24 May 1929. MEPO 3/861.

13 Statement of Barbara Smith, 23 May 1929. MEPO 3/861.

14 The police files contains at least one statement to this effect from all nine of the
   witnesses who had been in domestic service with the Duffs.

15 Report of Frederick Hedges, 28 May 1929. MEPO 3/861. Many years later Tom Sidney
   would write that the family all knew that Grace and Elwell were having an affair – by
   this time however, a great deal had happened to colour Tom's relationship with his sister,
   and whether he actively held that opinion in 1929 is open to question. It is also pertinent
   to recall that by the time Tom Sidney supposedly made this remark to Hedges, Edmund
   Duff had been dead for more than a year and there had been some speculation among
   the family that Dr Elwell might propose to Grace – which is very far from the same as
   their having had a love affair while Edmund was still living.

16 Statement of Grace Duff, 16 July 1929. MEPO 3/861.

17 This emerged with particular clarity during the hearing held on 1 May 1929, when
   Tom Sidney pointed out that he had not 'wished to speak of his sister Vera'. There are
   numerous similar indications in various statements and depositions in MEPO 3/861, and
   Hedges describes this as his method of obtaining statements in his own report dated
   23 March 1929.

18 Hedges remarks on Kathleen Noakes' illiteracy in his report dated 28 May 1929. MEPO
   3/861.

19 Report of Frederick Hedges, 12 June 1929. MEPO 3/861.

20 Statement of Margaret Neilson McConnell Sidney, 17 July 1929. MEPO 3/861.

21 Report of Frederick Hedges, 21 July 1929. MEPO 3/861.

22 Statement of Grace Mary Duff, 19 July 1929. MEPO 3/861.

23 Report of Frederick Hedges, 21 July 1929. MEPO 3/861.

24 More than forty years later Mary Duff recalled this episode and felt that from then on,
   her mother no longer trusted Tom. Richard Whittington-Egan, *The Riddle of Birdhurst
   Rise* (London, George G. Harrap & Co. Ltd, 1975), p. 284.

25 Statement of Thomas Sidney, 23 July 1929. MEPO 3/861. One of the minor oddities
   of the case is that Hedges never appears to have considered Margaret Sidney a suspect,
   although there was as much (or as little) evidence against her as existed against Tom,
   Grace or Kathleen Noakes. In Margaret's own statement to the police on 12 March
   1929, she mentioned dropping in at Violet's on the day of Mrs Greenwell's visit and her
   own and other witnesses' evidence makes it clear that she had also been in the house
   in the days immediately preceding Violet's death, and had called in at the Duffs' on the
   day Edmund died – moreover she presumably had access to the garden shed where her
   husband kept his Eureka Weed Killer.

26 Report of Frederick Hedges, 28 July 1929. MEPO 3/861.

27 Richard Whittington-Egan, *The Riddle of Birdhurst Rise* (London, George G. Harrap & Co. Ltd, 1975), p. 230, p. 285. There was a further possible source of antagonism between Grace Duff and the Revd Deane in that, according to Mary Duff, Vera Sidney had been deeply hurt by the vicar's allegations that her friendship with his wife was 'unhealthy'. Richard Whittington-Egan, *The Riddle of Birdhurst Rise* (London, George G. Harrap & Co. Ltd, 1975), p. 282. In Tom Sidney's memoir, he admits that Revd Deane was not a particularly good judge of character and based his disapproval of Grace principally on the fact that she was not a regular churchgoer. Thomas Sidney, *Echoes of the Past – An Autobiography* (privately published in the USA by M.N. Sidney, 1977), p. 74.

28 A cleaning and disinfecting agent based on hydrochloric acid.

29 Report of Frederick Hedges, 28 July 1929. MEPO 3/861.

30 Report of Frederick Hedges, 7 August 1929. MEPO 3/861.

31 Letter from Archibald Bodkin, 8 August 1929. MEPO 3/861.

32 Report of Frederick Hedges, 12 August 1929. MEPO 3/861.

33 Report of Frederick Hedges, 20 September 1929. MEPO 3/861.

34 Letter from Messrs Wontner & Sons, 16 August 1929. MEPO 3/861.

35 Report of Frederick Hedges, 20 September 1929. MEPO 3/861.

36 Letter from Archibald Bodkin, 24 September 1929. MEPO 3/861.

37 Report of Frederick Hedges, 9 October 1929. MEPO 3/861.

Chapter 9

1 Richard Whittington-Egan, *The Riddle of Birdhurst Rise* (London, George G. Harrap & Co. Ltd, 1975), p. 220.

2 Richard Whittington-Egan, *The Riddle of Birdhurst Rise* (London, George G. Harrap & Co. Ltd, 1975), p. 220.

3 Richard Whittington-Egan, *The Riddle of Birdhurst Rise* (London, George G. Harrap & Co. Ltd, 1975), p. 218.

4 Agatha Christie, *Ordeal by Innocence* (London, William Collins, Sons & Co. Ltd, 1958) p. 40. It has been suggested that Christie's inspiration for the book had its origins in the Croydon case.

5 Letter from Messrs Wontner & Sons, 16 August 1929. MEPO 3/861.

6 Deposition of Grace Duff, 22 April 1929. MEPO 3/861.

7 Deposition of Bernard Henry Spilsbury, 6 August 1929 and the *Croydon Advertiser & Surrey County Reporter*, 10 August 1929.

8 Statement by Kathleen Noakes, 11 March 1929. MEPO 3/861.

9 Statement by Kathleen Noakes, 16 April 1929. MEPO 3/861.

10 Statement by Gwendoline Mary Stafford Greenwell, 12 April 1929. MEPO 3/861,

11 Deposition of Gwendoline Mary Stafford Greenwell, 1 June 1929. MEPO 3/861.

12 Statement of Grace Duff, 18 April 1929. MEPO 3/861.

13 Deposition of Kathleen Noakes, 9 May 1929. MEPO 3/861.

14 Statement of Kathleen Noakes, 16 April 1929. MEPO 3/861.

15 Deposition of Grace Duff, 22 June 1929. MEPO 3/861.

16 The *Croydon Advertiser & Surrey County Reporter*, 29 June 1929.

17 Richard Whittington-Egan, *The Riddle of Birdhurst Rise* (London, George G. Harrap & Co. Ltd, 1975), p. 214.

18 Kathleen Noakes' statements confirm that she always heated up the whole pan of soup, not just each individual portion as required.

19 COR/1 130, Croydon Local Studies.

20 This occurred during the inquest on 6 June 1929. Deposition of Kathleen Noakes, 6 June 1929, MEPO 3/861 and the *Croydon Advertiser & Surrey County Reporter*, 8 June 1929.

21 The fact that Kathleen Noakes was obliged to work one month's notice is confirmed in deposition of Kathleen Noakes, 12 April 1929 and deposition of Grace Duff, 22 April 1929. MEPO 3/861.

22 Statement of Mary Keetley, 8 April 1929. MEPO 3/861.

23 Statement of Daisy Geer, 10 April 1929. MEPO 3/861.

24 These events are borne out by statements from both Grace Duff and Daisy Geer.

25 Like Violet Sidney, Miss Kelvey's name had undergone a slight change during the course of her life, her birth certificate stating Annie Maria, her death certificate Anna Maria, while some press reporters referred to her as Maria Ann.

26 Will of Anna Maria Kelvey. MEPO 3/861.

27 Statements given by Grace Duff, Dr Elwell and Jessie Bonfield (the Duffs' maid), together with reports by Frederick Hedges all support this. MEPO 3/861.

28 Statement of Francis Gaynor, 5 June 1929. MEPO 3/861.

29 Statement of Thomas Eadie Purdom, 5 June 1929 and statement of Robert Graham Elwell, 1 June 1929. MEPO 3/861.

30 Richard Whittington-Egan, *The Riddle of Birdhurst Rise* (London, George G. Harrap & Co. Ltd, 1975).

31 Statement of Marian Hartley, 31 May 1929 and statement of Gertrude Russell, 5 June 1929. MEPO 3/861.

32 Statement of Francis Gaynor, 8 June 1929. MEPO 3/861.

Chapter 10

1 *The Times*, 8 May 1884.

2 *The Times*, 19 December 1887.

3 Madeleine Smith was tried in 1857 for the murder of her lover Pierre Emile L'Angelier. The defence claimed that L'Angelier had committed suicide. The jury brought in a verdict of not proven. More than seventy years later, the case was still sufficiently notorious that Sir William Willcox was able to cite it (during the inquest into the death of Harry Pace in May 1928) as an example of a poisoning case, confident that ordinary members of the public would know who he was talking about.

4 Mary Ann Cotton was tried in 1873 for the murder of her step-son Charles Edward Cotton. She was found guilty and executed.

5 Florence Maybrick was tried for the murder of her husband James Maybrick in 1889. She was found guilty and sentenced to death, but the sentence was commuted to life imprisonment and she was released in 1904.

6 *The Times*, 7 April 1904 and 4 July 1904.

7 A good account of Edith Bingham's trial and the events leading up to it can be found in the *Lancaster Guardian*, 19 August 1911, 2 September 1911, 16 September 1911, 30 September 1911, 14 October 1911 and 28 October 1911.

8 This account of the Eliza Barrow murder is derived from Seddon F.H. Murder. DPP 1/17, National Archives.

9 This account of the Greenwood case is derived from Suspected Murder of Mabel Greenwood. MEPO 3/265B, National Archives, supported by accounts of the trial of Harold Greenwood reported in *The Times* throughout November 1920.

10 This account of the Black case is derived from Criminal Cases: Black, Edward Ernest. HO 144/1758/426469, National Archives.

11 This account of the Armstrong case is derived from Criminal Cases: Armstrong, Herbert Rowse. HO 144/1757/425994, National Archives.

12 Martin Beales, *Dead Not Buried – Herbert Rowse Armstrong* (London, Robert Hale Ltd, 1995), p. 13.

13 *The Times*, 9 February 1923, 16 February 1923 and 1 March 1923.

14 This account of the Morgan case is derived from *The Times* which covered the full proceedings over the period 1 March–17 April 1923.

15 *The Times*, 7 April 1923.

16 *Nolle prosequi* is a formal order to discontinue proceedings, usually applied for where there is insufficient evidence or where it is not deemed to be in the public interest to pursue a case.

17 This account of the King case is derived from *The Times*, which covered the case from 12 June–29 August 1924.

18 *The Times*, 23 November 1927 and 25 November 1927.

19 Criminal Trial of Mrs Pace. HO 144/10854, National Archives.

20 *The Times*, 30 August 1928.

21 This account of the Hearn case is derived from coverage in *The Times* 13-24 June 1931.

22 Cornwall was the country's leading producer of arsenic for many years.

23 This account of the Bryant case is derived from Criminal Cases: Bryant, Charlotte. HO 144/20180, National Archives and coverage in *The Times*, 11 February–16 July 1936.

24 This was the old Sturminster Union Workhouse, which in 1936 was still the place of last resort for local homeless people.

Chapter 11

1 In 1949 Frederick Radford killed himself after poisoning his wife Margery, who was dying from tuberculosis in a Surrey sanatorium. Keith Simpson, *Forty Years of Murder* (London, Harrap Ltd, 1978), pp. 220–2. In 1968 Percy Beevers committed suicide after murdering Adrienne Taylor of Wath-on-Dearne. *The Times*, 3-4 May 1968.

2 Percy Parsons' involvement as prime mover emerges during both the trial and press coverage of the Hearn case.

3 A series of articles written by Harold Greenwood – 'My Own Story' appeared in the *Illustrated Sunday Herald* from 14 November–19 December 1920.

4 This account is drawn from Criminal Cases: Armstrong, Herbert Rowse. HO 144/1757/425994, National Archives.

5 The United States Agency for Toxic Substances and Disease Registry established by experiment with human volunteers that urinary levels of arsenic drop rapidly with the first twenty-four to forty-eight hours of exposure, so that more than forty-eight hours after ingestion, the level of arsenic in the urine is invariably back at pre-test level. *Case Studies in Environmental Medicine – Arsenic Toxicity – Clinical Evaluation* available via www.atsdr.cdc.gov or the ATSDR at Atlanta, Georgia USA.

6 While there had never been any official acceptance that Herbert Rowse Armstrong was wrongly convicted of murdering his wife Katharine, the present writer would venture to suggest that anyone who troubles to read in full the trial transcript and case papers could not fail to come to the conclusion that not only did more than a reasonable doubt exist as to Armstrong's guilt, but that the conduct of his trial was a travesty of British justice.

7 *Liverpool Echo*, 25 July 1929.

8 *The Times*, 3 October 1928.

9 *Liverpool Echo*, 25 July 1929.

10 *The Times*, 13 August 1930.

11 *The Times*, 27 February 1926.

12 *The Times*, 4 December 1931.

13 *The Times*, 7 July 1928.

14 Robin Odell, *Exhumation of a Murder* (London, George G. Harrap & Co. Ltd, 1975) p. 180.

15 Willcox William, *Toxicology with Reference to its Criminal Aspects* (1938).

16 Figures derived from John J. Eddleston's list of all those executed in England and Wales throughout the twentieth century. John J. Eddleston, *Encyclopaedia of Executions* (London, Blake Publishing, 2002).

17 Douglas G. Browne & E.V. Tullett, *Bernard Spilsbury: His Life and Cases* (London, George G. Harrap & Co. Ltd, 1951), p. 128.

18 Further history and details of the Marsh test and its inventor can be found in any good book on the history of chemistry. The test depends on the reduction of arsenic by nascent hydrogen to gaseous arsine and stibine, which are decomposed by heat into their component elements and the metal is deposited on cooling. The hydrogen is usually liberated by the action of sulphuric acid or granulated zinc, or by electrolysis.

19 Katherine D. Watson, *Medical and Chemical Expertise in English Trials for Criminal Poisoning 1750-1914* (Oxford Brookes University, 2006)

20 An account of the Fenning case can be found in Leslie Hale, *Hanged in Error* (London, Penguin Books, 1961), pp. 17–31.

21 An account of the Russell & Leany case can be found in Leslie Hale, *Hanged in Error* (London, Penguin Books, 1961), pp. 32–41.

22 An account of the Smethurst case can be found in John Camp, *100 Years of Medical Murder* (London, Bodley Head, 1982) pp. 33–49.

23 The full effects of Taylor's well publicised mistake and confession can never be precisely quantified; some commentators have claimed they were minimal, but others, e.g. Robin Odell, *Landmarks in 20th Century Murder* (London, Headline Publishing, 1995) pp. 39–40, clearly considered them substantial.

24 The first dedicated 'forensic science' laboratory came into being at Hendon in 1935, operating under the auspices of the Metropolitan Police.

25 Details of the life and career of Sir William Willcox are derived from Philip H.A. Willcox, *The Detective-Physician: the Life and Work of Sir William Willcox* (London, Heinemann Medical Books, 1970) and Douglas G. Browne & E.V. Tullett, *Bernard Spilsbury: His Life and Cases* (London, George G. Harrap & Co. Ltd, 1951).

26 Douglas G. Browne & E.V. Tullett, *Bernard Spilsbury: His Life and Cases* (London, George G. Harrap & Co. Ltd, 1951), p. 134 and Robin Odell, *Exhumation of a Murder* (London, George G. Harrap & Co. Ltd, 1975), p. 147.

27 They were not involved in the trial of William King, which took place in Edinburgh and was thus under the jurisdiction of the Lord Advocate, rather than the Director of Public Prosecutions.

28 *The Illustrated Sunday Herald*, 14 November 1920.

29 At the trial of Herbert Rowse Armstrong, each of the medical experts appearing for the defence was asked whether they considered first Willcox, then Webster, then Spilsbury to be among the foremost experts in their field, the question and answer sessions being conducted in such a way that each witness in turn appeared to concede by implication that their own expertise was considerably less extensive. Criminal Cases: Armstrong, Herbert Rowse. HO 144/1757/425994, National Archives.

30 A particularly strong example occurred at the trial of Herbert Rowse Armstrong when, during his summing up, Mr Justice Darling said, 'Do you remember Dr Spilsbury? Do you remember how he stood and the way in which he gave evidence? … Did you ever see a witness who more thoroughly satisfied you that he was absolutely impartial, absolutely fair, absolutely indifferent as to whether his evidence told for one side or the other?' Filson Young (ed.), *The Trial of Herbert Rowse Armstrong* (Glasgow, William Hodge & Co., 1927). At the trial of Harold Greenwood, in his summing up, the judge described Willcox and Webster as 'recognised experts, who have no interest in the case…' *The Times*, 10 November 1920.

31 Seddon F.H. Murder. DPP 1/17, National Archives.

32 The John Bolton Memorial Lecture *Expert Evidence – The Problem or the Solution* delivered by The Rt Hon Attorney General, 25 January 2007.

33 Swee Teo Eng, *The Doctor as Expert Witness* (www.lawgazette.com)

34 W.J. Tilstone, K.A. Savage & L.A. Clark, *Forensic Science: An Encyclopaedia of History, Methods & Techniques* (New York, Abc-Clio Inc, 2006) p. 28. John Preece's conviction was declared unsafe and he was released after serving almost ten years of a life sentence.

35 Beverley Schurr, *Expert Witnesses and the Duties of Disclosure & Impartiality: The Lessons of the IRA Cases in England* (NSW Legal Aid Commission).

36 The letter in question appeared during the controversy over the conviction of Florence Maybrick for the murder (allegedly by arsenical poisoning) of her husband James. *The Times*, 13 August 1889.

37 *Hereford Evening News*, 16 April 1922.

38 Biographical details of Spilsbury's early career are derived from Douglas G. Browne & E.V. Tullett, *Bernard Spilsbury: His Life and Cases* (London, George G. Harrap & Co. Ltd, 1951).

39 The shortage of pathologists is confirmed by the memoirs of, among others, Professor Keith Simpson, who describes this same situation still prevailing when he first qualified in 1934. Keith Simpson, *Forty Years of Murder* (London, Harrap Ltd, 1978), p. 27.

40 According to his biographers Browne and Tullett, a newspaper once published a photograph of Spilsbury, captioned 'the handsomest man in London'.

41 An account of the Crippen case can be found in David James Smith, *Supper with the Crippens* (London, Orion Books, 2005).

42 Spilsbury was frequently likened to Sherlock Holmes in newspaper and magazine articles throughout the next two decades and was also referred to as 'the great medical detective'. The comparison continues to be made – as recently as 2006, *MQ Magazine*, 16 January 2006 referred to Spilsbury as 'Sherlock Holmes incarnate'.

43 Katherine D. Watson, *Medical and Chemical Expertise in English Trials for Criminal Poisoning 1750-1914* (Oxford Brookes University, 2006) p. 9. Watson acknowledges that she is repeating the views of Browne & Tullett in *Bernard Spilsbury: His Life and Cases* and that numerous other commentators have made similar claims.

44 Douglas G. Browne & E.V. Tullett, *Bernard Spilsbury: His Life and Cases* (London, George G. Harrap & Co. Ltd, 1951), pp. 387–8.

45 Details of the career of Dr Bronte can be found in his various obituaries.

46 Criminal Cases: Thorne, John Norman Holmes, HO 144/5193, National Archives.

47 For example, *The Law Journal* stated that the jury had arrived at their verdict by 'following the man with the biggest name' and that this sort of approach to pathological evidence was 'valueless'. A newspaper correspondent wrote: 'For some reason or other Sir Bernard Spilsbury has now arrived at a position where his utterances in the witness box receive unquestioning acceptance from judge, counsel and jury… But a reputation for infallibility … is quite out of place in medical and surgical matters…' Douglas G. Browne & E.V. Tullett, *Bernard Spilsbury: His Life and Cases* (London, George G. Harrap & Co. Ltd, 1951), p. 173.

48 Douglas G. Browne & E.V. Tullett, *Bernard Spilsbury: His Life and Cases* (London, George G. Harrap & Co. Ltd, 1951), p. 221.

49 Douglas G. Browne & E.V. Tullett, *Bernard Spilsbury: His Life and Cases* (London, George G. Harrap & Co. Ltd, 1951), p. 221.

50 By the time Merrett murdered his wife and mother-in-law, Spilsbury was dead, but his role did not go unremarked, with Sir Sidney Smith writing: '…the credit given to the misleading evidence of Spilsbury … allowed Merrett to live – and to kill again.' Robin Odell, *Landmarks in 20th Century Murder* (London, Headline Book Publishing, 1995), pp. 89–91.

51 Robin Odell, *Landmarks in 20th Century Murder* (London, Headline Book Publishing, 1995) p. 103.

52 P.D. James, *Death of an Expert Witness* (London, Faber & Faber, 1977) p. 94.

53 Criminal Cases: Thorne, John Norman Holmes. HO 144/5193, National Archives.

54 Robin Odell, *Landmarks in 20th Century Murder* (London, Headline Book Publishing, 1995), pp. 135–7.

55 Criminal Cases: Armstrong, Herbert Rowse. HO 144/1757/425994, National Archives.

56 Sir Bernard Spilsbury's Index Cards. PP/SP/1-8, Wellcome Collection.

57 The archive of Spilsbury's index cards at the Wellcome Collection does not provide an exhaustive list of every post-mortem he performed, but it can be assumed reasonably representative. Prior to the Seddon case there are no cards recording either any arsenical poisoning cases or any exhumations.

58 There are various remarks on record which Spilsbury made against Bronte, all implying professional incompetence – unfortunately, as Spilsbury continued to be lionised, some subsequent authors have taken them at face value – describing Bronte as 'hopeless' and 'inept', presumably without bothering to check what is recorded of his career in less partisan sources.

59 Keith Simpson, *Forty Years of Murder* (London, Harrap Limited, 1978), pp. 26–7.

60 Sir Patrick Hastings was among those who continued to express concern about Spilsbury's influence on court proceedings. During the trial of Elvira Barney in 1932, Hastings successfully applied to have Spilsbury kept out of the court, excepting for the duration of his own evidence, thereby preventing Spilsbury from being invited to comment on anything said by other witnesses. Douglas G. Browne & E.V. Tullett, *Bernard Spilsbury: His Life and Cases* (London, George G. Harrap & Co. Ltd, 1951), p. 183–5.

61 According to Spilsbury's biographers, 'These complaints seem in the main to belong to one period … when the lively appearance of Dr Bronte gave the Adullamites a rallying point.' Douglas G. Browne & E.V. Tullett, *Bernard Spilsbury: His Life and Cases* (London, George G. Harrap & Co. Ltd, 1951), p. 185.

62 *The Times*, 23 March 1932. Bronte's position as a well-known public figure is confirmed by the fact that his illness was deemed sufficiently newsworthy to be included in the column reserved for medical briefings on the 'great and the good'. The fact that Bronte was being treated in Middlesex Hospital was first noted in this section of *The Times* on 14 March 1932, alongside news of the Lord Chancellor, a member of parliament and a prominent churchman.

63 *The Medical Times*, April 1932.

Chapter 12

1 Douglas G. Browne & E.V. Tullett, *Bernard Spilsbury: His Life and Cases* (London, George G. Harrap & Co. Ltd, 1951), p. 207.

2 Richard Whittington-Egan, *The Riddle of Birdhurst Rise* (London, George G. Harrap & Co. Ltd, 1975), p. 242.

3 Douglas G. Browne & E.V. Tullett, *Bernard Spilsbury: His Life and Cases* (London, George G. Harrap & Co. Ltd, 1951), p. 117.

4 In his evidence at the Croydon hearings Spilsbury constantly emphasised that his conclusions were based on the findings of Ryffel and Roche Lynch.

5 Seddon F.H. Murder. DPP 1/17, National Archives.

6 Deposition of Thomas Sidney, 6 June 1929. MEPO 3/861.

7 This has been established by numerous bodies, including the Anthropology Research Facility, University of Tennessee, who have been running long-term studies on rates of human decomposition since 1980.

8 Sydney Smith, *Forensic Medicine* (London, J. & A. Churchill Limited 1925), pp. 32–3 explains the 'conditions affecting the rate of putrefaction', making it abundantly clear that the most significant of these is temperature.

9 The question arose at the trial of Norman Thorne. Criminal Cases: Thorne, John Norman Holmes. HO 144/5193, National Archives.

10 Temperature figures for Croydon, 19 February–22 March 1929, Air Ministry Climatological Returns, National Meteorological Archive.

11 Temperature figures for Croydon, 3 May 1928–18 May 1929, Air Ministry Climatological Returns, National Meteorological Archive.

12 Post-mortem of Edmund Duff, MEPO 3/861 and post-mortem of Katharine Armstrong, Criminal Cases: Armstrong, Herbert Rowse. HO 144/1757/425994, National Archives.

13 Temperature figures for Belmont Abbey, Hereford and Tenbury Wells, 25 February– 31 December 1931, Air Ministry Climatological Returns, National Meteorological Archive.

14 At Katharine Armstrong's post-mortem, the stench emanating from her coffin, coupled

by the sight of the corpse itself, quickly emptied the room of all but essential personnel. The shroud and grave clothes were partly rotted away, as was the flesh of hands, face, feet and various other areas. Mould was visible on some parts of the body, as were infestations of beetles and other insects. In spite of his post-mortem report describing 'advanced decomposition', Spilsbury testified in court that 'the body was in an unusually good state of preservation for the time elapsed since death.' Criminal Cases: Armstrong, Herbert Rowse. HO 144/1757/425994, National Archives.

15 Rentoul & Smith (eds), *Glaister's Medical Jurisprudence and Toxicology* (London, Churchill & Livingstone, 1973) p. 541.

16 On 6 May 1913 Spilsbury performed a post-mortem on a young woman who had deliberately swallowed weedkiller. His card on the case describes all the classic post-mortem signs of arsenical poisoning, including yellow staining to the stomach, intestines, duodenum etc., and ulceration of the oesophagus. Sir Bernard Spilsbury's Index Cards. PP/SP/2, Wellcome Collection. The contemporaneously accepted post-mortem appearances for arsenic are detailed in Sydney Smith, *Forensic Medicine* (London, J. & A. Churchill Limited 1925), pp. 465–6.

17 Petechiae are tiny flat red spots caused by local haemorrhage from small blood vessels.

18 These post-mortem indicators of acute arsenical poisoning are all described in both Sydney Smith, *Forensic Medicine – A Textbook for Students and Practitioners* (London, J. & A. Churchill Ltd, 1925) and Rentoul & Smith (eds), *Glaister's Medical Jurisprudence and Toxicology* (London, Churchill & Livingstone, 1973).

19 Post-mortem report in respect of Vera Sidney. MEPO 3/861.

20 Seddon F.H. Murder. DPP 1/17, National Archives.

21 Rentoul & Smith (eds), *Glaister's Medical Jurisprudence and Toxicology* (London, Churchill & Livingstone, 1973), p. 541.

22 The following account of events at the trial of Frederick Seddon is derived from Seddon F.H. Murder. DPP 1/17, National Archives.

23 Criminal Cases: Black, Edward Ernest. HO 144/1758/426469, National Archives.

24 Criminal Cases: Black, Edward Ernest. HO 144/1758/426469, National Archives.

25 Criminal cases: Greenwood, Harold. HO 144/11780, National Archives.

26 Criminal: Trial of Mrs Pace. HO 104/10854, National Archives.

27 *The Times*, 23 January 1922 and 3 February 1922.

28 *The Times*, 21 December 1921.

29 Criminal cases: Greenwood, Harold. HO 144/11780, National Archives.

30 *The Times*, 5 July 1920.

31 *The Times*, 13 October 1934.

32 Swee Teo Eng, *The Doctor as Expert Witness* (www.lawgazette.com).

33 *The Croydon Advertiser & Surrey County Reporter*, 10 August 1929.

34 Criminal Cases: Armstrong, Herbert Rowse. HO 144/1757/425994, National Archives.

Chapter 13

1 The episode devoted to the Sidney case in the occasional series *Julian Fellowes Investigates: A Most Mysterious Murder* first broadcast on BBC TV 16 October 2004.

2 Richard Whittington-Egan, *The Riddle of Birdhurst Rise* (London, George G. Harrap & Co. Ltd, 1975), p. 267-8. Whittington-Egan also describes Bronte as perspiring heavily while answering questions at the inquest and struggling to save face (pp. 121-2) but there is no contemporaneous documentary evidence to support the idea that Bronte was anything other than cool, calm and confident while giving his evidence.

3 By 1929 Candy was able to claim 'more than thirty years' of experience in analysis. Roche Lynch did not graduate until 1913. The *Croydon Advertiser & Surrey County Reporter*, 10 August 1929 and the Medical Register for 1927.

4 Richard Whittington-Egan, *The Riddle of Birdhurst Rise* (London, George G. Harrap & Co. Ltd, 1975), p. 267.

5 According to Rose Ellen Walker's death certificate, cause of death was chronic myocarditis and chronic interstitial nephritis. Rose Walker died at 1 Birdhurst Rise, a strange coincidence considering her accidental involvement in what would come to be known as 'the Birdhurst Rise case'. General Register Office of England death records.

6 Statement of Hugh Charles Herbert Candy, 13 July 1929, confirmed by original report dated May 1928. MEPO 3/861.

7 Calomel is another name for subchloride of mercury. John D. Comrie, *Black's Medical Dictionary* (London, A. & C. Black Limited, 1918), p. 122.

8 *The Croydon Advertiser & Surrey County Reporter*, 10 August 1929.

9 Report of Bernard Henry Spilsbury, 17 June 1929. MEPO 3/861.

10 Deposition of John Archibald Binning, 17 July 1929. MEPO 3/861.

11 Deposition of Gerard Roche Lynch, 13 July 1929. MEPO 3/861.

12 This account of the history of Edmund's last illness derives from deposition of Grace Duff, 1 June 1928 and deposition of Robert Graham Elwell, 1 June 1928. MEPO 3/861.

13 Calomel is a mercury-based purgative. Hugh Alistair McGuigan, *Textbook of Pharmacology and Therapeutics* (London, Saunders & Co., 1928).

14 Statement by Grace Duff, 2 May 1928. MEPO 3/861.

15 Deposition of Robert Matthew Bronte, 1 June 1928, based on post-mortem report dated 29 April 1928. MEPO 3/861.

16 Deposition of Robert Graham Elwell, 1 June 1928. MEPO 3/861.

17 Deposition of Robert Graham Elwell, 5 July 1929. MEPO 3/861.

18 Statement of John Duff, 18 July 1929. MEPO 3/861.

19 Deposition of Robert Matthew Bronte, 13 July 1929. MEPO 3/861.

20 Report of Frederick Hedges, dated 3 May 1928. MEPO 3/861.

21 Report of Frederick Hedges, dated 29 March 1929. MEPO 3/861.

22 Preliminary report of Gerard Roche Lynch, 28 May 1929. MEPO 3/861.

23 Different authorities give slightly differing figures; for example, the 1973 edition of *Glaister's Medical Jurisprudence and Toxicology* cites a normal figure of 0.027 parts per million of arsenic in the human heart, while Miami University's *Secondary School Chemistry* quotes the normal range as 0.001–0.078. The expected proportions of arsenic in other parts of the body are similarly variable.

24 The following table and accompanying information are derived from the report of Gerard Roche Lynch, 21 June 1929. MEPO 3/861.

25 His height is recorded in Spilsbury's post-mortem report.

26 Various different bodies produce very slightly differing results.

27 Amanda M. Czerniawski, *From Average to Ideal – The Evolution of Height and Weight Tables in the United States 1836-1943* (Social Science History, 2007) pp. 273–96.

28 Sydney Smith, *Forensic Medicine – A Textbook for Students and Practitioners* (London, J. & A. Churchill Ltd, 1925) p. 623. It is now generally accepted that the skeleton represents 13 per cent of a normal person's bodyweight.

Chapter 14

1 *The Times*, 20 June 1931.

2 Birkett's demolition of Gerard Roche Lynch is reported in full in *The Times*, 20 June 1931.

3 The research carried out in Basle in 1968 is reported in *The International Journal of Legal Medicine* Vol 64, No.2, 2 June 1968. The research carried out in 2000 is reported on numerous internet sites.

4 John Emsley, *The Elements of Murder – A History of Poison* (Oxford, Oxford University Press, 2005), p. 95.

5 Elson M. Haas, *Staying Healthy with Nutrition: The Complete Guide to Diet and Nutritional Medicine* (Berkeley, Celestial Arts, 1992), p. 239.

6 Mickey Sarquis, *Arsenic & Old Myths, Journal of Chemical Education* Vol.56 No.12, December 1979 provides a list of the natural arsenic content of various foodstuffs. Haddock contains more than twice the level of beef, while fresh shrimps contain more than seven times the level of haddock. Ronald Bentley & Thomas G. Chasteen, *Arsenic Curiosa and Humanity* (Universities of Pittsburgh & Sam Houston State, 2001) report the relatively high values of arsenic found in a study of Japanese males, which was attributed to the greater dietary use of fish and shellfish than is encountered in other societies.

7 www.atsdr.cdc.gov *Case Studies in Environmental Medicine – Arsenic Toxicity – Clinical Evaluation.*

8 Rentoul & Smith (eds), *Glaister's Medical Jurisprudence and Toxicology* (London, Churchill & Livingstone, 1973), p. 542.

9 Rentoul & Smith (eds), *Glaister's Medical Jurisprudence and Toxicology* (London, Churchill & Livingstone, 1973), Appendix III: Normal levels of trace elements in the human body.

10 Various sources suggest that fewer than one in ten deaths involved a coronial autopsy and fewer than one in ten of these would involve any chemical tests on organs, still less any specific test to establish the presence of arsenic.

11 Ronald Bentley & Thomas G. Chasteen, *Arsenic Curiosa and Humanity* (Universities of Pittsburgh & Sam Houston State, 2001), p. 6.

12 John Emsley, *The Elements of Murder – A History of Poison* (Oxford, Oxford University Press, 2005), pp. 102–3.

13 The saga of the arsenic in the ashes and professor Bone's approach to the court is derived from *The Times*, 29 May 1936, 30 June 1936 and 17 July 1936.

14 Anthony S. Wohl, *Endangered Lives – Public Health in Victorian Britain* (London, J.M. Dent & Sons Ltd, 1983), pp. 265–6.

15 Ronald Bentley & Thomas G. Chasteen, *Arsenic Curiosa and Humanity* (Universities of Pittsburgh & Sam Houston State, 2001), p. 3.

16 John Emsley, *The Elements of Murder – A History of Poison* (Oxford, Oxford University Press, 2005), p. 95.

17 John Emsley, *The Elements of Murder – A History of Poison* (Oxford, Oxford University Press, 2005), p. 101 and *The Times*, 4 December 1903.

18 *The Times*, 19 November 1926.

19 John Emsley, *The Elements of Murder – A History of Poison* (Oxford, Oxford University Press, 2005), p. 119.

20 The deaths of Roderick and Miriam Turley in the Forest of Dean in December 1931 may have been the cause of a gradual revolution in home decorating, with householders adopting the habit of stripping paper back to the plaster before redecorating. Old habits died hard, however, and stories of removing up to a dozen layers of wallpaper were still common in the 1960s. As rooms were often not repapered for five or more years, the lowest layers may well have been Victorian.

21 Statement of John William Bird, 12 July 1929. MEPO 3/861.

22 The instances of contamination specified here are derived from *The Times*, 14 January 1904, 15 January 1904, 4 April 1906, 15 May 1911, 13 April 1920, 19 December 1922, 24 September 1924, 6 January 1923 and 14 September 1931. Other cases of arsenic-contaminated foodstuffs which reached the courts included chocolate sauce, anchovy paste, flour, mineral water, bloater paste, wine, cakes, tinned salmon, bismuth, meat juice, milk powder, bread and a wide variety of sweets and confectionery.

23 *The Times* regularly carried stories about the American apple problem from 1925 onwards.

24 *The Times*, 8 March 1902.

25 A good explanation of the relationship between arsenic and tobacco can be found in John Emsley, *The Elements of Murder – A History of Poison* (Oxford, Oxford University Press, 2005), p. 99 and the *Arsenic Poisoning* section of www.patient.co.uk.

26 The 'very' heavy smoker description appears repeatedly in witness statements and in the statement made by Grace Duff on 3 June 1929; someone, presumably the policeman who typed the report, has underlined the word 'very'.

Chapter 15

1 Letter from Wontner & Sons, 16 August 1929. MEPO 3/861.
2 Report of Frederick Hedges, 12 August 1929. MEPO 3/861.
3 Criminal Cases: Armstrong, Herbert Rowse. HO 144/1757/425994, National Archives.
4 Report of John Henry Ryffel, dated 19 April 1929. MEPO 3/861.
5 Deposition of Bernard Henry Spilsbury, 22 June 1929. MEPO 3/861.
6 Report of Bernard Henry Spilsbury, 2 April 1929. MEPO 3/861.
7 Statement of Grace Duff, 7 March 1929. MEPO 3/861.
8 William R. Jack, *Wheeler's Handbook of Medicine* (London, E. & S. Livingstone, 1920), pp. 302–3.
9 Fowler's Solution was an arsenic-based patent medicine, invented by Dr Thomas Fowler in 1786. It was an extremely popular tonic for more than 150 years, recommended for a whole variety of ailments, including neuralgia, epilepsy, lumbago and skin disorders and was only removed from sale in the 1950s. Its fans included the author Charles Dickens and Queen Victoria's physician, Dr James Begbie.
10 Statement of Grace Duff, 18 April 1929. MEPO 3/861.
11 Deposition of Robert Graham Elwell, 18 April 1929 and statement of Robert Graham Elwell 11 March 1929. MEPO 3/861.
12 Statement of Kathleen Noakes, 7 March 1929. MEPO 3/861.
13 Statement of Clara Caroline Collett, 20 June 1929. MEPO 3/861.
14 Report of Bernard Henry Spilsbury, 2 April 1929. MEPO 3/861.
15 Supplementary report of Bernard Henry Spilsbury, 22 June 1929. MEPO 3/861.
16 Dilated cardiomyopathy is a condition in which the heart becomes weakened and enlarged and cannot pump blood effectively.
17 Statement of Grace Duff, 7 March 1929. MEPO 3/861.
18 General practitioners appeared as witnesses in every arsenic case mentioned in this volume. There is no evidence that any of them testified other than from memory (except in regard to drugs prescribed or dates of visits, which derived respectively from prescription and account books) and in a number of cases, including Elwell and Binning, doctors confirmed during the course of their evidence that they had no contemporaneous notes of the cases under consideration.
19 The *Croydon Times & Surrey County Mail*, 20 March 1929.
20 The 1929 epidemic cannot be accurately described as Norovirus, because the bacteria involved was not isolated, but the symptoms are similar. Norovirus has only been known since 1968 and is spread by faecally contaminated foods (usually as a result of poor hand washing or food hygiene) and by person to person contact.
21 This sequence of events is confirmed not only by Elwell's own statements, but also those of Kathleen Noakes, Grace Duff and the two nurses, Mary Keetley and Daisy Geer.
22 This account of Dr Elwell's descriptions of Vera's symptoms derives from his statements dated 11 March 1929 and 18 April 1929. MEPO 3/861.
23 Deposition of John Archibald Binning, 9 May 1929. MEPO 3/861.
24 The mesentery is a membrane which attaches various organs to the abdominal wall.
25 Report of Bernard Henry Spilsbury of post-mortem carried out on 22 March 1929. MEPO 3/861.
26 Statement of Mary Keetley, 8 April 1929. MEPO 3/861.
27 Criminal Cases: Black, Edward Ernest. HO 144/1758/426469, National Archives.
28 Deposition of John Henry Ryffel, 12 April 1929. MEPO 3/861.
29 Supplementary report of Bernard Henry Spilsbury, 22 June 1929. MEPO 3/861.
30 Deposition of John Henry Ryffel, 6 May 1929. MEPO 3/861.
31 Deposition of Robert Matthew Bronte, 6 May 1929. MEPO 3/861.

32 Report of Frederick Hedges, 28 May 1929. MEPO 3/861.

33 Keith Simpson, *Forty Years of Murder* (London, Harrap Limited, 1978), p. 28.

34 Deposition of John Henry Ryffel, 12 April 1929. MEPO 3/861.

35 None of the cases involving arsenical poisoning which were reported in the national press in 1927-9 involved evidence from Dr Ryffel.

36 Dr Gerard Roche Lynch appeared for the Crown against both Annie Hearn and Charlotte Bryant.

Chapter 16

1 *Sunday Express*, 21 July 1929.

2 The *Sunday People*, 30 June 1929.

3 *The Times*, 1 January 1924. Louis Darwal had been sentenced to penal servitude for life in 1878, but after Kohn-Abrest, Sicard and Paraf established that at least 3mg of arsenic might normally be found in the human body, he successfully applied to have his sentence quashed and was awarded FF20,000 in damages.

4 *Sunday Express*, 7 April 1929.

5 The *Croydon Advertiser & Surrey County Reporter*, 25 May 1929

6 Statement of Clara Caroline Collett, 20 June 1929. MEPO 3/861.

7 Amy Sidney was not called to make a statement on the subject, but both Tom and Grace mention their aunt's supposition and given that the letter was extremely gloomy in tone and content, such a conclusion would not be surprising. According to Tom Sidney, his uncle, William Sidney, separately entertained a theory that Violet had killed herself: Richard Whittington-Egan, *The Riddle of Birdhurst Rise* (London, George G. Harrap & Co. Ltd, 1975), pp. 279–80. Tom and Grace's subsequent protestations that their mother would not have taken her own life appear to be entirely consistent with the level of disbelief often expressed by relatives of a suicide. For example, when John Watson, the ex-chief constable of Bristol, committed suicide in Eastbourne in 1930, his close family used the same arguments, indeed virtually the same words, to refute the idea that he had killed himself, in spite of the fact that he self-evidently had. *Bristol Times & Mirror*, 21, 22 and 26 January 1931.

8 Deposition of Grace Duff, 22 April 1929. MEPO 3/861.

9 According to Tom, in 1897 there were still three maids and a governess living in. Thomas Sidney, *Echoes of the Past – An Autobiography* (privately published in the USA by M.N. Sidney, 1977), p. 2.

10 Deposition of Grace Duff, 22 April 1929. MEPO 3/861.

11 Kathleen Noakes originally gave notice in October to leave on 29 November 1928, but later agreed to stay to 'oblige Miss Vera'. Deposition of Kathleen Noakes, 12 April 1929. MEPO 3/861.

12 Tom and Margaret Sidney and Grace Duff all variously confirmed the timings and length of their own and each others' visits to Violet. Tom confirmed that the death of Violet's last close personal friend had taken place just before Christmas 1928 in his deposition, 4 April 1929. MEPO 3/861.

13 There are numerous references to the prolonged spell of harsh weather. In its edition of 19 January 1929, the *Croydon Advertiser & Surrey County Reporter* reports two separate incidents in which elderly ladies had collapsed in the street, with the extreme cold being attributed as the cause. On 16 February 1929 *The Times* reported that there had been hundreds of broken limbs due to falls on the ice.

14 Statement of Robert Graham Elwell, 11 March 1929 and statement of Grace Duff, 9 March 1929. MEPO 3/861.

15 Statement of Grace Duff, 9 March 1929 and statement of Kathleen Noakes, 7 March 1929. MEPO 3/861.

16 The letter to Lucille Dagron is reproduced in Thomas Sidney, *Echoes of the Past – An Autobiography* (privately published in the USA by M.N. Sidney, 1977), p. 76. The supporting remarks appear in deposition of Grace Duff, 22 April 1929; deposition of Thomas Sidney, 4 April 1929 and statement of Kathleen Noakes, 7 March 1929.

17 Deposition of Robert Graham Elwell, 22 April 1929. MEPO 3/861.

18 Deposition of Grace Duff, 22 April 1929. MEPO 3/861.

19 Deposition of Margaret McConnell Sidney, 26 July 1929. MEPO 3/861. As she was already acknowledged to be ill and was being treated by her doctor, Violet might have assumed that Dr Elwell would simply oblige with a certification of death due to natural causes.

20 Deposition of Grace Duff, 22 April 1929. MEPO 3/861.

21 Deposition of Robert Graham Elwell, 22 April 1929. MEPO 3/861.

22 Deposition of Grace Duff, 22 April 1929. MEPO 3/861.

23 *The Times* 19 January 1897.

24 *The Times* 12 December 1911.

25 The police search appears to have focussed on medicinal and household items rather than cosmetics. The only things included in the list of items removed on 6 March which could be considered cosmetic are an empty Eau de Cologne bottle and a bottle of 'Astringent Quinine lotion for growth and improvement of hair'. The police search on 22 July did include, among the thirty items removed, two which were obviously for cosmetic purposes – one tin of 'Oatdine for the complexion', and one box of white powder labelled 'Special Powder of the Dermal Research Institute', together with four items which may have been cosmetic – two packets of unidentified white powder, one 'china pot containing a sponge and white powder' and one 'wooden box containing a sponge and white powder'. From the descriptions of Violet's cluttered cupboards and her tendency to hoarding, it is reasonable to deduce that this by no means covered all the cosmetic preparations she was liable to have owned at the time of her death. Statements of Samuel Clarke, 14 March 1929 and 22 July 1929. MEPO 3/861.

Chapter 17

1 The case of Annie Maria Luck is reported in *The Times*, 20-22 August 1929.

2 Report of Reginald Morrish, 14 August 1933. This was her uncle Willie, who according to Tom later changed his mind and concluded that Violet had murdered Edmund and Vera, before taking her own life. Thomas Sidney, *Echoes of the Past – An Autobiography* (privately published in the USA by M.N. Sidney, 1977), pp. 72–3. Tom also mentions on p. 77 that numerous friends who knew Grace well were absolutely convinced of her innocence, and on p. 109 says himself that poisoning anyone would have been completely out of keeping with her character – a remark which has separately been made to the current author by people who knew Grace in later life.

3 The story of Binning's remark the day after Vera's death appears in deposition of Thomas Sidney, 22 June 1929 and again in his deposition on 12 July 1929. MEPO 3/861.

4 Deposition of Thomas Sidney, 12 July 1929. MEPO 3/861.

5 Deposition of John Archibald Binning, 16 July 1929. MEPO 3/861.

6 Report of Frederick Hedges, 13 March 1929. MEPO 3/861.

7 Statement of Robert Graham Elwell, 11 March 1929. MEPO 3/861.

8 Dr Binning does not feature at all in *Julian Fellowes Investigates: A Most Mysterious Murder*.

9 Richard Whittington-Egan, *The Riddle of Birdhurst Rise* (London, George G. Harrap & Co. Ltd, 1975), p. 228, p. 236.

10 Richard Whittington-Egan, *The Riddle of Birdhurst Rise* (London, George G. Harrap & Co. Ltd, 1975). The 'report' appears between pp. 237–47 and all quotations in this chapter emanating from John Binning are taken from it unless otherwise stated.

11 Report of Frederick Hedges, 23 March 1929. MEPO 3/861.

12 Report of Frederick Hedges, 4 April 1929. MEPO 3/861.

13 Tenesmus is a strong desire to empty the bowel, which results in continual painful straining. Binning believed it to be particularly associated with arsenic poisoning.

14 Dr Binning's 'report' contains two separate references to alleged clairvoyance connected to the Sidney case – that Vera Sidney's death had been accurately foreseen by a fortune teller and that his own peril of being poisoned by Grace Duff had occasioned a 'psychic storm' for one of his other patients.

15 Report of Frederick Hedges, 12 June 1929. MEPO 3/861.

16 Report of Frederick Hedges, 21 July 1929. MEPO 3/861.

17 T.A. Critchley, *A History of Police in England and Wales* (London, Constable & Co. Ltd, 1978), p. 206.

18 T.A. Critchley, *A History of Police in England and Wales* (London, Constable & Co. Ltd, 1978), p. 203, p. 210.

19 Report of Frederick Hedges, 13 March 1929. MEPO 3/861.

20 Richard Whittington-Egan, *The Riddle of Birdhurst Rise* (London, George G. Harrap & Co. Ltd, 1975), pp. 234–5.

21 Richard Whittington-Egan, *The Riddle of Birdhurst Rise* (London, George G. Harrap & Co. Ltd, 1975), p. 285.

22 Richard Whittington-Egan, *The Riddle of Birdhurst Rise* (London, George G. Harrap & Co. Ltd, 1975), p. 246.

23 Richard Whittington-Egan, *The Riddle of Birdhurst Rise* (London, George G. Harrap & Co. Ltd, 1975), pp. 217–18.

24 Richard Whittington-Egan, *The Riddle of Birdhurst Rise* (London, George G. Harrap & Co. Ltd, 1975), p. 217.

25 Statement of Margaret Neilson McConnell Sidney, 17 July 1929. MEPO 3/861.

26 Richard Whittington-Egan, *The Riddle of Birdhurst Rise* (London, George G. Harrap & Co. Ltd, 1975), p. 283.

27 Deposition of Grace Duff, 20 July 1929, MEPO 3/861, and Richard Whittington-Egan, *The Riddle of Birdhurst Rise* (London, George G. Harrap & Co. Ltd, 1975), p. 281. Tom describes Grace as an attractive, lively extrovert, who had many beaux before she married. Thomas Sidney, *Echoes of the Past – An Autobiography* (privately published in the USA by M.N. Sidney, 1977).

28 Undated letter to Mary Keetley from Grace Duff. MEPO 3/861.

29 Jessie Llewellyn died on 13 June 1928 and the inquest dragged on throughout July and August, reported in detail by *The Times* among others. Her family doctor and several relatives thought she had been poisoned with arsenic, but the eventual verdict was death by natural causes.

30 *The Times*, 19 January 1929.

31 A good account of the Chapman case and Dr Grapel's involvement can be found in *The Times*, January- March 1903.

32 Their overlapping careers are confirmed by the Medical Register, in which Dr Francis Gaspar Grapel's practice was listed at 282 London Road, Croydon, well into the 1920s.

33 Richard Whittington-Egan, *The Riddle of Birdhurst Rise* (London, George G. Harrap & Co. Ltd, 1975), p. 282.

34 Statement of Evelyn King, 19 July 1929. MEPO 3/861.

35 This picture of family life derives from the statement of John Duff, 23 April 1929; statement of Grace Mary Duff, 23 April 1929; statement of Evelyn King, 19 July 1929; statement of Thomas Sidney, 16 July 1929; statement of Margaret Neilson McConnell Sidney, 19 July 1929; statement of Marian Hartley, 31 May 1929 and statement of Clara Caroline Collett, 20 June 1929. MEPO 3/861.

36 Richard Whittington-Egan, *The Riddle of Birdhurst Rise* (London, George G. Harrap & Co. Ltd, 1975), p. 223.

37 Deposition of Grace Duff, 22 April 1929. MEPO 3/861.

38 Statement of Amy Clarke, 7 May 1929. MEPO 3/861.

39 The *Croydon Advertiser & Surrey County Reporter*, 14 September 1929.

40 Details of Grace and her family derive from the General Register Office of England records of births, deaths and marriages and Calendar of Wills held by the Principal Probate Registry. In 2009 old family friends confirmed to the author that the case overshadowed the rest of Grace's life, and continued to cause distress to her surviving children after her death. Mary, Alastair and Lorna Duff are now all deceased.

41 Thomas Sidney, *Echoes of the Past – An Autobiography* (privately published in the USA by M.N. Sidney, 1977).

42 In 2009 this was confirmed to the author by Tom's daughter, Mary-Virginia Christakos, and his grandson, Paul Christakos, who both felt that Tom had never fully accepted his sister's guilt. He was never able to reconcile the Grace he had always known with the cold-blooded poisoner which so many people encouraged him to believe she had become.

43 Ships Passenger Indices held at the National Archives confirm that Tom regularly made the crossing back to England, both before and after the Second World War, but according to his own comments in *Echoes of the Past – An Autobiography* (privately published in the USA by M.N. Sidney, 1977) and the recollections of his daughter Mary-Virginia Christakos, he never set eyes on his sister again.

44 R v. Ward, Court of Appeal, 1992.

SELECT BIBLIOGRAPHY

Beales, Martin, *Dead Not Buried – Herbert Rowse Armstrong* (London, Robert Hale,1995)

Browne, Douglas G. & Tullett, E.V., *Bernard Spilsbury: His Life and Cases* (London, Harrap, 1951)

Emsley, John, *The Elements of Murder – A History of Poison* (Oxford, Oxford University Press, 2005)

Hale, Leslie, *Hanged in Error* (London, Penguin Books, 1961)

Odell, Robin, *Landmarks in 20th Century Murder* (London, Headline Publishing, 1995)

Sidney, Thomas, *Echoes of the Past – An Autobiography* (published privately, 1977)

Simpson, Keith, *Forty Years of Murder* (London, Harrap, 1978)

Smith, Sydney, *Forensic Medicine – A Textbook for Students and Practitioners* (London, J. & A. Churchill, 1925)

Whittington-Egan, Richard, *The Riddle of Birdhurst Rise* (London, Harrap, 1975)

ALSO BY THE SAME AUTHOR

Edwardian Murder: Ightham and the Morpeth Train Robbery

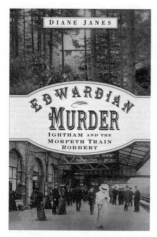

Caroline Luard was shot near Ightham in Kent in 1908. Within weeks, her husband, Major General Charles Luard, committed suicide amid rumours that he was about to be arrested. In 1910 John Nisbet, a colliery cashier, was shot and robbed on a train running between Newcastle and Morpeth. This second killing was brought home to a fellow citizen of Newcastle, John Dickman, but the conviction relied on circumstantial evidence and even after Dickman's execution, some considered the Nisbet murder unsolved.

Speculation increased following the publication of a memorandum written in 1950 by C.H. Norman, the official shorthand writer at John Dickman's trial, which alleged that Dickman had been the victim of a conspiracy which involved the earlier, unsolved murder of Mrs Luard.

This meticulously researched book, which includes previously unpublished information, is the definitive investigation into the murders of Caroline Luard and John Nisbet.

Comments from reviewers on Amazon.com

'This book sets the standard for historical crime studies...'

'...an absorbing read, and I found it almost impossible to put down...'

INDEX